Professional Hairdressing

The official guide to Level 3

Professional Hairdressing

The official guide to Level 3

Fourth Edition

Martin Green and Leo Palladino
with a contribution from Theresa Bullock

THOMSON

City & Guilds

Australia · Canada · Mexico · Singapore · Spain · United Kingdom · United States

HABIA

THOMSON

Professional Hairdressing, Level 3 – Fourth Edition

Copyright © 2004 Martin Green, Leo Palladino and Theresa Bullock

The Thomson logo is a registered trademark used herein under licence.

City & Guilds name and logo are the registered trade marks of The City and Guilds of London Institute and are used under licence.

For more information, contact Thomson Learning, High Holborn House, 50–51 Bedford Row, London WC1R 4LR or visit us on the World Wide Web at: http://www.thomsonlearning.co.uk

British Library Cataloguing-in-Publication Data
A catalogue record for this book is available from the British Library

ISBN 1-86152-940-6

First edition published 1994 by Macmillan Press Ltd
Second edition 1997
Third edition 2001 published by Thomson Learning
This edition published by Thomson Learning 2004
Reprinted 2004 by Thomson Learning

Typeset by Meridian Colour Repro Ltd, Pangbourne-on-Thames, Berkshire

Printed in Italy by G. Canale & C.

Contents

Health, safety and security 1

Consultation 31

Finance and resources 225

Creative business promotion 261

Foreword

Professionalism. If there was ever a word to sum up the changes in hairdressing since the first edition of *Professional Hairdressing – The Official Guide to Level 3*, this is it. Our vision in developing the first set of standards for Level 3 has made an incredible impact on the growing professionalism of the hairdressing industry.

I remember discussing the concept of this book with Martin Green and Leo Palladino in a hotel lobby somewhere in London. Usually when someone begins to discuss 'professionalism', they continue to say how events have moved far beyond their imagination. Let me tell you that in this case it's far from the truth; Martin Green had a wondrous grip on events and would talk for hours on ideas and strategies not just for the book but for the industry as well.

The one thing I've learnt about our authors is their passion for the industry, but it's not enough to be passionate; a wealth of knowledge, experience working in salons and communicating with colleagues and clients are all essential for a book to work well. Handling problems and dealing with difficulties are balanced by the euphoric feeling of seeing a perfect cut and an ecstatic client!

Martin and Leo show once more their intact vision and, with the timely contribution from Theresa Bullock, the phrase *Professional Hairdressing* is more than a book title. I feel this fourth edition is actively placed to become a 'must read' for all hairdressing professionals irrespective of the years spent in the salon. It's not a one-time read book. Read it, practise it, write on it – but most of all, use it.

Alan Goldsbro
Chief Executive Officer
Hairdressing and Beauty Industry Authority

Preface

If an introduction should give a preamble, an insight, or a taster of what's to come, then this book is about self-improvement. This self-improvement comes about as a result of an increase in expectation. Your customers want more. Not only are they prepared to pay for it, but they will also tell you if they are not totally satisfied.

Customer expectation is far greater than before and this principal factor has fuelled the change culture of business for over a decade. We all hear about changes in systems and practices in everyone's work. We are led to believe that change initiates improved efficiency, minimises costs and streamlines operations. When involved in these processes, change is the only thing that we all see and people 'naturally' resist change. We all gravitate to the norm or 'comfortable' yet boring routines. It needn't be like that though; the big picture is quite different. *These changes are necessary in order to meet customer needs*. Business competes to attract customers and once it has *found* them, it will survive only if it manages to keep them. Hairdressing is constantly changing and, like many businesses allied to the fashion industry, it responds to the challenges of the '*I want*' and '*I want it now*' culture.

This book fails if the strong message of communication does not come through. It's the one thing that successful and experienced hairdressers do really well. Improve your communication skills and you too, will reap the benefits. The technical aspects and procedures of the craft can be learnt; it may be daunting, but it is achievable. However, if you fail to develop the way in which you interact with others your hard efforts will be wasted. The new Level 3 qualification is about building on experiences and combining them with a greater understanding of people. These are the new changes and the new challenges and, what's more, they are here to stay.

Acknowledgements

The authors and publishers would like to thank the following for providing images for the book: Alison Stewart, Alistair Hughes, American Express, Andrew Jose, Anthony Mascolo, Antoinette Beenders, Aveda, Belavance Colour by Labothene International -- Germany, Best of British, BLM Health, Bob's Hair Company, Brendan O'Sullivan Creative Director – Regis International Ltd, Bruno Miarli, Charles Worthington, Charlie Taylor, Cheynes Training (www.cheynestraining.com), Chris Moody, City & Guilds, Claudia Woolley @ Saks Hair & Beauty, Clynol, Desmond Murray, Dome Cosmetics (www.domecosmetics.com), Dr. A.L. Wright, Dr. John Gray, Dr. M.H. Beck, Echoes Hair & Beauty, Essensuals: Sacha Mascolo-Tarbuck, Francesco Group, Gemis, Goldwell Professional Haircare, Great Lengths www.greatlengths.net, Guillaume Vappereau @ Guy Kremer International, Guy Kremer, Hair and Beauty Industry Authority, Hair Direct, Hair Flair, Helena Royal @ Regis, ICL, Ishoka Young Image Team, Ishoka-Derek Grant, Ishoka-Phillip Bell, Jackie McShannon and Anders, James Kimber Salon – Birmingham, Jason and India Miller, Charlie Miller, Joanna Myers and Michelle Josling, Karly Whitaker (Sarah Hodge Hairdressing, Somerset and Devon), Lee Preston, Lesley Fairley (Boilerhouse, Newcastle), London Hair Academy, L'Oréal, Mahogany, Mane Connection, Mark Hill, Mark Pearson @ Creator, Martine Finnegan, Maurice Medcalf, Neville Daniel, Nick Malenko, Midlands Hairdresser of the Year, Pat Dixon at Classics Hair & Beauty, Pat Wood, Patrick Cameron, Pierre Alexandre, Ray Nightingale and Connor Kelly at Nightingales, Redken, Regis, Richard Ward Hair & Beauty, London, Robin Callender at McMillan, Royston Blythe – Wolverhampton, S. Lewis, Saks: Covent Garden – flagship for the sales group, Saks: Premier Collection, Sean Hanna and Fiona Connolly, Sharon Forrester, The Controller of Her Majesty's Stationery Office, Toni & Guy, Trevor Sorbie, Umberto Giannini, Vidal Sassoon, Wella UK Ltd.

Special thanks to Corrine Godfrey for her contributions and assistance in helping the authors to produce the final manuscript ahead of schedule.

Every effort has been made to trace all copyright holders, but if any have been inadvertently overlooked the publishers will be pleased to make the necessary arrangements at the first opportunity.

John Rawson PR images: pages 42, 187, 268 and 270: Hair by Roberta Kneller at Bobs Hair Company, Grimsby, photography by John Rawson, styling by FiAn, make-up by Chris Atkinson; page 269: Hair by Clive Boon at Boons, Retford, photography by John Rawson, styling by FiAn, make-up by Chris Atkinson; page 31: Hair by Allan Edwards of Glasgow, photography by John Rawson, styling by FiAn, make-up by Chris Atkinson; pages 35 and 36: Hair by Lisa Neill at Kaliks, Aberdeen, photography by John Rawson, styling by FiAn, make-up by Chris Atkinson; page 102: Hair by Philip Cristie at Unity, Aberdeen, photography by John Rawson, styling by FiAn, make-up by Chris Atkinson; page 182: Hair by Adrian Allen at Red Hair Couture, Wath-upon-Dearne, photography by John Rawson, styling by FiAn, make-up by Chris Atkinson; page 187: Hair by Zullo and Pack in Nottingham, photography by John Rawson, styling by FiAn, make-up by Chris Atkinson.

NVQ – an introduction

National Vocational Qualifications (NVQs) have a common structure and design; that is to say, they all follow a particular format for all occupations and vocational sectors. Each vocational qualification is structured the same way and is made up of a number of individual units and elements. Each unit will address a specific task or area of work, and, where a number of tasks are involved within that area of work, the unit is subdivided into a number of smaller components. These components are called elements.

Units and elements

The unit of competence is the smallest component of an NVQ that can be credited by certificate: i.e. it is the smallest part of a full NVQ that can be awarded to a candidate. An NVQ is made up of a number of units each covering specific areas of work. The unit comprises of a unit title and one or more individual elements. An NVQ can be made up of mandatory units, or mandatory and optional units. For example, reducing risks to health and safety at

Unit structure

Unit G6

Promote additional products or services to clients

Element G6.1   Identify additional products or services that are available

Element G6.2   Inform clients about additional products or services

Element G6.3   Gain client commitment to using additional products or services

Element structure

work is essential and therefore a mandatory unit. Certain occupations involve technical diversity. Therefore there can be a different emphasis within jobs at the same level. In these situations, optional units provide an alternative. Optional units are often separated into two or more option groups and from these the candidate is able to make selections appropriate to their own needs.

Each unit consists of a number of main outcomes known as elements. These are the smallest meaningful activity that has been identified during the process of NVQ development.

The element title

This is a brief statement that outlines the task in hand. Element titles are always expressed in '*Do this*' language, e.g. *Identify additional products or services that are available*.

Performance criteria

The performance criteria are a *list* of essential actions (*not necessarily in order*) that must be carried out so that the task can be completed competently, i.e. a definitive list of what needs to be done. During training these performance criteria form the smallest components of method. However, just learning to carry out a procedure in a 'robotic' fashion does not mean that the person understands what they are doing or why they are doing it. The object of NVQs is to learn and acquire skills, and skills are derived from the combination of method and understanding.

Performance criteria for G6.1

> Element G6.1 Identify additional products or services that are available **by**
>
> a) working with others to keep your information regarding your salon's products or services up-to-date.
>
> b) checking with others when you are unsure of new product or service details.
>
> c) identifying appropriate products or services which may match individual clients' needs.

Range statements

> **Range:** Your performance must cover the following situations
>
> 1 **Additional products and services**
>   a) use of products or services which are new to your client
>   b) more use of the same products or services your client has used before
> 2 **Products or services outside your salon**

Range

The range statements provide a number of conditions or applications in which the elements must be performed; quite simply, under what particular circumstances, on what occasions, or in what special situations the activity must take place.

Knowledge and understanding

National Vocational Qualifications are not only about doing. You will realise that however practical you are about carrying out your work well, you cannot do it well without understanding what you are doing and why you're doing it. The terms 'theory', 'learning' and 'principles' generally refer to essential knowledge and understanding.

Units and elements often share similar components. For example, some of the performance criteria used within the elements: *Style hair using thermal techniques, Style and dress hair to achieve a variety of looks* and *Style and dress long hair* are the same. Similarly, the knowledge that is essential and underpinning one element will often occur in another. This duplication may at first seem unnecessary, but occurs because of the modular, stand-alone, design of NVQs. This can be useful for accelerating the learning process, particularly when knowledge or skills learnt in one activity are applicable to other tasks. Recording these learnt experiences is further made easy by simply cross-referencing the evidence in the candidate's portfolio.

Assessment requirements

The assessment process is designed to establish at what point the candidate is deemed competent and specific methods of assessment are drafted for each element. At the end of each element there is a specification of the *type* and *how much* evidence is required.

Evidence requirements (example Unit G6)

Simulation is not allowed for any performance evidence within this unit. You must supply all the evidence from work you have carried out with clients in your workplace.

You must prove that you have worked to offer additional products or services to clients over a period of time with different clients on different occasions. The additional products or services offered must include:

- Use of products or services which are new to your customer
- More use of the same products or services your customer has used before.

You must prove that you:

- Regularly follow agreed salon procedures for offering additional products or services to your clients
- Create your own opportunities for encouraging your clients to use additional products or services
- Identify what your customer wants by seeking information directly and by collecting information from spontaneous customer comments.

The products or services outside your own area of responsibility may include:

- Those offered by other sections of your salon

or

- Products or services which you have not supplied before.

The information which you provide to your clients may be given verbally or in written form.

Your evidence must show that you have applied the knowledge and understanding requirements when you are dealing with your clients.

Assessment guidance

The following situations will provide potential sources for the collection of evidence. However, there may be a variety of other appropriate sources.

- Observed performance, for example
  1 Greeting visitors/clients on arrival at workplace and visitors from within or inside the organisation.
  2 Putting visitors/clients at ease.
  3 Finding out reasons for visit, business, appointment, information.
  4 Referring visitors/clients to other staff when the requirements are beyond their own capability or authority.

Health, safety and security

Saks: Covent Garden

What do I need to learn?

You need to know and understand:

- **Your expected duties, legal responsibilities and key contacts for health and safety at your salon**

- **The types of hazards that exist in your salon and how _you_ should deal with them**

- **Safe working practices and your salon's health and safety policy and procedures**

Unit G1 Mandatory
Ensure that your own actions reduce risks to health and safety.

Element G1.1 Identify the hazards and evaluate the risks in your workplace.

Element G1.2 Reduce the risks to health and safety in your workplace.

What does it mean?

This chapter will explain how you can help your manager/employer to maintain a healthy and safe working environment for you, your work colleagues and other business customers and visitors.

What do I need to do?

- **You need to ensure that your actions at work do not create any risks to health and safety.**
- **You mustn't ignore any significant risks within the working environment.**
- **Make sure that you *report* any potential hazards with salon equipment, or in connection with staff, clients and other people.**

Other info

Related topics and other useful information:

- **COSHH**
- **Risk assessment**
- **Personal health, hygiene and safety at work**
- **Safe use of salon equipment**
- **Emergency procedures (fire, first aid, etc.)**
- **Maintaining salon security**
- **Display screen equipment (DSE regs)**
- **Manual handling**
- **RIDDOR**
- **Employers liability compulsory insurance**

Science bit!

- **Antiperspirants – how do they work?**
- **Infection and disease**
- **Electrical fuse ratings**

Key words

- **Hazard**, something with potential to cause harm
- **Risk**, the likelihood of a hazard occurring

 This feature appears within the text at points where essential knowledge and understanding are addressed for candidates undertaking Technical Certificates.

Started it ✓	I know who is responsible for H+S and to report to them any hazards in the workplace ✓	I understand and follow the salon's policy in respect to H+S practices and procedures ✓	I always recognise hazards and potential risks at work and take appropriate action ✓
I can identify the main areas of potential risk at work ✓	I understand all the relevant H+S regulations applicable to work ✓	I always carry out working practices according to the salon's policy ✓	I've covered most of it! ✓
I understand the implications of cross-infecting others ✓	I can handle, use and work with materials, products and equipment safely ✓	I understand the necessity of personal hygiene and presentation ✓	I know the salon's policy and procedures in the event of fire or accidents ✓
I know what would be considered unsafe practices at work ✓	Done it all ✓		**CHECKER BOARD** ✓

Introduction

This mandatory unit comprises of two elements:

G1.1   Identify the hazards and evaluate the risks in your workplace.

G1.2   Reduce the risks to health and safety in your workplace.

The chapter covers the essential information in supporting these tasks and extends to a wide range covering other related information. This includes aspects of legislation and general security of the working environment.

You will need to show that you understand the health and safety requirements in the workplace. This includes monitoring your own work routines and workspace so that hazards are quickly identified and potential risk to others in being harmed is minimised.

The *Health and Safety at Work Act 1974*, is the main piece of 'umbrella' legislation under which all other regulations are made. Employers have a legal duty under this Act to ensure, so far as reasonably practicable, the health, safety and welfare at work of all the people for whom they are responsible and the people who may be affected by the work they do.

This Act also requires all employees to take reasonable care of themselves or others who may be affected by their working practices. It expects them to co-operate and support their employers in fulfilling their obligations in complying with current health and safety requirements.

Safety of the environment

You share the responsibility with your employer for the safety of all the people in the salon.

You need to be aware of:

1 *Environmental hazards* such as:
   - wet or slippery floors
   - cluttered passageways or corridors
   - rearranged furniture
   - electrical flexes (e.g. a trailing electric cable is a hazard; if it lies across a passageway there is a high risk of somebody tripping over it whereas if it lies along a wall the risk is much less.)

2 *Hazards to do with equipment and materials* such as:
   - worn or faulty electrical equipment
   - incorrectly labelled substances such as cleaning fluids; leaking or damaged containers (e.g. toxic or flammable chemicals are a hazard and may present a high risk. However, if they are properly kept, securely stored and correctly handled the risk is greatly reduced.)

3 *Hazards connected with people* such as:
   - visitors to the salon
   - handling procedures
   - intruders

Simply being aware of potential hazards is not enough. You also have a responsibility to contribute to a safe working environment, so you must take steps to check and deal with any sources of risk. You can fulfil your role in two ways:

☀ Active learning

Find out your salon's policy in respect of the following procedures.

1 What constitutes safe working (good) practices?

2 How should hazardous substances be stored, dispensed and used?

3 What are the salon's rules regarding smoking, consuming food and drink on the premises and policy in respect to alcohol and other drugs?

4 What takes place during the event of an emergency occurring?

5 What are the salon's expectations in respect to personal presentation and hygiene?

Key skills: Communication

2.1 Take part in discussions

2.2 Produce written materials

2.4 Read and respond to written materials

1   Deal directly with the hazard, which means that you have taken individual responsibility. This will probably apply to obvious hazards such as:

- trailing flexes – *roll them up and store them safely*
- cluttered doorways and corridors – *remove objects and store them safely or dispose of them appropriately*
- fire – *follow the correct procedures to raise the alarm and assist with evacuation*

2   Inform your manager or supervisor, which means that it becomes an organisational responsibility. This applies to hazards that are beyond your responsibility to deal with such as:

- *faulty equipment* – dryers, tongs, straightening irons, kettles, computers, etc.
- *worn* floor coverings or broken tiles
- *loose or damaged fittings* – mirrors, shelves or backwashes
- *obstructions* too heavy for you to move safely
- *fire*

Remember: Checklist	
Hazards:	**Check for:**
Floors	☐ Are they slippery or wet?
Doorways	☐ Are they clear of obstacles?
Electrical flexes	☐ Are they loose or trailing?
Chemicals	☐ Are they labelled and stored correctly?
Equipment	☐ Is it worn or in need of attention?

Working safely in the salon

You have a duty to your employer and your colleagues to keep the working environment safe. You need to be alert, spotting potential hazards and preventing accidents, thus helping to avoid emergency situations arising. Suppose, for example, that someone had carelessly blocked a fire door with a recently delivered stock order. You could take the initiative and remove a possible hazard by moving the box to a safe and secure location. If you notice a potential hazard that you cannot easily rectify yourself, tell your supervisor immediately. Imagine, for instance, that someone accidentally tripped over a trailing lead from a hand dryer while it was plugged in, wrenching the lead from the dryer handle onto a wet floor. Under no circumstances should you enter the wet area and try to retrieve the trailing lead, but you should tell a senior member of staff at once so that she can shut off the power at the mains supply.

Obstructions

It is dangerous to obstruct areas used as thoroughfares such as doorways, corridors, stairs and fire exits. In an emergency people might have to leave the salon, or part of it, in a hurry – perhaps even in the dark. It could be disastrous if someone injured themselves or fell in these circumstances. So always be on the lookout for any obstruction in these areas. If you see something that could present a risk, move it away as quickly as you can.

Spillage and breakages

Take care when you have to clear up spilled chemicals or damaged equipment. First of all find out what has been spilled or dropped. Is this something that needs special care and attention when handling? Does personal protective equipment need to be worn? (see p. 22)

Disposal of waste

General salon waste

Everyday items of salon waste should be placed in an enclosed waste bin fitted with a suitably resistant polyethylene bin liner. When the bin is full, the liner can be sealed using a wire tie and placed ready for refuse collection. If for any reason the bin liner punctures, put the damaged liner and waste inside a second bin liner. Wash out the inside of the bin itself with hot water and detergent.

Disposing of sharps

Used razor blades and similar items should be placed into a safe screw-topped container. When the container is full it can be discarded. This type of salon waste should be kept away from general salon waste as special disposal arrangements may be provided by your local authority. Contact your local council offices for more information.

General health and safety checklist	Yes	No	Go to p.
Has your salon got a written health and safety policy?			12–20
Who is in charge of health and safety in your salon?			20
Has your salon done a risk assessment?			12–22
Do you know what COSHH means?			20–23
Do you know where the first aid kit is?			15–18
Do you know where the accident book is?			16
Do you know the emergency procedures?			12–18
Do you carry out routine checks/inspections?			19–29

General salon hygiene and routine maintenance

The salon

It is important that you develop an awareness of health and safety risks and that you are always aware of any risks in any situation. Quite simply, a tidy salon is easier to clean so get into the habit of clearing up your work as you go.

Floors and seating

Floors should be kept clean at all times. This means that they will need regular mopping, sweeping or vacuuming. When working areas are damp-mopped during normal working hours, make sure that adequate warning signs are provided close to the wet areas.

The salon's seating will be made of material that is easily cleaned. It should be washed regularly with hot water and detergent. After drying, the seats can be wiped over with disinfectant or an antiseptic lotion.

Saks: Covent Garden

Working surfaces

All surfaces within the salon, including the reception, staff and stock preparation areas, should be washed down at least once each day. Most salons now use easily maintained wipe-clean surfaces, usually some form of plastic laminate. They can be cleaned with hot water and detergent, and after the surfaces are dry they can be wiped over with a spirit-based antiseptic which will not smear. Don't use scourers or abrasives as these will scratch plastic surfaces. Scratched surfaces look dull and unattractive as well as containing minute crevices in which bacteria will develop.

Mirrors

Glass mirrors should be cleaned every morning before clients arrive. Never try to style a client's hair while he or she sits in front of a murky, dusty or smeary mirror. Glass surfaces should be cleaned and polished using either hot water and detergent or a spirit-based lotion that evaporates quickly without smearing.

Salon equipment

Towels and gowns

Each client must have a fresh, clean towel and gown. These should be washed in hot soapy water to remove any soiling or staining and to prevent the spread of infection by killing any bacteria. Fabric conditioners may be used to provide a luxurious softness and freshness.

Styling tools

Most pieces of salon equipment, such as combs, brushes and curlers, are made from plastics. These materials are relatively easy to keep hygienically safe if they are used and cleaned properly.

Combs should be washed daily. When not in use they should be immersed in an antibacterial solution. When needed they can be rinsed and dried and are then ready for use.

If any styling tools are accidentally dropped onto the floor, do not use them until they have been adequately cleaned. Don't put contaminated items onto work surfaces as they could spread infection and disease.

Handle non-plastic items, such as scissors and clipper blades, with care. If they need cleaning use surgical spirit by carefully wiping over the flat edges of the blades. Although most of these items are made of special steels, don't immerse them in sterilising fluids. Many of them contain chemicals that will corrode the precision-made surfaces of the blades.

Regularly used clippers in the hairdressing salon will require frequent routine checks for both safety and efficiency. Hair will get trapped between the blades, which reduces cutting performance, and constant vibration may loosen the cutting edges. The macerated hair between the blades will increase friction between the cutting surfaces and reduce the amount of movement of the upper, cutting edge. This will need routine checking and lubricating. Accurate resetting, alignment, lubrication and retightening of the blades is essential, so make sure that only trained individuals carry out this regular, routine maintenance.

Preventing infection

A warm, humid salon can offer a perfect home for disease-carrying bacteria. If they can find food in the form of dust and dirt, they may reproduce rapidly. Good ventilation, however, provides a circulating air current that will help to prevent their growth. This is why it is important to keep the salon clean, dry and well aired at all times. This includes clothing, work areas, tools and all equipment.

Some salons use sterilising devices as a means of providing hygienically safe work implements. *Sterilisation* means the complete eradication of living organisms. Different devices use different sterilisation methods, which may be based on the use of heat, radiation or chemicals.

Ultraviolet radiation

Ultraviolet (UV) radiation provides an alternative sterilising option. The items for sterilisation are placed in wall- or worktop-mounted cabinets fitted with UV-emitting lightbulbs and exposed to the radiation for at least 15 minutes. Penetration of UV radiation is low, so sterilisation by this method is not guaranteed.

Remember

Personal presentation is an essential factor in creating a professional image.

Remember

On every occasion, before using clippers, make sure you check the alignment and positioning of the blades. Frequent use will not only impair their effectiveness, but the constant vibration may loosen the blades.

Good practice

All salons carry out a risk assessment of the substances they use. Any substances that have been identified as potentially hazardous to health will have special handling instructions. These instructions, along with any necessary personal protective equipment (PPE), must be 'publicly' available within the salon.

Chemical sterilisation

Chemical sterilisers should be handled only with suitable personal protective equipment, as many of the solutions used are hazardous to health and should not come into contact with the skin. The most effective form of sterilisation is achieved by total immersion of the contaminated implements into a bath of fluid. This principle is widely used in the sterilisation of babies' feeding utensils.

Disinfectants reduce the probability of infection and are widely used in general day-to-day hygienic salon maintenance. *Antiseptics* are used specifically for treating wounds. Many prepackaged first-aid dressings are impregnated with antiseptic fluids.

Personal hygiene and appearance

Remember

Always wear gloves

When? On any occasion where you come into contact with chemicals

Why? Because gloves are a protective barrier against infection

Always wash hands

When? Before work, after eating, using the toilet, coughing, sneezing or blowing your nose

Why? Because your hands are one of the main sources of spreading infection

Always wear protective clothing

When? Always wear a plastic apron for any salon procedure involving chemicals

Why? This will prevent spillages onto your clothes, particularly when colouring and perming

Hairdressing is a personal service industry and your clients will judge your personal and professional standards by the way in which you present yourself. Remember, hairdressing is an image-conscious industry. We strive to provide a high-quality service that gives clients well-cut, well-styled and well-groomed hair, so that they feel pleased and confident and have greater self-esteem. Would you give clients confidence if you turned up for appointments with stained overalls, unkempt hair and dirty hands and nails?

Hands and nails

Your hands should always be perfectly clean. Dirt on your hands and under your nails will harbour bacteria. By spreading germs you could infect other people. Your hands need washing not only before work but also several times throughout the day. Where hands regularly come into contact with water or detergents, the skin may lose its moisture, become dry and crack. Cracked, broken skin allows germs to enter and infection may follow. To prevent this from happening, you should regularly moisturise your skin after washing. If your hands are often in water (for example, in shampooing or conditioning), you may find it helpful to use a *barrier cream*. Barrier creams cover the skin with an invisible barrier which greatly reduces the penetration of hairdressing cleansing and conditioning agents. (Many trainees have given up hairdressing after developing the skin condition called *dermatitis*, in which the hands become sore, cracked, itchy and red. At this stage work becomes painful and medical advice should be sought.)

Long nails not only trap dirt but can also cause discomfort to clients. In certain hairdressing procedures it is quite possible that longer nails could even scratch or damage the skin. The risk of spreading infection and disease can be prevented by keeping nails short and neat. Clean, well-manicured nails without splits or tears are hygienic and safe.

Body

Taking a daily shower/bath is necessary to remove the build-up of sweat, dead skin cells and surface bacteria. Skin in areas such as the armpits, feet and genitals have more sweat glands than elsewhere and the warm, moist conditions provide an ideal breeding ground for bacteria. Regular washing is therefore essential if body odour (BO) is to be prevented.

Mouth

Unpleasant breath is offensive to clients. Bad breath (halitosis) is the result of leaving particles to decay within the spaces between the teeth. You need to brush your teeth after every meal. Bad breath can also result from digestive troubles, stomach upsets, smoking and strong foods such as onions, garlic and some cheeses.

Personal appearance

In addition to personal cleanliness, your personal appearance is an important factor too. The effort you put into getting ready for work reflects your pride in the job. It is alright for you to have your own individual look, provided that you appreciate and accept that there are professional standards of dress and appearance that must be followed – a sort of personal code of practice.

Clothes

Clothes or overalls should be clean and well ironed. It is sensible to wear clothes made from fabrics that are suitable not only for your intended work but also for the time of year. Clothes that are restrictive or tight will not allow air to circulate around your body and will prevent you from keeping cool and fresh; they could lead to uncomfortable perspiration or possibly BO. Apart from the clothes that other people see, remember that a daily change of underwear is essential.

Shoes

Wear shoes that have low heels. They should be smart, comfortable and made of materials suitable for wearing over long periods of time. Remember that hairdressing involves a lot of standing and your feet can therefore get tired, hot, sweaty and even sore. It is worth wearing shoes that allow your feet to 'breathe', as ventilated feet remain cool and comfortable throughout the working day.

Hair

Your hair reflects the image and expected standards of the salon in which you work. It should be clean, healthy and manageable. Don't let long hair fall over your face, as this will obstruct good communication with the clients and your poor body language may give them the wrong message.

Jewellery

Only the minimum of jewellery should be worn in the salon. Rings, bracelets and dangling necklaces will get in the way of normal day-to-day duties and will make the client uncomfortable. In many hairdressing operations, such as shampooing and conditioning, jewellery can catch and pull at the client's hair as well as provide unhygienic crevices for dirt and germs to lurk in.

Posture

Bad posture will lead to fatigue or even longer term injury. Adopting the correct posture is essential for trainees and competent hairdressers alike. An incorrect standing position will put undue strain on both muscles and ligaments, as well as giving your clients an impression of an uncaring, unprofessional attitude towards work.

Posture fatigue will occur when a part of the body is out of line with another part immediately below. Hairdressers have to be on their feet a great deal. Therefore adopting a good posture is a requirement of the job. You will achieve correct posture when your head, shoulders, upper torso, abdomen, thighs and legs distribute your body's weight in a balanced, equally proportioned way, over feet that are positioned forward and slightly apart. Dropping a shoulder will shift your body's weight over one foot. This will cause curvature of the spine, applying strains on muscles and ligaments, as well as exerting pressures on the intervertebral discs in your

TECH. CERT. **Remember: Infection and disease**

We all carry large numbers of micro-organisms inside us, on our skin and in our hair. These organisms, such as *bacteria*, *fungi* and *viruses*, are too small to be seen with the naked eye. Bacteria and fungi can be seen through a microscope, but viruses are too small even for that.

Many micro-organisms are quite harmless, but some can cause disease. Those that are harmful to people are called *pathogens*. Flu, for example, is caused by a virus, thrush by a fungus and bronchitis often by bacteria. Conditions like these, which can be transmitted from one person to another, are said to be *infectious*.

The body is naturally resistant to infection; it can fight most pathogens using its inbuilt immunity system, so it is possible to be infected with pathogenic organisms without contracting the disease. When you have a disease, the *symptoms* are the visible signs that something is wrong. They are the results of the infection and of the reactions of the body to that infection. Symptoms help you to recognise the disease.

Infectious diseases should always be treated by a doctor. Non-infectious conditions and defects can often be treated in the salon or with products available from the chemist.

spine. This will at least be uncomfortable and at worst dangerous, possibly starting a longer term back problem or injury.

Your posture while sitting should be restful. Your back should be supported all the way down. This does not mean that chairs must have a continuous back or contoured, moulded panels, but that your sitting position should provide your body with support so that the pelvis and not the base of the spine takes the body's weight. Avoid sitting with crossed legs as this will restrict blood circulation. It will result in numbness and a sensation of 'pins and needles'.

Fire safety

Under the *Fire Precautions Act 1971*, a fire certificate is required for business premises if:

- more than 20 people are employed on one floor at any one time
- more than 10 people are employed on different floors at any one time

Where premises are shared with other businesses, the employers must include everyone collectively.

All premises must be provided with an adequate means of escape in case of fire and a means of fighting fire, whether or not a fire certificate is required. All fire exits need to be clearly marked with the appropriate signs and all doors must be capable of being opened easily and immediately from the inside.

Every employer must carry out a fire risk assessment covering the premises. This should address the following key aspects:

- Assessment of fire risks within the premises as required under the Management of Health and Safety Regulations 1999.
- The installation of suitable fire detection equipment, e.g. smoke alarms.
- The installation of a suitable warning system (this could be an automatic fire alarm system).
- Checks that everyone can get back safely from the premises in the event of fire and that all means of escape including passageways, stairwells, etc. are kept clear of obstructions at all times. Where necessary adequate emergency lighting should be installed.
- The provision of adequate firefighting equipment.
- The provision of adequate training for employees so that everyone knows what to do in the event of fire.
- Regular checks and maintenance of all fire safety equipment.
- Regular reviews of the fire safety arrangements.

HEALTH AND SAFETY FOR HAIRDRESSERS

FIRE RISK ASSESSMENT CHECKLIST

HABIA

	Item	Yes/No	If yes, how is this controlled? If no, outline problem areas	Additional control measures required
1.	Are all sources of fuel kept to a minimum and stored safely? · Do not store next to ignition sources such as hot radiators. Remove rubbish regularly and store safely.	No	Aerosols stored on shelves above radiator.	Store aerosols in well ventilated stock cupboard away from heat and direct sunlight.
2.	Are all electrical hand tools regularly inspected/tested? · Electrical faults can cause overheating and result in fires.	Yes	Staff inspect before use. Formal inspection every six months. Contractor PAT test annually.	
3.	Is the salon electrical wiring inspected regularly by a competent person? · See section 8.	No	Only hand tools tested by contractor.	Arrange for contractor to test wiring when carrying out PAT testing of portable appliances.
4.	Is the use of adaptors/extension leads kept to a minimum? · Adaptors/extension leads can overheat.	Yes	No adaptors in salon. One extension lead which can only be used with permission of manageress.	
5.	Are all cables run so that they cannot be damaged? · Damaged cables can result in fuel such as hair, paper etc. catching fire.	No	Cable to washing machine runs across staff room floor.	Install new power point in kitchen

---

Active learning

Your workplace will have its own fire safety procedures. Find out what and where the information is displayed and what action should be taken.

Key skills: Communication

2.4 Read and respond to written materials

Remember

Classes of fire

There are four classifications of fire:

Class A Fires involving solid material, i.e. paper, wood, hair, etc.

Class B Fires involving liquids such as petrol, paraffin, etc.

Class C Fires involving gases, i.e. propane, butane

Class D Fires involving metals

Fire

Fires occurring in salons would be more likely to arise from either an electrical fault, a gas escape, or smoking. Faulty or badly maintained *electrical equipment*, such as hand dryers or hood dryers, may malfunction, overheat, and even ignite. *Gas appliances*, such as ovens or hobs, present a possible risk if left unattended. Staff cooking facilities need to be closely monitored to prevent gas being left on, whether lit or not. *Smoking* can cause fires when lit cigarettes are dropped, discarded or left unattended to smoulder in ashtrays. Your salon will have set fire safety procedures, which must always be followed.

Raising the alarm

In the event of fire breaking out, your main priorities are to:

- *Raise the alarm*. Staff and customers must be warned and the premises must be evacuated.
- *Call the fire brigade*. Do this even if you believe that someone else has already phoned. Dial 999, ask the operator for the fire service, and give the telephone number from where you are calling. Wait for the transfer to the fire service, then tell them your name and the address of the premises that are on fire.

Firefighting

If the fire is small, you may tackle it with an extinguisher or fire blanket. Under the Fire Precautions Act 1971, all premises are required to have firefighting equipment, which must be suitably maintained in good working order. Different types of fire require different types of fire extinguisher.

Types of fire extinguisher

1   **Water**. These are *red* with a label to indicate its type and can only be used for Class A fires. The standard size is 9 litres (2 gallons). (The main problem with this type of extinguisher is the subsequent damage caused by the water and that it cannot be used on electrical fires.)

2   **Foam**. These used to be *cream/buff*, but are now *red* with a *cream/buff label*, and used for Class B fires and small Class A fires. The standard capacity is 9 litres (2 gallons). (This type of extinguisher has the same problems as water extinguishers.)

3   **Carbon dioxide (CO_2)**. These used to be *black*, but are now *red* with a *black label* and can be used on all fires but are particularly suitable for Class B and electrical fires. They are available in a range of sizes depending on the weight of CO_2 contained.

4   **Dry powder**. These used to be *blue*, but are now *red* with a *blue label* and can be used on all classes of fire, but are particularly suitable for Class B, C and electrical fires. They are available in a range of sizes from 0.75kg to 4 kg. The main disadvantage is that the residual powder has to be cleaned up and the powder can cause damage to electronic equipment.

5   **Vaporising liquids (BCF)**. This type of fire extinguisher is no longer available, but may continue to be used until its expiry date. These used to be *green* and can be used on all classes of fire, but are particularly suitable for Class B, C and electrical fires. The main disadvantage is that the vapour is toxic, particularly in confined spaces.

Fire escape

All premises must have a designated means of escape from fire. This route must be kept clear of obstructions at all times and during working hours the fire doors must remain unlocked. The escape

If you weren't shown how to use an extinguisher during your induction, ask your manager to demonstrate how to use it. Remember that all extinguishers are noisy when they are discharged and this can be quite a shock so be careful not to drop it.

Key skills: Communication

2.1 Take part in discussions

2.4 Read and respond to written materials

route must be easily identifiable, with clearly visible signs. In buildings with fire certificates, emergency lighting must be installed. These lighting systems automatically illuminate the escape route in the event of a power failure and are operated by an independent battery back-up.

Fire safety training

It is essential for staff to know the following fire procedures:

- fire prevention
- raising the alarm
- evacuation during a fire
- assembly points following evacuation

Training is given to new members of staff during their induction period. This training must be regularly updated for all staff and fire drills must be held at regular intervals.

Dealing with accidents (first aid)

The *Health and Safety (First Aid) Regulations 1981* require employers to provide equipment and facilities which are adequate and appropriate in the circumstances for administering first aid to their employees. Remember that any first-aid materials used from the kit must be replaced as soon as possible. All accidents and emergency aid given within the salon must be documented in the accident book.

Contents of the first-aid box

No. of employees	*1–5*	*6–10*	*11–50*
Contents			
First-aid guidance notes	1	1	1
Individual sterile adhesive dressings	20	20	40
Sterile eye pads	1	2	4
Sterile triangular bandages	1	2	4
Safety pins	6	6	12
Medium size sterile unmediated dressings	3	6	8
Large size sterile unmediated dressings	1	2	4
Extra-large size sterile unmediated dressings	1	2	4

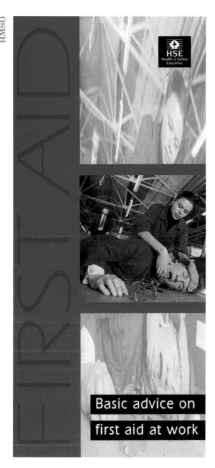

Recording accidents and illness

All accidents must be recorded in the accident book. The recording system should always be kept readily available for use and inspection. When you are recording accidents, you will need to document the following details:

- date, time and place of incident or treatment
- name, and job of injured or ill person
- details of the injury/ill person and the treatment given
- what happened to the person immediately afterwards (e.g. went home, hospital)
- name and signature of the person providing the treatment and entry

General guidance on first aid

The following basic information is available in leaflet form from HSE ISBN 0 7176 1070 5 (priced packs of 20).

Basic rules for first aiders

REMEMBER: YOU SHOULD NOT ATTEMPT TO GIVE ANYTHING MORE THAN BASIC FIRST AID!

When giving first aid it is vital that you assess the situation and that you:

- take care not to become a casualty yourself while administering first aid (use protective clothing and equipment where necessary)
- send for help where necessary
- follow this advice from the HSE

What to do in an emergency

Check whether the casualty is conscious. If the casualty is unconscious or semi-conscious:

- check the mouth for any obstruction
- *open the airway* by tilting the head back and lifting the chin using the tips of two fingers

If the casualty has stopped breathing and you are competent to give artificial ventilation, do so. Otherwise *send for help* without delay.

Unconsciousness

In most workplaces expert help should be available fairly quickly, but if you have an unconscious casualty it is vital that his or her airway is kept clear. If you cannot keep the airway open as described above, you may need to turn the casualty into the recovery position. *The priority is an open airway.*

Wounds and bleeding

Open wounds should be covered – *after washing your hands* if possible. Apply a dressing from the first-aid box over the wound and press firmly on top of it with your hands or fingers. The pad should be tied firmly in place. If bleeding continues, another dressing should be applied on top. *Do not remove the original dressing.* Seek appropriate help.

Minor injuries

Minor injuries of the sort which the injured person would treat themselves at home can be treated from the contents of the first-aid box. The casualty should wash his or her hands and apply a dressing to protect the wound and prevent infection. In the workplace special metallic and/or coloured or waterproof dressings may be supplied according to the circumstances. Wounds should be kept dry and clean.

Suspected broken bones

If a broken bone is suspected *obtain expert help. Do not move casualties* unless they are in a position which exposes them to immediate danger.

Burns

Burns can be serious. If in doubt seek medical help. Cool the part of the body affected with cold water until the pain is relieved. Thorough cooling may take ten minutes or more, but this must not delay taking the casualty to hospital.

Certain chemicals may irritate or damage the skin, some seriously. Treat in the same way as for other burns. It is important that irrigation continues, even on the way to the hospital if necessary. Remove any contaminated clothing which is not stuck to the skin. Make sure that you *avoid contaminating yourself* with the chemical.

Eye injuries

Eye injuries are potentially serious. The casualty will be experiencing intense pain in the affected eye, with spasm of the eyelids. Before attempting to treat, *always protect yourself with surgical gloves.*

If there is something in the eye, irrigate the eye with clean, cool water or sterile fluid from a sealed container to remove loose material. *Do not attempt to remove anything that is embedded.*

If chemicals are involved, flush the open eye with water or sterile fluid for at least 10 to 15 minutes. Apply an eyepad and send the casualty to hospital.

Remember

Essential basic first aid rule

Always protect yourself with surgical gloves when administering first aid. Washing hands is not sufficient!

Special hazards

Electrical and gassing accidents can occur in the workplace. You must assess the danger to yourself and not attempt assistance until you are sure it is safe to do so. If the casualty has stopped breathing and you are competent to give artificial ventilation and cardiac resuscitation, do so. Otherwise *send for help without delay*.

Illness

Many everyday ailments can arise at work. Giving medicines is not within the scope of first aid at work. Application and common sense and reassurance to the casualty are the most valuable help that you can give. If in doubt about the seriousness of the condition, seek expert help.

Record keeping

(See p. 16.)

Salon security

Effective salon security is essential and your employer is required by law to provide secure business premises. Moreover, insurance companies would either refuse to insure a salon where adequate precautions were not taken, or would demand premiums so high that no salon could afford them. In order for your employer to establish and maintain the security of people and their belongings, money, equipment and premises, set procedures will have been laid down and put into action.

The potential threats to salon security come from either external or internal sources, both in and out of business hours.

External provisions

No salon can make its premises totally burglar proof, but steps may be taken to deter entry by unauthorised people and to minimise any damage they might do. As long as reasonable measures have been taken, insurance will not be withheld. Security devices should be fitted such as:

- five-lever mortice locks ('deadlocks') to all external doors. These locks are rebated (cut out of both the door and the frame), not surface-mounted like latch locks, and require keys both to lock and unlock them
- locking catches or bolts on all external opening windows
- security bars or grilles on potentially vulnerable points of entry
- burglar alarms that sound in the event of forced intrusion or damage

Remember

In addition to the advised security features, particular attention should be paid to:

- never leaving money or valuables on the premises overnight
- strict control of the number and location of keys and designated key holders
- switching off all electrical or gas appliances, especially at the end of the day

During normal hours of business, be very alert to the following risks:

- people in areas without the relevant authority
- unauthorised people asking for private or business information
- security of details relating to customers and staff

Internal provisions

Good practice: Security checklist

- Don't leave valuables in the salon overnight
- Don't leave money in the till
- Leave the till drawer open overnight
- Lock all doors, windows and cupboards
- Secure all data / information relating to staff and clients

Unfortunately, outside intruders are not the only threat to the salon's security. Pilfering by staff and clients is also a possibility. Don't let yourself think that taking the occasional product home is a 'perk' of the job. Unless it has been paid for or you have permission, *it is theft*. Your salon may have its own policy in respect to staff purchases. Always ask. Theft at work is defined as an act of *gross misconduct*. A thief faces instant dismissal if your employer exercises her disciplinary rights. Your employer will have taken preventative steps to minimise the risk of theft. Procedures will be set in place to monitor till transactions, stock movements and personal items and valuables.

Money missing from the till will show up during the daily cashing up and book-keeping exercises. Shortfalls will be noticed when the number of clients attended, services and treatments provided and retail items sold do not tally with the available money and cash equivalents, the till rolls and the expected cumulative totals and daily reports and transaction breakdowns.

Missing items of stock will be noticed during normal stock control procedures, in routine situations where stock is not available as expected, and during spot checks and searches.

Personal possessions of both clients and staff also need protecting from theft. Make sure that these are kept safely away from risk situations. Clients' handbags, jewellery and any other valuables should remain with them at all times. Valuable items or money belonging to staff should be securely stored during working hours, or kept with the individual, perhaps in an overall pocket.

Legal framework (health and safety legislation)

This section will provide you with an outline of the main health and safety regulations that affect hairdressers and their work. The *Health and Safety at Work Act 1974* is the legislation that covers a variety of safe working practices and associated regulations. You do not need to know the contents of this Act, but you should at least be aware of the existence of relevant regulations made under its provisions:

- Management of Health and Safety at Work Regulations 1999
- Workplace (Health, Safety and Welfare) Regulations 1992

- Personal Protective Equipment at Work Regulations (PPE) 1992
- Control of Substances Hazardous to Health Regulations 1999 (COSHH)
- Electricity at Work Regulations 1989
- Health and Safety (First Aid) Regulations 1981
- Reporting of Injuries, Diseases and Dangerous Occurrences Regulations 1995 (RIDDOR)
- Health and Safety (Information for Employees) Regulations 1989
- Fire Precautions Act 1971
- Fire Precautions (Workplace) (Amendment) Regulations 1999
- Health and Safety (Display Screen Equipment) Regulations 1992
- Manual Handling Operations Regulations 1992
- Provision and Use of Work Equipment Regulations (PUWER) 1998

Management of Health and Safety at Work Regulations 1999

The main regulation requires the employer to appoint competent personnel to conduct risk assessments for the health and safety of all staff employed or otherwise and other visitors to the business premises. Staff must be adequately trained to take appropriate action, eliminate or minimise any risks. Other regulations cover the necessity to set up procedures for emergency situations, reviewing the risk assessment processes. In salons where five or more people are employed, there is the added obligation to set up a system for monitoring health surveillance, should the risk assessments identify a need. Main requirements for management of health and safety are as follows:

- Identification of any potential hazards
- Assessing the risks which could arise from these hazards
- Identifying who is at risk
- Eliminating or minimising the risks
- Training staff to identify and control risks
- Regular reviewing of the assessment processes

Young workers at risk

There is also a requirement to carry out a risk assessment for young people. Any staff member who is under school leaving age must have a personalised risk assessment kept on file. This would be applicable for those on work experience or Saturday staff.

Remember

Potential areas of risk to young people

- Manual handling
- Electricity and electrical equipment (clippers, etc.)
- Scissors and razors
- Dermatitis
- Chemicals

Remember

Website help from HSE direct COSHH Essentials

Easy online steps to control health risks from chemicals

COSHH Essentials has been developed to help firms comply with the COSHH regulations. The COSHH Essentials website is easy to use and available free as part of hsedirect – a database of all health and safety legislation and HSE's priced guidance.

For more information visit: www.coshh-essentials.org.uk

HEALTH AND SAFETY FOR HAIRDRESSERS

COSHH ACTION PLAN

HABIA

Staff Member Responsible:		Date:		Review Dates:		
Problem requiring attention	Priority High/Med/Low	Action to be taken	Staff Member Responsible	Completion Date		Result
				Target	Actual	
Staff complaining that Xedos Acid Perm is making clients and staff feel nauseous and faint.	HIGH	Contact manufacturer for advice. Look for alternative product. Do not use this product.	Mary Murphy	30/11/98	22/11/98	Manufacturer can only suggest using product in well ventilated area. Product will not be used in salon again. Newline Acid Perm has been ordered and the manufactuer has not experienced any bad reactions with this. Staff to be trained to monitor its use carefully and report any problems to Mary Murphy.

EXAMPLE

HSIP 2c

Electricity at Work Regulations 1989

The Electricity at Work Regulations 1989 cover the installation, maintenance and use of electrical equipment and systems in the workplace. Equipment must be adequately checked by a qualified electrician on a yearly basis. An electrical testing record should be kept for each piece of equipment, which should clearly show:

- electrician's/contractor's name, address, contact details
- itemised list of salon electrical equipment along with serial number (for individual identification)
- date of inspection
- date of purchase/disposal

Health and Safety (First Aid) Regulations 1981

(See p. 15.)

Reporting of Injuries, Diseases and Dangerous Occurrences Regulations 1995 (RIDDOR)

Under these regulations there are certain diseases and groups of infections that if sustained at work are noticeable by law. So if any employees suffer a personal injury at work which results in either:

- death
- major injury
- more than 24 hours in hospital
- an incapacity to work for more than three calendar days

you must report them to the incident contact centre. In addition to this, if a member of the public or salon visitor is injured within the salon and taken to hospital, this is also reportable.

Remember: Science bit!

Electrical fuses

Different items of electrical equipment have differing power consumption ratings. This is measured in watts (1000 watts = 1 kilowatt).

A powerful, salon hand drier would typically be rated at 1300 watts (1.3kw)

The power rating of the washing machine may be more than 2.2kw

What fuse should I use?

Up to 750 watts	a 3 amp fuse
750 to 1200 watts	a 5 amp fuse
1200 to 3000 watts	a 13 amp fuse

Certain industrial diseases are reportable using form F5208A and these include occupational asthma or dermatitis (but only if supported and notified by the employee's doctor).

Other accidents that occur within the salon must also be recorded. Entries must be kept up to date within the *accident record book* (see p. 16).

Health and Safety (Information for Employees) Regulations 1989

The regulations require the employer to make available to all employees, notices, posters and leaflets in either the approved format or those actually published by the Health & Safety Executive (HSE).

The Health and Safety Law leaflet is available in packs of 50 from HSE Books Box 1999, Sudbury, Suffolk CO16 6FS tel. 01787 881165. Other useful HSE publications are:

- *Essentials of Health and Safety at Work* (ISBN 0 7176 0716)
- *Writing your Health and Safety Policy Statement* (ISBN 0 7176 0425)
- *Successful Health and Safety Management* (ISBN 0 7176 0425)

- *A Guide to RIDDOR* (ISBN 0 7176 0432 2)
- *Step by Step Guide to COSHH Assessment* (ISBN 0 11886379 7) or online information @ www.cosh-essentials.org.uk
- *First Aid at Work* (ISBN 0 7176 0426 8)

Fire Precautions Act 1971 and Fire Precautions (Workplace) (Amendment) Regulations 1999

(See pp. 12–15.)

Health and Safety (Display Screen Equipment) Regulations 1992

These regulations cover the use of computers and similar equipment in the workplace. Although not generally a high risk, prolonged use can lead to eye strain, mental stress and possible muscular pain. As more hairdressing salons now use information technology it is becoming a major consideration for employees.

It is the employer's duty to assess display screen equipment and reduce the risks that are discovered. They will need to plan the scheduling of work so that there are regular breaks or changes in activity and provide information training for the equipment users. Computer users will also be entitled to eyesight tests which will be paid for by the employer.

Manual Handling Operations Regulations 1992

These regulations apply in all occupations where manual lifting occurs. They require employers to carry out a risk assessment of the work processes and activities that involve lifting. The risk assessment should address detailed aspects:

- any risk of injury
- the manual movement that is involved in the task
- the physical constraints that the loads incur
- the work environmental constraints that are incurred
- the worker's individual capabilities
- steps and/or remedial action to take in order to minimise the risk

Provision and Use of Work Equipment Regulations (PUWER) 1998

These regulations refer to the regular maintenance and monitoring of work equipment. Any equipment, new or secondhand, must be suitable for the purpose that it is intended. In addition to this they require that anyone using this equipment must be adequately trained.

Good practice: PUWER

- Is all salon equipment checked regularly?
- Are maintenance logs kept for items of equipment?
- Has introduced secondhand equipment been checked?
- Have all the staff been trained to use the equipment?

Code of Hygiene for Hairdressers and Barbers (HABIA)

All hairdressers and barbers are subject to various pieces of legislation paramount among which are the *Health and Safety at Work Act 1974*, *South Yorkshire Act 1974*, *South Yorkshire Act 1980* (registration) and the Byelaws. This code is intended as a guidance to fulfilling these obligations.

General

1 All premises must be kept in a clean condition.
2 All fixtures and fittings should be of such material as to be easily cleanable, e.g. fabric covered chairs not suitable. All surfaces should be wiped down with a disinfectant regularly throughout the day.
3 All tools or instruments which come into contact with a customer must be sterilised before use on each customer (see below for appropriate methods).
4 All towels and other items which come into contact with customers must be clean and used only once before being washed on a high temperature cycle.
5 All gowns should be washed regularly and should any contamination or soiling with blood etc. occur that gown should not be reused until it has been washed on a high temperature cycle.
6 Solid soap, powder puffs, alum blocks or sponges should not be used.
7 A shaving brush must only be used for the first lather, once shaving has commenced the brush cannot be used.
8 Styptics should only be applied using disposable pads, e.g. cotton wool or swabs.
9 Powder should be applied using a spray.
10 Where clippers are used they must be sterilised between customers and if the skin is cut the clipper blades must be removed immediately, washed carefully and then sterilised.
11 The use of razors should be restricted to either disposable or cut-throat razors with disposable blades (e.g. Magic or Alcoso). The blades must be discarded after each customer and the holder washed and sterilised.
   - Electric razors should not be used because of sterilisation difficulties
   - Cut throat razors with integral blades must not be used
   - The disposable razors and blades must be discarded in an approved 'Sharps Disposal' box clearly marked 'Danger Contaminated Needles'
   - These boxes must be disposed of only to an authorised incinerator
   - Details of a suitable collection service are available from the Environmental Services Directorate

Personal hygiene

1 Hands should be washed before every client.
2 Any skin problems, cuts or boils must be covered with a waterproof, impervious dressing. Dermatitis or similar condition on the hands or arms should be covered using disposable seamless gloves changed for each customer.

3   Clean, washable overalls must be worn and must be changed if contaminated or soiled by any blood or other body fluid. Dirty overalls should be washed on a high temperature programme.

Disinfection and sterilisation procedures

1   All equipment once used should be disinfected or sterilised (according to contamination) before reuse and should be divided into plastic items – combs, brushes, etc., and metal items – scissors, razors, etc.

2   The plastic items should be rinsed and all hair removed. Any items contaminated by blood or body fluid must be handled with care to ensure that the contaminated area does not come into contact with any broken skin.

3   These should then be placed in a solution of hypochlorite until required.

4   The metal equipment should be sterilised, ideally in an autoclave.

Autoclaves may be automatic and go through a cycle with appropriate holding times, otherwise the times and temperatures shown in the table must be achieved.

Temperature	Holding times
121°C	15 minutes
126°C	10 minutes
134°C	3 minutes

An alternative to an autoclave is to boil all equipment for 30 minutes in a boiler specially designed for instruments.

The third alternative method for dealing with metal instruments is to rinse away visible contamination. Care must be taken to avoid touching any contamination, especially with areas of broken skin. The instruments must then be placed in a solution of glutaraldehyde for at least 30 minutes. It is advisable to use disposable razors.

Disinfectants

The two most commonly used disinfectants are hypochlorite and glutaraldehyde. These do not sterilise, i.e. kill all known germs, but do reduce the number to the extent that there is very little danger of infection.

● *Hypochlorite* (sold commercially as Milton or bleach) is corrosive to metals and therefore can only be used for wiping down work surfaces, chairs, etc. and for soaking combs, brushes, etc. The solution should be made up freshly each day with a dilution of one part Milton to ten parts water or one part good quality bleach to one hundred parts water.

● *Glutaraldehyde* (sold commercially as Cidex or Totacide) can be used for wiping down all surfaces including metals and for soaking metal implements. The solution can be made up weekly according to manufacturers' instructions.

Self-test section

Quick quiz: a selection of different types of questions to check your knowledge

Q1   A .... is something with potential to cause harm.   Fill in the blank

Q2   Risk assessment is a process of evaluation to ensure safe working practices.   True or False

Q3   Select all that apply. Which of the following are environmental hazards: Multi-selection

Boxes of stock left in the reception area	☐	1
Stock items upon the shelves	☐	2
Wet or slippery floors	☐	3
Shampoo backwash positions	☐	4
Salon work stations	☐	5
Trailing flexes from electrical equipment	☐	6

Q4   First-aid boxes should contain paracetamol tablets.   True or False

Q5   Which of the following regulations relate to the safe handling of chemicals?   Multi-choice

PPE	☐	a
RIDDOR	☐	b
COSHH	☐	c
OSRPA	☐	d

Q6   All salons must have a written health and safety policy.   True or False

Q7   Which of the following records must a salon keep up to date by law: Multi-selection

Telephone book	☐	1
Accident book	☐	2
Appointment book	☐	3
Electrical equipment annual test records	☐	4
Health and safety at work checklist	☐	5
Fire drill records	☐	6

Q8   The .... regulations require employers to provide adequate equipment and facilities in case of an accident occurring.   Fill in the blank

Q9   What colour is the label on a *dry powder* filled fire extinguisher?   Multi-choice

Red	☐	a
Cream	☐	b
Black	☐	c
Blue	☐	d

Q10   A *dry powder* filled fire extinguisher can be used on all classes of fire.   True or False

Consultation

Alan Edwards of Glasgow. Photography by John Rawson

What do I need to learn?

You need to know and understand:

- **The principles of positive communication, i.e. correct body language, listening skills, attention to detail and good customer care**

- **The technical aspects of hair and skin analysis and how that influences future actions**

- **How to negotiate and gain professional respect, whilst mutually benefiting from the relationship**

- **How to eliminate ambiguity arising from the use of technical language and terms**

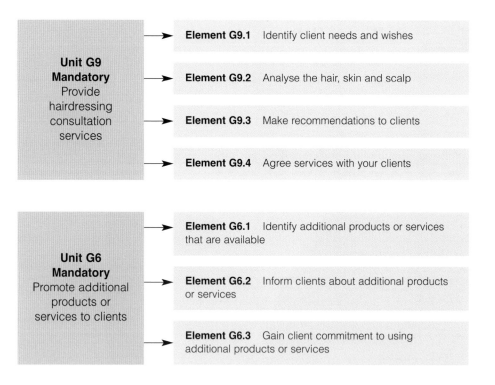

Unit G9 Mandatory Provide hairdressing consultation services	Element G9.1	Identify client needs and wishes
	Element G9.2	Analyse the hair, skin and scalp
	Element G9.3	Make recommendations to clients
	Element G9.4	Agree services with your clients

Unit G6 Mandatory Promote additional products or services to clients	Element G6.1	Identify additional products or services that are available
	Element G6.2	Inform clients about additional products or services
	Element G6.3	Gain client commitment to using additional products or services

What does it mean?

This chapter will explain how to carry out thorough, professional client consultation, combining the skills of effective communication with comprehensive analysis, enabling sound technical advice, routes to further services and treatments and product promotion.

What do I need to do?

- **You need to be able quickly to gain sufficient information so that only suitable courses for action are taken.**
- **You need to gain customer confidence and trust so that a professional bond is created and maintained.**
- **You need to be able to maximise the relationship by enhancing and stimulating an ongoing business.**

Other info

Related topics and other useful information:

- **Hair tests**
- **Image analysis for consultation**
- **Promotion and selling**
- **Limiting and influencing factors**
- **Data protection**
- **Equal opportunities**
- **Consumer rights**

Ray Nightingale and Connor Kelly at Nightingales, for Schwarzkopf

Why a good communicator?

Good communicators use a mixture of skills in their daily routines. This mix or 'toolbag' of skills comprises the following essential components.

1   **Excellent listening skills**. This is the ability to hear and understand what the client is saying. This is particularly useful when the one requiring/initiating a change is not the client in the chair.

2   **A good speaker**. Long silent pauses can often be uncomfortable. Knowing when it is right to speak or keep quiet is an invaluable interpersonal skill. During normal consultation you, the hairdresser, will be taking the lead. You will be asking questions; i.e. trying to elicit enough information in the time span available to make the right judgements. You will be weighing up what the client wants balanced against the limitations arising from the analysis. You will be getting the client to agree on the various possible options and planning the necessary course of action.

In day-to-day, routine interactions with your client the balance changes. More often than not the client will have plenty to say, particularly when you ask them about what has happened since their last visit.

3   **'Reading' skills**. The ability to *read* situations, to understand what has been said or not said, is exceptionally useful. There are times when your client will look a certain way or say something that makes you think. In these situations, your ability to read the situation, i.e. perceptiveness in picking this up and responding appropriately, may have a crucial impact on your long-term relationship.

Body language

We have always relied upon our ability to speak and hear as the natural way of communicating. In fact we use all of our senses to communicate. (Marketers are particularly interested in using all the sensory channels as a way of getting the message across.) But do we use all of our senses equally? The way we use our sight is probably at the top of the list. This is the fastest but very often unreliable way of drawing conclusions.

In the animal world the main form of communication and interaction from one creature to another is through body language. The cat that is alarmed at being confronted by a dog on the street turns sideways on and hunches up. This makes him look larger than he actually is. Size means everything. You pull the dog away sharply and when you get home he sulks; he gets right in your view and turns his back to you. The positioning, posturing and mannerisms of animals all mean something, conveying very clear and strong messages.

We too express our interest and attitudes by non-verbal communication through eye contact, posture and general body positioning. So it is very important that we send the right message, particularly when dealing with clients and potential customers.

Mark Pearson at Creator

Mark Pearson at Creator

Richard Ward Hair & Beauty, London

Eye contact

Always maintain eye contact when in conversation with your client. Where possible, maintain the same eye level. For example, when you carry out a consultation with the client and she is seated, sit beside her or opposite her. Standing over or above her and looking down will convey a feeling of authority, and might appear as if you are trying to assert yourself and take control. This is threatening, intimidating and definitely the wrong signal to send to a potential client.

Body zones

People have a comfort zone. This the space around the body with which they feel at ease. Obviously this space or distance from the body of this space is notional and it varies from person to person. Within a close, intimate relationship, shared proximity may be welcome, but an uninvited invasion of this space is at best very uncomfortable and at worst menacing or threatening.

Posture/body position and gestures

Much has been written on the subject of body language and the psychological effects that it has on those *reading it*. This is far too complex a subject to address in a few simple paragraphs. It is a skill that develops over time and once learnt is never forgotten. However, there are certain obvious rules that can help to convey the right message and create a right impression:

- Slouching in the salon or at reception looks very unprofessional.

- Folded arms and the crossing of arms on the chest are protective gestures and portray a closed mind or show defensiveness.

- Open palms as a gesture supporting explanation or information, with hands at waist height, with palms upwards, indicate that the person has nothing to hide. This is interpreted as openness or honesty.

- Scratching behind the ear or the back of the neck whilst listening indicate that the listener is uncertain or does not understand. Rubbing the nose whilst listening can indicate that you don't believe what you are hearing.

- Talking with your hand in front your mouth may lead the listener to believe you are not being honest. You're hiding yourself behind your gestures.

These forms of communication are only an indication of feelings and emotions. In isolation they may not mean anything at all. However, collectively they can convey a very clear message. Make sure that you send the appropriate signals and look interested, keen, ready to help and positive. Above all show you can listen.

Active learning

Body language

During your break ask your fellow staff members to identify a range of body language gestures. Create a table to record this information. Then later collectively deliberate on the meaning of each gesture. *Is everyone getting the same message?*

Key skills: Communication

2.1 Take part in discussions

2.2 Produce written materials

2.3 Use images

2.4 Read and respond to writtten material

Desmond Murray

Why interested in people?

Having an interest in other people is essential. Anyone who enters the industry thinking 'I like hairdressing, I always have, ever since I used to style my doll's hair. I can even cut my family's hair, and they think it's OK too' is unfortunately going to learn a hard lesson very quickly. This may be a great starting point, having the interest and basic practical dexterity is very useful, but it's like a one-way street. Hairdressing is not just a practical service carried out in isolation, it is also about developing an *interactive community*. An employer who creates a business develops a community by default. Consciously or subconsciously the community of clients that he develops has one shared interest. These clients (many of whom have found the salon from links through other external groupings such as friends, work associates, club memberships, etc.) have *bought into* the salon's overall image, synergy, ambience, range of technical services and the staff employed within the establishment.

However, in order to retain the goodwill and loyalty of the clientele, they need to be stimulated. This can only take place when an interaction occurs. Therefore, the stylist plays the key role in maintaining that bond. Clients do not remain with stylists who do not *continue* to stimulate them. Conversely, a hairdresser cannot be all things to all people so often it is teamwork, the collective application of *customer care* afforded by all the staff members, that strengthens the communal bond. The relationship exists because of shared interests. From this we start to see that good technical skills, i.e. hairdressing practical skills, are not enough; they are only part of the story. A sincere *genuine interest* in other people is essential.

Why willing to keep learning?

The truism that you never stop learning is a little bit overplayed and in an occupation where you constantly meet people it is the general fact. Hairdressing is constantly changing. It changes in many ways. From the fashion point of view it is near the leading edge. The main *drivers* for 'street fashion' are:

- *the music industry* – leading bands and artists are *produced* and *groomed* by professional stylists. It is the job of the *style director* to create a unique image that applies to the artist. Behind that image is a theme or thread, a working brief that the stylist must keep to. Hence, from the many layers of *paint* that are applied to create the overall image, i.e. clothes, make-up and hair, the final media image is produced.

- *film and media industry* – stars and celebrities are born out of prime-time TV. Some will be presenting the news or forecasting the weather. Others will be from the nation's favourite soaps. The really big 'mega stars' are featured in the best 'blockbuster' films. Again, these personalities and their 'public' images have been professionally manufactured.

- *the fashion industry* – at the highest level are the couture fashion houses, the main *label names* and *big brands*, e.g. Versacci, Lagerfeld, Paul Smith, Morgan, etc. These companies design and manufacture fashion itself, taking it round the world for display on stage in New York, Paris, London, Milan and Tokyo. The themes produced within these *high fashion* collections create the basis for the high street shops.

The one thing that they all have in common is media publicity. This is communicated via network broadcasting, video, DVD and popular magazines. This constant exposure to the public *creates* fashion and, at its basic, diluted level, it is recreated in the hair stylist's chair. It's not that hairdressers cannot achieve the same wonderful images as portrayed by the media, but their work is unfortunately more about the client's own lifestyle, confidence and skills. This is reflected during consultation and is the happy medium between *suitability*, *wearability* and *durability*.

So the ever-changing fashion world is just one thing to contend with, but without changing fashions hairdressing would be extremely boring or might not exist at all. People may choose to just grow their hair longer, never having it cut, or conversely just shave it off in front of the mirror at home. The more we work with people, our clients, the more we learn about them too.

 Active learning

Hair fashions are derived from current trends:

1 Choose one 'supermodel' and *collect* over two fashion seasons a range of visual images from newspapers, magazines, internet, etc.

2 Create a *case study* of the individual's progress, media coverage and fashion shows. See how, and provide supporting *explanation* of why, the portrayed images change and develop over that time.

Key skills: Communication

2.1 Take part in discussions

2.2 Produce written materials

2.3 Use images

2.4 Read and respond to written material

Desmond Murray

Why an ability to empathise?

Clients don't come to the salon just when there is a celebration. Because hair grows at an even rate, they are likely to arrive when all sorts of things are going on in their lives and in yours too. It's easy to have sympathy. As hairdressers we do it every day. We can all relate to the *stories* told by our fellow staff over lunch or during breaks – the stories about our clients in certain situations and circumstances. That's life. However, having the ability to put yourself in somebody else's shoes is quite difficult. It's easy to say 'how sad', or 'you poor thing', but beware because true sincerity is an emotion that is easily *read* through your body language.

Handling clients

Discuss with your fellow staff members how different client personalities will affect the style and method of consultation. Discuss also how you can vary the consultation delivery to ensure that a mutually beneficial outcome is derived.

Key skills: Communication

2.1 Take part in discussions

2.2 Produce written materials

2.3 Use images

2.4 Read and respond to written material

The close bond that forms between client and hairdresser is often tested at times like these. Not all clients can be upbeat all of the time. Due to modern living, people's lives have become more stressful. As a result there is an increase in *ambient negativity*. From the clients' point of view, the visit to the salon is not just about having their hair done, it's a lot to do with the feel-good factor too. As hairdressers we must recognise this. The hairdresser's role seems to involve a number of occupations – a little bit of social worker, a touch of psychologist, a bit of entertainer and a huge companion. In order to be this well-rounded individual, we need to *have and show* empathy. It is an extremely useful personal attribute for supporting and understanding others.

Why prepared to give service?

What is the difference if any between customer care and customer service?

Some people may think there's no difference at all, while others would disagree. The two are inextricably linked. If we think about terms another way and add an extra word before each, they may make a little more sense:

- *provide* customer service
- *maintain* customer care

So we have to do one in order to achieve the other. I think we can all agree that we need to *keep* our customers. Without the repeated business of clients coming back on a regular basis we would not remain in work for very long. So our aim is to retain our clients and therefore maintain our customer care. Customer care is like being a *good shepherd*. We *farm* our *flock* by initially *going to market* to get them, developing, nurturing and tending to their needs and *fencing out* the predators, i.e. fending off the competition. If we get it right, we develop a long-lasting and fruitful relationship. If we get it wrong, one or two will stray away, setting a path for others to follow. From this simple analogy we can see that in order to keep our clients we constantly have to work at it. If we are to retain any goodwill, loyalty and professional respect we have to commit ourselves to providing customer service.

How is this done? Gaining new clients is not easy to start with. How do they find us? One way or another we have to invest in our future. We would have had to have spent a great deal of time, money, or both, trying to attract new people. New customers find us from the salon's image and reputation, its location, advertising campaigns, or personal recommendation – that all important word of mouth from already satisfied existing clients.

When the new potential customers make their first visit, they get to sample what we can offer. However, be warned. The professional standards you employ in the way you conduct that initial meeting set down the *basis* for your ongoing relationship. Maintain that service level and the client stays with you. Reduce that standard and the competition picks off another one.

Clive Boon at Boons. Photograph by John Rawson

Roberta Kneller at Bobs Hair Company. Photograph by John Rawson

Why confident amongst others?

Working in the salon is like performing in public. You are on show all the time not only to your own clients, but also to all the other salon visitors. You have to remain confident during consultation, particularly when meeting a new customer, because the pressure is really on. You have to take the lead in these situations because of the feelings that the potential customer is already experiencing. For her it is always quite a daunting challenge because she will have to:

● enter unfamiliar surroundings
● meet new people
● put her trust in your knowledge and understanding
● explain in her own words what she would like

Therefore *you* will need to:

● break the ice immediately and put her at ease
● take control of the situation and steer the consultation process
● eliminate ambiguity arising from talking at cross-purposes or using technical jargon
● optimise the process to turn it into a mutually beneficial outcome

Why highly self-motivated?

Motivation is the key. By being self-motivated we inspire those around us with whom we come into contact. Lack of motivation is a downward spiral: the less we contribute, the less we want to. Others see this and the rot sets in. We hear about demotivated people all the time, people not happy at work, troubled at home. Do other people talk about us and our workplace in the same way? If they do we have a serious problem. Even if they are right, the damage to the business could be irreparable.

The positive outlook is the only way of carrying on. Unfortunately our customers get to know and understand our mood swings only too well. As mentioned earlier, we are like actors on a stage. If we drop our mask for a moment the message will have been received and be a short time away from broadcast.

Why a good memory?

You may have done NVQ Level 2 some time ago. In covering that particular qualification you will have learned many scientific aspects of hairdressing that, if forgotten, will have a potentially disastrous impact on both you and the business. For example, if you forget to conduct the variety of tests such as skin tests, perm tests, incompatibility tests, etc. the consequences could be disastrous. You carry out these procedures as a matter of course. They are linked to practical procedures and are essential. So now you are thinking 'I do this all the time'. Good. That's one example of using your memory, but as far as the clients are concerned this is part and parcel of the job.

Remember

Being highly self-motivated affects others too. The way in which we conduct ourselves at work has a direct, positive impact on those around us. Conversely, poor motivation spreads like a disease!

Active learning

Motivation

Discuss with your fellow staff members the benefits of self-motivation and the impact that it has on the whole team. Then discuss the disadvantages of demotivation and the impact it will have. Summarise and record your findings.

Key skills: Communication

2.1 Take part in discussions

2.2 Produce written materials

The truly great hairdresser will take this further. Because they have a genuine interest in each and every client, they will remember exactly what is going on. Here is an example. A client makes a repeat visit back to the salon following an initial visit and introduction two months previously. During that first consultation the stylist prescribes an initial reshaping and home care regimen to follow up the professional salon treatment, thus allowing the client to grow her hair over the next six months to the target length. She sits in the styling chair only to find that the same stylist says, 'Well what can I do for you today, a restyle cut and blow-dry?' The in-depth consultation and agreed plan for the future have been completely forgotten. The stylist's professional standing is compromised and a loyalty has been broken. It's as sensitive as that.

This is just the beginning. Through repeated visits we begin to learn more about our client's background, place of work, social interests and family, as they too learn more about us. Being able to remember where you left off during the last visit is perceived by the client to be an incredible personal skill. They are impressed that you have taken that much notice of them and their life. This will lift their beliefs in your professionalism and set you aside from the rest. It works!

Why not afraid to be an individual?

In life some lead and others follow. The professional bond that exists between you and your customers is very special. You may work in a shop but you are not just a retailer. Your clients will go into a clothes shop and browse through the rails. When they find something that interests them, they will quickly make up their minds about its suitability, how much wear it will give them and whether they can afford it. Regardless of the person who then comes up to sell the item to them, they have already *bought into* the idea so handling of the sale is fairly circumstantial.

This is not the same in hairdressing. Clients buy from hairdressers that they identify with and respect. In the majority of situations it is easier to take control of the communication during the salon visit, rather than letting the client take the lead. This occurs quite naturally for those who are more individualistic.

When children are at school age they tell their parents and friends that they want to be an individual, they want to be different. This is seldom the case. They have to have the same trainers or particular shoes. They need to look a certain way to fit in. Very few children want to stand out in a crowd. So in their search for individuality they find comfort and security by doing exactly the same as everyone else.

Later in life as adults we find that strong characters and individualistic personalities are often alluring. This change of view develops with maturity. It is less important for people to fit in and therefore there is a wider acceptance of people who are different. We may have developed a good rapport with our own customers, but we don't know how others perceive us. What we do know is that our personality has played a big part in maintaining our clients' goodwill and continuing relationship.

Why have a variety of interests and personal experience?

Clients may admire what you do for them in the salon; otherwise they wouldn't return. However, your hairdressing skills are plain to see. You don't need to bang on about technical issues. Very few people are inspired by 'know-it-alls'. They are interested in you as a person. It's difficult for others to see us in any other context than what we do. This is a naturally occurring physiological pattern. Most of us tend to create patterns as a way of remembering things. That's why certain images conjure up linked thoughts, or smells invoke certain situations. Likewise we often compartmentalise people. When we see someone in an unconnected situation we temporarily misplace them saying, 'I didn't recognise you without your work uniform on.'

People are interested in all sorts of social activities, sports and leisure pastimes. It's OK to be into extreme sports, butterfly collecting or wood carving. It stimulates good conversation, genuine interest and the real life experiences that we all like to talk about.

Good practice: Customer expectations

During consultation with your client, take a little extra time to find out what specific service expectations are required.

1 What aspects of customer service are already delivered?

2 What aspects are omitted? Of these, which would it be feasible to introduce? Would she be happy to pay for these additions?

About the client

Introduction

Customer expectation has never been higher. The latter part of the 1990s and through to the present day have seen a major change in the way that businesses relate and communicate with their customer base. Information Technology is now the driver of successful businesses and dominates the core activities of all business operations, giving companies that competitive edge. This advantage has automated many of the traditional business systems, enabling companies to react faster to a changing environment. However, this technology still remains to make any significant impact on the majority of hairdressing businesses, save the larger chains and groups which account for less than 10 per cent of the sector.

There are two significant factors that underline this strange anomaly. At present, in this transition away from the traditional

Lee Preston

Saks Premier Collection

Colour co-ordination

The other aspect of the subjective analysis has already been addressed by the fashion industry. However, very little information is available in text for hairdressing and recently it has been of particular interest to the colour manufacturers, e.g. Wella, L'Oréal, Matrix, etc. Obviously, these companies benefit from hairdressers' practical procedures involving colour. You too can benefit by understanding more about colour co-ordination, colour psychology and their applications with your customers.

So what is colour co-ordination and how is it applied to hairdressing? Understanding your client's needs and being able to make an informed opinion about a suitable course of action is far more challenging at a higher professional level. It is doubtful that your client has any understanding of the number of variables you must take on board in order to make the right decision and come up with the perfect solution.

People and *art and design* are permanently linked. This is not an 'arty' claim or 'soundbite' but an observation on life. The simplest way that this statement is proven is by the clothes that we wear. We all know that the image we portray is conjured up by the total, visual expression we convey to others. So therefore the *sum total* of our image is made up from a formula of elements or components, each varying in weight and value.

As an art and design aspect, clothes convey colour, shape, form and quality. These are easily changed and a new vision can be created. So outwardly the visual expression is modified for functional or aesthetic reasons. Equally as important is the feeling gained inwardly – the way that clothes can make us feel about ourselves.

Hair styling is one of the elements that makes up the sum total of our image. It differs from clothing because it is a permanent physical aspect of our bodies. It can be changed, managed, looked after or neglected. But other than shaving it off, it is the basis, the starting point, of that visual formula. In order to get colour right, we need to understand some fundamental principles, technical applications and, at a higher level, have the knowledge about why some colours work while others do not. The fundamental principles and techniques are covered in Chapter 5 on colouring (p. 129).

Colour suitability

Colour can be measured by a number of different variables. The amounts of these variables collectively will give an overall effect. These terms are illustrated overleaf in hairdressing perspectives as opposed to the graphic design and print industry.

In the tonal table we see that we have added further dimensions to the fundamental principles of depth and tone. It is illustrated this way to reveal other qualities that we should take on board.

Next we examine the difference between warm tones and cool tones.

Tonal table

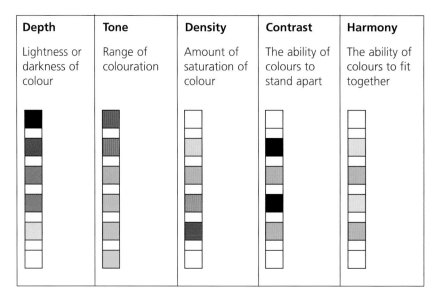

Depth	Tone	Density	Contrast	Harmony
Lightness or darkness of colour	Range of colouration	Amount of saturation of colour	The ability of colours to stand apart	The ability of colours to fit together

Warm and cool tones

From the warm/cool tones above we see that the *warm shade* contains gold/orange tones whereas the *cool shade* is a red/violet. Where we would normally consider red to be a hot shade, we see that certain reds have cool hues. The reason for this is the colour's basic make-up; i.e. a red with an orange or golden yellow base remains warm, whereas a red with a pink or mauve base is cool.

Warm–cool range

Active learning

Warm and cool tones

With another stylist, get out your manufacturer's permanent tint shade chart and together work through the ranges and decide collectively whether each shade is cool or warm. Then summarise and record your findings.

Key skills: Communication

2.1 Take part in discussions

2.2 Produce written materials

2.3 Use images

Structure of hair and skin

Hair

The cross-section taken through the hair lengthways shown in the diagram provides us with a microscopic view of the three specific layers.

The *cuticle* is the outer layer of colourless cells which forms a protective surface to the hair. It regulates the chemicals entering and damaging the hair and protects the hair from excessive heat and drying. The cells overlap like tiles on a roof with the free edges pointing towards the tips of the hair. The amount of layers is proportional to hair texture. Hair with fewer layers of cuticle is finer than coarser hair types which have several layers. Hair in good condition has a cuticle that is tightly closed, limiting the ingress of moisture and chemicals. Conversely, hair that is in a dry or porous condition has damaged or partially missing cuticle layers. One simple indicator of cuticle condition relates to the time taken to blow dry hair. Hair in good condition will dry quickly in proportion to the amount of hair on the head (*density*). The closely packed cuticle allows the drier to chase the water from the hairshaft. Porous hair absorbs moisture and therefore takes far longer to dry and is unfortunately subjected to more heat, which exacerbates the problem.

The *cortex* is the middle and largest layer. It is made up of a long fibrous material which has the appearance of rope. If looked at more closely, each of the fibres is made up of even smaller chains of fibres. The *quality* and condition of these bundles of fibres will determine the hair's strength. The way in which they are *bonded* together has a direct effect upon curl and ability to stretch (*hair elasticity*). It is within this part of the hair that the natural hair colour is distributed. These pigments are diffused throughout the cortex and their colour(s) and rate of distribution determine the colour that we can see. It is also in this layer that both synthetic colours and permanent waves make the permanent chemical changes.

The *medulla* is the central, most inner part of the hair. It only exists in medium to coarser hair types and is often intermittent throughout the length. The medulla does not play any useful part in hairdressing processes and treatments.

Parts of the hair shaft

Hair cuticle   Cortex   Medulla

Capillaries

Umberto Giannini

Chemical properties of hair

The bundles of fibres found in the cortex are made from molecules of *amino acids*. There are about 22 amino acids in hair and the molecules of each contain atoms of elements in different proportions. Overall, the elements in hair are in approximately these proportions:

> **Chemical bonds within the hair:**
> **carbon: 50% hydrogen: 7% nitrogen: 18%**
> **oxygen: 21% sulphur: 4%**

The amino acids combine to form larger molecules, long chains of amino acids called *polypeptides*, or, if they are long enough, *proteins*. One of the most important of these is **keratin**. Keratin is an important component of nails, skin and hair. It is this protein which makes them flexible and elastic. Because of the keratin it contains, hair can be stretched and compressed, curled and waved.

In hair, keratin forms long chains which coil up like springs. They are held in this shape by cross-links between chains. The three kinds of link are *disulphide bridges (sulphur bonds)*, *salt bonds* and *hydrogen bonds*. Salt bonds and hydrogen bonds are relatively weak and easily broken, allowing the springs to be stretched out. This is what happens in curling. The normal, coiled form of keratin is called *alpha-keratin*. When it has been stretched, set and dried it is called *beta-keratin*. The change is only temporary. Once the hair has been made wet or has gradually absorbed moisture from the air, it relaxes back to the alpha state. Disulphide bridges are much stronger but these too can be altered, as in perming.

Cheynes Training

Physical properties of hair

Hair *naturally* contains a certain amount of water that lubricates it, allowing it to stretch and recoil. Hair that is dry and in poor condition is less elastic. Hair is *hygroscopic*; it absorbs water from the surrounding air. How much water is taken up depends on the dryness of the hair and the moistness of the atmosphere. Hair is also *porous*. There are tiny tube-like spaces within the hair structure and the water flows into these by *capillary action*, rather like blotting paper absorbing ink. Drying hair in the ordinary way evaporates only the surface moisture, but drying over long periods or at too high a temperature removes water from within the hair, leaving it brittle and in poor condition. Damaged hair is more porous than healthy hair and easily loses any water, which makes it hard to stretch and mould.

Curled hair returns to its former shape as it takes up water, so the drier the atmosphere, the longer the curl or set lasts. Similarly, curling dry hair is most effective just after the hair has been washed because, although the surface is dry, the hair will have absorbed water internally. Blow-styling and curling with hot irons, heated rollers, hot combs and hot brushes all have similar temporary effects.

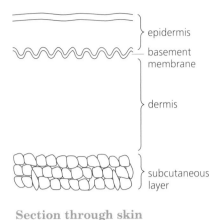

epidermis

basement membrane

dermis

subcutaneous layer

Section through skin

The skin

The skin is the largest organ of the body and if laid flat would cover an area of about 21 square feet. It forms the barrier to a multitude of external forces and is made up of many layers.

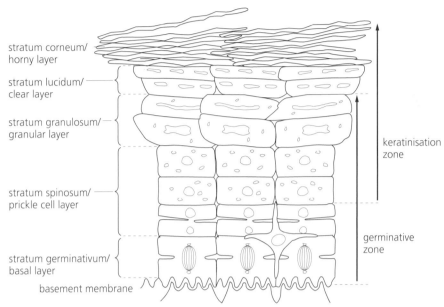

stratum corneum/ horny layer

stratum lucidum/ clear layer

stratum granulosum/ granular layer

keratinisation zone

stratum spinosum/ prickle cell layer

germinative zone

stratum germinativum/ basal layer

basement membrane

The epidermis

The epidermis is the front line of defence. This outer protective layer of the skin is called the *stratum corneum* and is a hard, cornified layer, consisting of 15 to 40 layers of flattened skin cells or corneocytes, which constantly migrate up from deeper regions and fully replace themselves about once a month. The *corneocytes* are filled with keratin and a fatty *lipid* that make a barrier to prevent loss of water through the skin.

Beneath the stratum corneum lie *keratinocytes* which produce keratin and form the building blocks of the epidermis. In the same area, *langerhans cells* scout for invading pathogens while *melanocytes* produce the pigment **melanin** that protects the skin from UV radiation. *Merkel* or nerve cells send messages via the nerve receptors to the brain to register sensation.

The dermis

The dermis is the thickest layer of the skin. It is here that the hair follicle is formed. The dermis is made up of elastic and connective tissue and is well supplied with blood and lymph vessels. The skin receives its nutrient supply from this area. The upper part of the dermis, the *papillary layer*, contains the organs of touch, heat and cold, and pain. The lower part of the dermis, the *reticular layer*, forms a looser network of cells.

Alison Stewart, Glenrothes, Fife

The subcutaneous fat

The subcutaneous fat lies below the dermis. It is also known as the *subcutis*, or occasionally as the *hypodermis*. It is composed of loose cell tissue and contains stores of fat. The base of the hair follicle is situated just above this area, or sometimes in it. Subcutaneous tissue gives roundness to the body and fills the space between the dermis and muscle tissue that may lie below.

The hair follicle

Hair grows from a thin, tube-like space in the skin called a hair follicle.

Cheynes Training

- At the bottom of the follicles are areas well supplied with nerves and blood vessels, which nourish the cellular activity. These are called *hair papillae*.
- Immediately surrounding each papilla is the *germinal matrix* which consists of actively forming hair cells.
- As the new hair cells develop, the lowest part of the hair is shaped into the *hair bulb*.
- The cells continue to take shape and form as they push along the follicle until they appear at the skin surface as *hair fibres*.
- The cells gradually harden and die. The hair is formed of dead tissue. It retains its elasticity due to its chemical structure and keratin content.

Oil glands

The oil gland, or *sebaceous gland*, is situated in the skin and opens out into the upper third of the follicle. Oil or *sebum* is secreted into the follicle and onto the hair and skin surface.

Sebum helps to prevent the skin and hair from drying. By retaining moisture it helps the hair and skin to stay pliable. Sebum is slightly acid – about pH 5.6 – and forms a protective antibacterial covering for the skin.

Sweat glands

The sweat gland lies beside each hair follicle. These are appendages of the skin. They secrete sweat which passes out through the sweat ducts. The ends of these ducts can be seen at the surface of the skin as sweat *pores*. There are two types of sweat gland: the larger, associated closely with the hair follicles, are the **apocrine glands**; the smaller, found over most of the skin's surface, are the *eccrine glands*.

Sweat is mainly water with salt and other minerals. In abnormal conditions sweat contains larger amounts of waste material. Evaporation of sweat cools the skin. The function of sweat, and thus the sweat glands, is to protect the body by helping to maintain the normal temperature.

The hair muscle

The hair muscle, or *arrector pili*, is attached at one end to the hair follicle and at the other to the underlying tissue of the epidermis. When it contracts it pulls the hair and follicle upright. Upright hairs trap a warm layer of air around the skin. The hairs also act as a warning system; for example, you soon notice if an insect crawls over your skin.

Hair growth

Hair is constantly growing. Over a period of between one and six years an individual hair actively grows, then stops, rests, degenerates and finally falls out. Before the hair leaves the follicle, the new hair is normally ready to replace it. If a hair is not replaced then a tiny area of baldness results. The lives of individual hairs vary and are subject to variations in the body. Some are actively growing while others are resting. Hairs on the head are at different stages of growth.

Stages of growth

The life cycle of hair is as follows:

Robin Callender, at McMillan Hair

- **anagen** is the active growing stage of the hair, a period of activity of the papilla and germinal matrix. This stage may last from a few months to several years. It is at this stage of formation at the base of the follicle that the hair's thickness is determined. Hair colour too is formed in the early part of anagen.

- **catagen** is a period when the hair stops growing but cellular activity continues at the papilla. The hair bulb gradually separates from the papilla and moves further up the follicle.

- **telogen** is the final stage, when there is no further growth or activity at the papilla. The follicle begins to shrink and completely separates from the papilla area. This resting stage does not last long. Towards the end of the telogen stage, cells begin to activate in preparation for the new anagen stage of regrowth.

Hair growth stages

The new anagen period involves the hair follicle beginning to grow down again. Vigorous papilla activity generates a new hair at the germinal matrix. At the same time the old hair is slowly making its way up and out of the follicle. Often the old and new hair can be seen at the same time in the follicle.

In some animals most of the hairs follow their life cycle in step, passing through anagen, catagen and telogen together. This results in moulting. Human hair, however, develops at an uneven rate and few follicles shed their hair at the same time. (If all hairs fell at the same time we would have bald periods.)

Hair texture

Individual hair thickness is referred to as hair texture and the main types are:

- very fine hair
- fine hair
- medium hair
- coarse hair

The main differences between the hair textures relate to the number of layers of cuticle.

Indicators of hair in good condition

Moisture levels within the hair are essential for maintaining good condition. We can see the evidence of this moisture from the shine that we associate with great looking hair. 'Bad hair' denotes poor condition and the lack of shine is due to the unevenness of the hair's surface, i.e. the cuticle. A roughened cuticle surface is an indicator of either physical or chemical damage. Each of these states is difficult to correct. In mild cases of dryness, treatments can be applied to improve the hair's manageability and handling. In more serious situations of porous hair, the hair's ability to resist the ingress of chemicals and moisture is severely impaired. There are no long-lasting remedies for this so regular reconditioning treatments must be used.

Properties of good condition hair

- shine and lustre
- smooth outer cuticle surface
- strength and resistance
- good elasticity
- good natural moisture levels

Properties of poor condition hair

- raised or open cuticle
- damaged, torn hair shaft

Remember

Hair texture

The more layers of cuticle that the hair has, the greater its resistance to absorbing moisture and chemicals. Therefore coarse hair in good condition can often take longer to perm than finer hair types.

- split ends
- low strength and resistance
- over-elastic/stretchy
- dry, porous lengths or end

Hair damage
Physical

- harsh or incorrect usage of brushes and/or combs
- excessive heat from styling equipment

Chemical

- hydrogen peroxide levels too strong
- bleaching products
- perm products either too strong or over-processing
- chlorine from swimming pools

Weathering

- excesses of sun and sea salts

Hair and skin tests

To minimise the likelihood of problems arising, there are a number of tests that you can carry out to help diagnose the condition and likely reaction of your client's skin and hair. These tests will assist you to decide what action to take before, during and after the application of hairdressing processes. You will need to record all these results onto the client's record file.

Good practice: Sensitivity test (also known as patch test or skin test)

The sensitivity test is used to assess the reaction of the skin to chemicals or chemical products. In the salon it is mainly used before tinting. Some people are allergic to external contact of chemicals such as PPD (found in permanent tint). This can cause dermatitis or, in more severe cases, permanent scarring of skin tissue and hair loss. Some are allergic to irritants reacting internally, causing asthma and hay fever. Others may be allergic to both internal and external irritants. To find out whether a client's skin reacts to chemicals in permanent tints, the following test should be carried out at least 24 hours prior to the chemical process.

Good practice: Sensitivity test (also known as patch test or skin test) (cont.)

Note: Skin testing is not just for new clients, it has now been found that clients can develop a sensitivity to chemicals through prolonged use of the same or similar products. Therefore periodic testing for adverse reactions is essential and should be carried out routinely from time to time.

1 Mix a little of the tint to be used with the correct amount of hydrogen peroxide – as recommended by the manufacturer.

2 Clean an area of skin about 8mm square behind the ear or in the fold of the arm. Use a little spirit on cotton wool to remove the grease from the skin.

3 Apply a little of the tint mixture to skin.

4 Cover the tint patch with a simple dressing to protect it. Ask your client to report any discomfort or irritation that occurs over the next 24 hours. Arrange to see your client at the end of this time so that you can check for signs of reaction.

5 If there is a *positive response*, i.e. a skin reaction such as inflammation, soreness, swelling, irritation or discomfort, do not carry out the intended service. Never ignore the result of a skin test. If a skin test showed a reaction and you carried on anyway, there may be a more serious reaction which could affect the whole body.

6 If there is a *negative response*, i.e. no reaction to the chemicals, then carry out the treatment as proposed.

Warning: In recent years there have been a growing number of successful personal injury claims made against salons where the necessary precautions have not been taken.

Skin test

Remember: Typical example of chemical incompatibility

Henna is still widely used throughout the world as a hair and skin dyeing compound. In the UK people using natural henna will often add other ingredients such as coffee, wine, lemon juice, etc. to intensify the final colour. However, other countries also add compounds to henna; e.g. India and Turkey sometimes add iron ore deposits which are crushed into the powder to increase the 'reddening' effect. If this mix subsequently comes into contact with hydrogen peroxide (either through tinting or perming), a chemical reaction will take place. In the exchange that takes place permanent damage and breakage will occur.

Robin Callender at McMillan Hair

Strand test

A strand test or hair strand colour test is used to assess the resultant colour on a strand or section of hair after colour has been processed and developed. It is carried out as follows:

1 Most colouring products just require the time recommended by the manufacturer – check their instructions.
2 Rub a strand of hair lightly with the back of a comb to remove the surplus tint.
3 Check whether the colour remaining is evenly distributed throughout the hair's length. If it is even, remove the rest of the tint. If it is uneven, allow processing to continue, if necessary applying more tint. If any of the hair on the head is not being treated, you can compare the evenness of colour in the tinted hair with that in the untinted hair.

Colour test

This test is used to assess the suitability of a chosen colour, the amount of processing time required and the final colour result. Apply the tint or bleaching products you propose to use to a cutting of the client's hair and process as recommended.

Test cutting

In this test a piece of hair cut from the head is processed to check its suitability, the amount of processing required and the timing, before the process is carried out. The test is used for colouring, straightening, relaxing, reducing synthetic colouring, i.e. decolouring, bleaching and incompatibility.

Test curl

This test is made on the hair to determine the lotion suitability, the strength, the curler size, the timing of processing and the development. It is used before perming.

Curl check or test

This test is used to assess the development of curl in the perming process. The test is used periodically throughout a perm and for final assessment of the result.

Peroxide test

This test is made on hair that has been decoloured or stripped of its synthetic colour. The test is used to assess the effectiveness of the process and to check that no synthetic pigment remains. Any synthetic colour remaining will oxidise later and darken again within two or three days. If the hair darkens after testing, remove all the chemicals from the test section, then reapply the decolourant. It may take several applications to strip all of the unwanted colour.

Remember

Sensitivity test and PPD

This test is used to assess the client's tolerance of chemicals introduced to the skin – PPD.

The abbreviation stands for *paraphenylenediamine*, the main ingredient within permanent colour that is a known irritant to skin and eyes and can cause an allergic reaction.

Guillaume Vappereau at Guy Kremer

Incompatibility test

Perm lotions and other chemicals applied to the hair may react with chemicals that have already been used such as home-use products. The incompatibility test is therefore used to detect chemicals/elements which could react with hairdressing processes such as colouring and perming. The test is carried out as follows:

1 Protect your hands by wearing gloves.
2 Place a small cutting of hair in a small dish.
3 Pour into the dish a mixture of 20 parts of 6 per cent hydrogen peroxide and one part ammonium thioglycolate (general purpose perm solution). Make sure that you are not bending over the dish to avoid splashing the chemicals on to your face or inhaling any resultant released fumes.
4 Watch for signs of bubbling, heating or discolouration. These indicate that the hair already contains incompatible chemicals. The hair should not be permed, tinted or bleached if there are any signs of reaction. Perming treatment might discolour or break the hair and could burn the skin.

Elasticity test

This test is carried out on a dry single hair and used to determine how much the hair will stretch and then return to its original position. It is an indicator of the internal condition of the hair's bonded structure and ability to retain moisture. By taking a hair between the fingers and stretching it you can assess the amount of spring it has. If the hair breaks easily, care needs to be taken before applying any hairdressing process and further tests are indicated – a test curl or a test cutting, for example. Natural healthy hair in good condition will be elastic and more likely to retain the effects of physical curling, setting or blow shaping longer. It will also take chemical processes more readily. Hair with little elasticity will not hold physical shaping or chemical processes satisfactorily.

Porosity test

This test is used to assess the ability of the hair to absorb moisture or liquids – another indicator of condition. If the cuticle is torn or broken, it will soon lose its moisture and become dry. It may be able to absorb liquids quicker, but its ability to retain them is reduced. If the cuticle is smooth, unbroken and tightly packed, it may resist the passage of moisture or liquids. By running the fingertips through the hair, from points to roots, you can assess the degree of roughness. The rougher the hair, the more porous it will be and the faster it will absorb chemicals.

Remember: Hair's natural moisture levels

The natural moisture levels in hair play a significant part in the way that hair responds to treatments and styling. If the natural levels can be retained following perming, colouring and bleaching the client's hair will remain manageable, easier to detangle and able to hold thermal styling effects for far longer.

Deplete those natural levels and the hair becomes porous and will tangle easily, is less manageable and not able to hold a set for long. Pre-chemical treatments help to reduce the hair's moisture reduction.

Hair and scalp diseases, conditions and defects

Diseases of the hair and scalp may be caused by a variety of infectious organisms. Signs or symptoms are presented which enable us to recognise them. Initial examination during consultation should be carried out before any hairdressing procedure is applied. If this precaution is not taken, there is a danger of cross-infection where both hairdresser and clients may contract and spread disease. Other hair and scalp conditions or defects may be due to abnormal formation or the result of a variety of chemical and physical causes. They are not infectious.

 ## *Infectious diseases*

Bacterial diseases

Condition	Symptoms	Cause	Treatment	Infectious
Folliculitis Inflammation of the hair follicles	Inflamed follicles, a common symptom of certain skin diseases	A contact bacterial infection, or due to chemical or physical action	Medical referral	Yes
Impetigo A bacterial infection of the upper skin layers	At first a burning sensation, followed by spots becoming dry; honey-coloured, crusts form and spread	A staphylococcal or streptococcal infection	Medical referral	Yes
Sycosis A bacterial infection of the hairy parts of the face	Small, yellow spots around the follicle mouth, burning, irritation and general inflammation	Bacteria attack the upper part of the hair follicle, spreading to the lower follicle	Medical referral	Yes
Furunculosis Boils or abscesses	Raised, inflamed, pus-filled spots, irritation, swelling and pain	An infection of the hair follicles by staphylococcal bacteria	Medical referral	Yes

Impetigo

Sycosis

Furunculosis

Viral diseases

Condition	Symptoms	Cause	Treatment	Infectious
Herpes simplex (cold sore) A viral infection of the skin	Burning, irritation, swelling and inflammation precede the appearance of fluid-filled blisters, usually on the lips and surrounding areas	Possibly exposure to extreme heat or cold, or a reaction to food or drugs; the skin may carry the virus for years without exhibiting any symptoms	Medical referral	Yes
Warts (verrucae) A viral infection of the skin	Raised, roughened skin, often brown or discoloured. There may be irritation and soreness. Warts are common on the hands and face	The lower epidermis is attacked by the virus, which causes the skin to harden and skin cells to multiply	Medical referral	Yes

Herpes simplex

Warts

Animal (parasitic) infestations

Condition	Symptoms	Cause	Treatment	Infectious
Head lice (pediculosis capitis) Infestation of the hair and scalp by head lice	An itchy reaction to the biting head louse, 'peppering' on pillowcases and minute egg cases (nits) attached to the upper hair shaft close to the scalp	The head louse bites the scalp feeding on the victim's blood. Breeding produces eggs, which are laid and cemented onto the hair shaft for incubation until the immature louse emerges	Referral to a pharmacist	Yes

Condition	Symptoms	Cause	Treatment	Infectious
Scabies An allergic reaction to the itch mite	A rash in the skin folds around the midriff and on the inside of the thighs, extremely itchy at night	The itch mite burrows under the skin where it lays eggs	Medical referral	Yes

A head louse

A louse egg (nit)

Fungal diseases

Condition	Symptoms	Cause	Treatment	Infectious
Tinea capitis Ringworm of the head	Circular bald patch of grey or whitish skin surrounded by red, active rings; hairs broken close to the skin, which looks dull and rough. The fungus lives off the keratin in the skin and hair. This disease is common in children	Fungal infection of the skin or hair	Medical referral	Yes

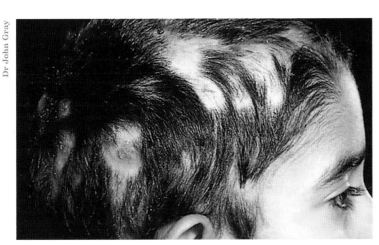

Tinea capitis

Non-infectious diseases

Conditions of the hair and skin

Condition	Symptoms	Cause	Treatment	Infectious
Acne Disorder affecting the hair follicles and sebaceous glands	Raised spots and bumps within the skin, commonly upon the face in adolescents	Increased sebum and other secretions block the follicle and a skin reaction occurs	Medical treatment required	No
Eczema and dermatitis In its simplest form a reddening of the skin	Ranging from slightly inflamed areas of the skin to severe splitting and weeping areas with irritation and soreness	Many possible causes, eczema often associated with internal factors, i.e. allergies or stress. Dermatitis a reaction or allergy to external factors	Medical treatment required	No
Psoriasis An inflamed, abnormal thickening of the skin	Areas of thickened skin, often raised and patchy. Often on the scalp and also at the joints (arms and legs)	Unknown	Medical treatment required	No

Acne

Eczema

Psoriasis

Conditions of the hair and skin

Condition	Symptoms	Cause	Treatment	Infectious
Dandruff (Pityriasis capitis) Dry scaling scalp	Dry, small, irritating flakes of skin. If moist and greasy it sticks to the skin and the condition *scurf* results	Fungal (yeast-like) infection, or physical or chemical irritants	Anti-dandruff treatments	No
Seborrhea Excessive greasiness of the skin exuding on to the hair	Very greasy, lank hair and greasy skin, making styling difficult	Over-production of sebum	Astringent shampoos	No

Alopecia (hair loss)

Condition	Description	Treatment
Alopecia areata	The name given to balding patches over the scalp. Often starts around or above the ears, circular in pattern ranging from 1–2.5cm in diameter	Trichological referral
Traction alopecia	Hair loss as a result of excessive pulling at the roots from brushing, curling and straightening. Very often seen with younger girls tying, plaiting or braiding long hair	None
Alopecia totalis	Complete hair loss sometimes as a result of alopecia areata spreading and joining up across the scalp	Trichological referral
Cicatrical alopecia	Baldness due to scarring of the skin arising from chemical or physical injury. The hair follicle is damaged and permanent baldness results	
Male pattern alopecia	Male baldness or thinning of hair occurring in teens or early 20s. Hair recedes at the hairline or loss at the crown area. Condition is hereditary (passed on in families)	Remedies currently being developed

Dr A L Wright

Alopecia areata

Defects of the hair

Condition	Symptom	Cause	Treatment
Split ends (fragilitas crinium) Fragile, poorly conditioned hair	Dry, splitting hair ends	Harsh physical or chemical treatments	Cutting off or special treatment conditioners
Monilethrix Beaded hair	Beadlike swellings along the hair shaft, hair often breaks at weaker points	Irregular development of the hair forming during cellular production	None

Condition	Symptom	Cause	Treatment
Trichorrhexis nodosa Nodules forming on the hair shaft	Areas of swelling at locations along the hair shaft, splitting and rupturing the cuticle layer	Harsh physical or chemical processing	None, although cutting and conditioning may help
Sebaceous cyst Swelling of the oil gland	Bumps, lumps and swellings on the scalp containing fluid, soft to the touch	Sebaceous gland becomes blocked allowing a build-up of fluid to take place	Medical referral
Damaged cuticle Broken, split, torn hair	Rough, raised, missing areas of cuticle; hair loses its moisture and becomes dry and porous	Harsh physical or chemical processes	None, although cutting and conditioning may help

Fragilitis crinium

Damaged hair

Monilethrix

Trichorrhexis nodosa

Damaged hair cuticle

The client's influencing features and factors

The aim of consultation is to arrive at a suitable hairstyle or hair colour which is pleasing to the client. It should be done in a way that gives the client confidence in both the salon and in you. The process should be inspiring.

It is necessary to study the 'complete picture' when you first meet the client. This is to make sure that you have enough information to advise her properly. Your aim is not to alter what the client wears or her self-image, but to harmonise with these to achieve satisfaction. Consider all the aspects of the client's existing image and ask yourself what your impression is. Is there anything that doesn't work? Is the client happy with the existing style? She may point to areas which you feel are wrong or unnecessary, so you need to be able to express your technical appraisal in a clear, simple way without any ambiguity. The use of technical jargon and trade terms will only lead to confusion or misrepresentation.

Consultation is customised for the client. It is personal and individual on each and every occasion. We therefore have to consider technical and personal image aspects:

- cutting and final shape of the hair
- volume or colour which will enhance the style
- finishing options of blow drying or dressing the hair
- hair type, hair growth, natural colour and face shape
- her personal image, lifestyle and personality
- amount of time she can give to her hair

Expression

Facial expression is an important part of communication. Even if your client looks disgruntled or is scowling, you will need to use a friendly, pleasant expression to encourage her to relax. Facial expression reflects the client's mood or how she is feeling. You need to pick up on these expressions and react to them appropriately. This will help to understand the client's wants and needs more easily.

Hair and hair growth patterns

Hair is the frame for the face. The length, quantity, quality and texture of the hair all contribute to the total image. Fine hair often lacks body; most clients want fullness and volume which will last. Cutting methods to achieve this include volumising techniques where body can be created by using longer layers levelled in line with the client's baselines and face shape. You should also consider proportioning the hair weight. By setting hair or using light perms, you can create bulk and volume which give foundation to shape and style.

Hair fashion is constantly changing and the client who wears a hairstyle which is of the moment wants to give the impression of being in touch with trends. Sometimes clients want up-to-the-minute hairstyles to keep a youthful image or to make themselves feel confident. Others will often choose a particular image that complements their career and lifestyle. Television presenters, solicitors and newscasters may go for fashionable but *classic* looks. Models will display the current themes. Those in artistic careers may choose *dramatic* styles.

Good practice

- Always make and maintain eye contact with your client.
- Be aware of your client's expressions and react appropriately.

Good practice

- Look at the amount and quality of your client's hair.
- Remember that clients with fine hair want volume.
- Look at the proportion, partings and distribution of the hair.
- How much natural movement has the hair got? Will it impede the styling plan?
- Are there any strong growth patterns to contend with?

Double crown

Cowlick

Nape whorls

Widow's peak

Growth patterns

The hair's **movement** refers to the amount of curl or wave within the hair lengths. However, its growth pattern denotes the direction from which it protrudes from the scalp. Natural hair fall can be seen on wet and dry hair and strong directional growth will have a major impact on the lie of the hair when it is styled. So it is essential that it is taken into account during consultation.

double crown – the client with a double crown will benefit from leaving sufficient length in the hair to overfall the whole area. If it is cut too short, the hair will stick up and will not lie flat.

nape whorl – a nape whorl can occur at either or both sides of the nape. It can make the hair difficult to cut into a straight neckline or tight 'head-hugging' graduations. Often the hair naturally forms a V-shape. Tapered neckline shapes may be more suitable, but sometimes the hair is best left long so that the weight of the hair overfalls the nape whorl directions

cowlick – a cowlick appears at the hairline at the front of the head. It makes cutting a straight fringe difficult, particularly on fine hair, because the hair often forms a natural parting. The strong movement can often be improved by moving the parting over so that the weight overfalls the growth pattern. Sometimes a fringe can be achieved by leaving the layers longer so that they weigh down the hair.

widow's peak – the widow's peak growth pattern appears at the centre of the front hairline. The hair grows upward and forward, forming a strong peak. It is often better to cut the hair into styles that are dressed back from the face, as any 'light fringes' will be likely to separate and stick up.

Face and head shape

The basic, natural shape of the head, face and features are what form the underlying structure in styling. The proportions of the hair mass and distribution in relation to the face and head are vital in choosing a style. The outer hair shape should fit the face shape to achieve a suitable hair arrangement.

The contours of the head are its focal points. Those on the side of the head are formed by the parietal and temporal bones. Those on the back of the head and nape are formed by the **occipital** bones, which can be **concave** or **convex**: curving inwards or outwards. The frontal bone forms the forehead shape. It is the beginning of the profile, which follows along the nose to the lips and chin. This can vary in shape and may be concave or convex.

The face shape is made up of straight or curved lines, and sometimes a mixture of the two. Straight, fine shapes appear angular and chiselled or firm and solid. They can be triangular, rectangular, square or diamond shaped. Curved line shapes appear soft and may be round, oval, pear shaped or oblong. Shapes which have some straight and some curved lines are defined as heart shaped or soft square shaped.

Remember

Head shapes can have a major impact on the final profile of the style you are attempting to create. For example, a flatter crown or back of the head is made more noticeable when a contoured, layered cut is selected as the chosen hairstyle.

To create a pleasant balance, the hairstyle and face shape need to be compatible. An angular hair cut will not suit a soft, rounded face. A soft hair shape will not complement a chiselled face. Hair shape outlines can be made to look quite different from the front by simply changing a parting from side to centre. Side partings tend to make the face appear wider, whilst centre partings close down the width of a wide forehead.

An oval face shape suits any hair style. Round faces need height to reduce the width of the face. A centre parting can also help to reduce width. Long facial proportions are improved with short, wider hairstyles. Square-shaped faces need round shapes with texture on to the face to soften them. Longer lengths beyond the jaw line improve the balance and proportion.

Ears, nose and mouth

Often ears are out of balance, which can affect the cut if you use them as a guide. Generally, large ears or even large lobes are accentuated by hair cut short or dressed away from the face. It is often better to leave hair longer over the ears unless it is an essential part of the style's impact.

Your client may wear a hearing aid and this may be a sensitive issue. Some clients wish to have all signs of an aid hidden, but others do not mind and even display it. You should discuss this with your client carefully and with sensitivity; she may feel too embarrassed to bring up the subject herself. The size of the aid will need careful consideration when completing the total image.

The position, shape, size and colour of the nose and mouth are very important in the facial expression. The angles that are created can be softening or harsh and must not be ignored when the image is being planned. Hair shape and make-up can contribute to create the required effect.

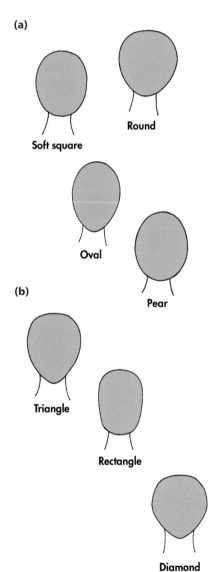

Face shapes
(a) Soft
(b) Straight or cornered

Remember: Facial features

- What is the shape, position and size of the client's ears?
- What is the shape and size of the client's nose and mouth?
- Are these features a major concern to your client?
- What shape is your client's facial and head shape?
- Are there any significant features that need to be accounted for?
- Small faces need 'opening up' while larger faces need narrower framing effects.

Make-up

Make-up can enhance features, define eyes and mask or disguise features or blemishes. How the client uses make-up may give a clue to her personality, dress sense and style. In business, a well made-up person is seen to be finished, groomed and in control. Without make-up a person may appear to be 'off duty' or as if she has not made an effort.

Lipstick reflects the colour depth of the skin and eyes, creates light on the face and defines the lips. Shiny lipstick is most suitable for someone with a glitzy image. Matt lipstick is more suitable for the quieter person, or when a natural look is required. Lip balm or gloss looks natural and keeps lips soft.

Make-up can create a range of images: soft and kind; bold and extrovert. It can make people feel different about their appearance and so boost confidence if it is properly applied.

Eyes

We already know the importance of maintaining eye contact when communicating with the client, showing that you are listening to each other. But eyes play a major part in the selection of hairstyles too. Heavy fringes can accentuate and frame or they can obstruct vision.

Eye colour is a guide to the natural colouring of the client. This is a useful pointer when choosing hair colour. Eye shape is another element to be considered when choosing which style to create. Ideally, eye, head and face shape should all be complemented by the hairstyle and colour.

The eyebrows frame the eyes. Their shape, size and colour are all significant. A very harsh appearance is created if the eyebrows are removed and various other effects are created by adding shapely lines. Eyelash and brow tinting help to balance facial effects and give the eyes more definition.

Spectacles should be considered when you are deciding on a hairstyle. Frame and lens colour, size and shape have a major impact upon styling and therefore must be taken into account.

Neck and shoulders

The length, fullness and width of the neck will affect the fall of the back and nape hair. Longer necks allow better positioning of long hair. They are complemented by high, neat lines; for example, mandarin collars or polo-neck tops. Short necks need to be uncluttered, with short hair and low collars. Long and thin necks are more noticeable with short styles and will therefore be better suited to longer hair around them. Shorter necks can be counterbalanced with height or upswept hair styles.

Body shape

The body shape also needs to be considered. You need to carefully balance the amount, density and overall shape of the hair to your client's physical body shape. This is particularly important if your client considers her shape or size a particularly important factor. For example, a small, clinging hairstyle would look wrong on a large body shape.

Lifestyle, personality and age

Remember that people are constrained by what they do for a living or what they like to do in their spare time. Usually, people who work in environments where they have face-to-face contact with clients have to be more particular about the image they portray. This is a very important factor in style selection.

From a leisure point of view, you should consider whether the client does a lot of sport or exercise. If so, the hairstyle will have to be versatile and able to withstand a lot of washing. Also, think about how the style could be handled to create a number of different effects when the client is going out. If you are styling for a special occasion, it is worth asking what dress will be worn. A beautiful gown needs to be accompanied by an elegant hairstyle. However, this style will need to be altered for normal wear.

- Many clients want practical and manageable styles for work.
- Nurses, doctors and caterers, among others, may require styles which keep the hair off the face, or they may have to wear face and head coverings at work.
- Dancers, athletes and skaters, among others, need hairstyles which will not get in their eyes and obscure their vision.
- Fashion models may require elaborate styles for special photographic or modelling sessions or displays.

Character and personality can often override physical features when you are choosing a style for your client. A self-confident client will be able to wear looks that a self-conscious client cannot. Make sure you take this into account so that mistakes are not made. Is your client confident and outgoing or shy, timid and retiring, not wishing to stand out in a crowd? Is she professional and businesslike?

And what age group does your client fall in to? There are basic rules that apply to people at certain ages:

children – simple, practical shapes

teenager – something slightly different, especially from older styles, fashionable

young married – something suitable for work, attractive styles

parents – practical and attractive styles, often shorter styles

middle aged – softening shapes to disguise wrinkles

senior age – softening shapes

young businessmen – fashionable cuts

older men – simple, practical styles

You should note this, but remember we live in a community that is progressive, which can throw off convention and which welcomes visual change.

Manageability

Different styles need different amounts of commitment from the client once she leaves the salon. You need to take these factors on board when consulting with the client to make sure that she will carry on being happy with the style you both choose until it is time for her next visit.

Using visual aids in consultation

Pictures

'A picture paints a thousand words' – the term is a cliché but very true. There are many forms of communication and most of them are covered one way or another within the consultation process. We have already stressed the importance of **body language**, the unspoken form of communication that implies much about ourselves and other people.

We know how to speak with clients, we know what to ask and what not to ask. We listen, hear and confirm back to the client. The whole discussion forms a naturally developing contract, an obligation that will be performed, so it is vitally important that we summarise and agree throughout the whole process.

This natural form of check and recheck enables you to move forward. It covers each feature and factor bit by bit. The same feelings are felt by the client. By covering and confirming each aspect, you convey professionalism and competence, which ultimately concludes with you gaining the client's trust.

'Hairdressers don't like clients taking in pictures' – we've all heard that one and it's rubbish too. As hairdressers we needn't develop a complex about it though; it is simply one of those fallacies that clients have. It is a psychological thing; in order for clients to feel more comfortable they say this about hairdressers as it covers a little bit of their embarrassment.

Pictures are an immensely important visual aid and another form of language that hairdressers understand very well. One reason for this is their understanding of visual/spatial imagery. However, there is a vast difference between what the client sees in a photo and what the hairdresser will see.

A client brings in this photo as an example for her own hairstyle. What aspects of this image does she find appealing? What is the client deriving from the image?

Hair by Anne McCuigan. Photograph by John Rawson

- mood
- attitude
- sex appeal
- colour contrasts
- fun 'clubbin' hairstyle
- perimeter shape

What do you, as the hairdresser, see?

- a textured, above the shoulder length bob
- no fringe
- unrealistic hair across the face
- false inference of hair colour produced by photographic lighting
- limited flexibility for work/social wear

From this example you can see that great images convey a lot more than hairstyles. We don't expect the client to understand the technical aspects of the style. She doesn't. She is buying into an ambience. You see something with a trained eye that is quite different. Yes we all find good imagery stimulating, but as hairdressers we are trained to strip off those veneers in order to make sense of what we are seeing.

From a handful of aspects in the client's column, way down the list is the reason for coming to the salon. In identifying this we certainly don't want to devalue our profession. It is simply an example of our client's expectation. She may be wanting to change many things in her life. We can only focus on one, for which we want to benefit commercially. However this visual aid is very useful. It provides the basis, the fundamental roots, from which constructive conversation will bloom.

Colour charts

Colour charts are extremely useful for hairdressers. We rely on them every day. However, they are not always a very helpful medium for the client. We tend to treat others as we would want to be treated ourselves. This is a good philosophy, but there are times when our expectation of others is a little over-optimistic. Generally speaking, clients have very little ability for self-visualisation. This could be confirmed another way. Think about shopping. How often do women shop in pairs? Other people's comments, assistance and points of view are very important. The reason is obvious. If we need more reassurance about what we are doing we have to involve someone else; ideally someone else who knows us, our likes and dislikes, and most important of all someone who can objectively comment about our decision-making process.

The colour chart is a useful tool for hairdressers and a nice colouring book for clients. Unless you can help the client visualise the amount, intensity, density and saturation of the resultant colour, the visual aid will have little or no impact on the decision-making process of whether to buy colour or not.

Computer-generated images

The internet is a valuable medium for conveying information about hair and hairstyles. Many salons have their own websites. The ease of using computer-generated images and uploading them to salon sites is proving a very cost effective advertising medium. However, there is very little information technology used for graphical purposes within salons. Although many software packages are available for generating makeover effects, very little use is made of this medium at present. The constraints of cost, training and operator time are still barriers to salons that want to harness this technology.

After the consultation

Style or service selection

You and the client will select the required style or service together. To avoid disappointment, you must ensure that she knows exactly what is entailed, what it will cost and how long it will take. Remember, the purpose of consultation is to create a commercial opportunity.

Good practice: Consultation checklist

- ☑ Listen carefully to what is requested
- ☑ Use visual aids to assist the consultation process
- ☑ Communicate the possible effects
- ☑ Explain why certain effects are not possible
- ☑ Give good reasons for suggested actions
- ☑ Ensure that the client understands what is being said
- ☑ Agree on a final and suitable course of action
- ☑ Assure and reassure throughout
- ☑ Make it clear if follow-up appointments are necessary
- ☑ Carry out the agreed service or treatment
- ☑ Encourage the client to rebook the next visit before she leaves
- ☑ Maintain the client's goodwill and safety throughout the appointment
- ☑ Record the details for future reference

Promoting the business further

The services and treatments that a salon provides to its clients form the basis of the business functions. This particular business model is built on two specific factors:

- maintaining client satisfaction
- retaining client loyalty

For the majority of all salons these two factors are directly linked and are therefore essential for a business to succeed. It is possible to make a really good job of satisfying our clients, but unless they return within a reasonable time scale their annual contribution to the salon will be drastically reduced. So we need to stimulate the client's loyalty by encouraging them to:

- return on a regular basis
- buy into other services, products and treatments
- share their experiences with their family, friends and work associates

We should bear in mind that the bond built between client and stylist is purely a business arrangement. Hairdressing may be a very social occupation but the clients are not your friends. Businesses exist by charging the highest prices that their customers will afford. We leave the marketing to the employer or his agents, as they will have already targeted a *specific profile* for the types of customer that the business will serve. So how do we serve that target group? We serve them by selling:

- ourselves
- hairdressing services and treatments
- retail
- salon image

Selling ourselves

Contrary to popular belief, good communication far outweighs technical excellence for a busy, popular stylist. So you don't have to be a brilliant hairdresser to do well. Hairdressing is changing very quickly and not just by fashions and trends. *Customers expect more.* They have a right to anyway. People's opinions in respect to *accountability*, *responsibility* and *recourse* have changed greatly in the last few years. People have learned not to take second best or let corporations push them around. Therefore competition between companies is fierce. Our customers want us to be able to shoulder these aspects and the quicker they find that these are not only on offer but *actively* demonstrated, the faster respect and loyalty will develop.

Good customer service is customer focused. It is centralised upon the needs of the client and reflected in all the features involved within routine salon operations: telephone response time, meeting and greeting, refreshments and magazines, visually pleasing interiors and polite and friendly staff. Why do clients come to our salon? To have their hair improved – this part is obvious. Beyond this they want to feel better emotionally, they want to be uplifted. So in order to feel better they need to look good, and that's where you come in. Have you ever considered what the client undergoes before you start the service? Your client's hair is vitally important to her and she is passing on the stewardship to you – a safe pair of hands!

Services and treatments

The clients that are recommended to us form a particularly special group. They have found us through the network of already satisfied customers. The product of our work, the way in which we communicate and our personality have all preceded us. Our satisfied customers feel confident enough in our expertise to promote us to their friends and colleagues.

If recommendation is such a powerful channel of communication, why don't we use it more? Well we can. The perfect time to talk about the variety of services and treatments available to clients is when they are in the chair in front of us. Recommendation is the simplest way of extending the range of services to our clients and enhancing the professional relationship.

Excellent communicators are good listeners, they understand how to ask the right questions and listen effectively to responses, building on the information given to them.

Retail

How well do you sell?

As Britain's largest and oldest trading activity, retailing should be easy. If it were there would be more millionaires around and fewer cracks about pushy salesmen ('so many doors slammed in their faces they've all got flat noses and turned up toes'). But the plain truth is that while more than a million businesses carry out some form of retailing, only about one retail worker in twenty has received adequate training.

In hairdressing, fierce competition and the rise of professional home haircare products have meant that retailing is no longer a neglected area. Innovative stylists, salons and suppliers have led this important turnaround.

Good practice: Good selling

- Listening, asking questions, showing interest
- Using the client's name
- Empathising (putting yourself in the client's place), establishing a bond
- Recognising non-verbal cues (dilated pupils = 'I approve'; ear-rubbing = 'I've heard enough')
- Identifying needs; helping clients reach buying decisions
- Knowing your products/services
- Highlighting the results or user benefits; demonstrating these where possible
- Thinking positively, talking persuasively, projecting confidence and enthusiasm

Standardising the way in which clients are handled before any service or treatment is carried out will eliminate many of the pitfalls encountered in providing public service. This can be done by implementing a full pre-treatment consultation program within the salon.

reservations once again. Consult with the manager or salon owner before proceeding if the customer insists this is the service they want.

Ask the client medical and lifestyle questions pertinent to the treatment they want. If the hair style requires a maintenance regime, brief them thoroughly. Make sure they know exactly what they are letting themselves in for. Some salons give clients a questionnaire, which is not only useful to glean information, but can also help defend any subsequent actions by the client.

If in doubt, leave it out

No one likes to turn down business, but if you think a client will leave the salon looking like a 'bad hair day' you could say something like: 'In my professional opinion, I am convinced that this style will not suit you. Another hairdresser may well do it for you, but I want you to be a regular client and I would like you to leave this salon feeling happy. Please be guided by my expertise.' Then suggest alternatives. The client will trust you and respect you for it.

Complaint summary

If the final effects are not what was thought to have been agreed, or not what was expected, the client will have due reasons for complaint. Use the following checklist as a guide.

- Listen carefully to the client's complaint.
- Resolve the problem immediately or as soon as possible.
- Do not allow the disagreement to affect the salon environment and act sensibly and with decorum at all times.
- Record the complaint.
- Refer to senior staff if necessary.
- Refer to the management so that they can inform the insurers if necessary.
- If the client is not happy, she may want to take legal action. This must be dealt with by the management.

Active learning: Handling complaints

Discuss with your fellow staff members how different client complaints could be handled. Then as a group activity 'act out' the four different scenarios in a role play.

Key skills: Communication

2.1 Take part in discussions

2.4 Read and respond to written material

Self-test section

Quick quiz: a selection of different types of questions to check your knowledge

Q1   The three stages of hair growth are anagen, ... and telogen.   Fill in the blank

Q2   The cortex is the outermost layer of the hair.   True or False

Q3   Select all that apply. Which of the following are infectious diseases?   Multi-selection

Impetigo	☐	1
Scalp ringworm	☐	2
Alopecia	☐	3
Head lice	☐	4
Psoriasis	☐	5
Eczema	☐	6

Q4   The natural colour of hair depends on the amount of melanin within it.   True or False

Q5   Which of the following is commonly known as split ends?   Multi-choice

Trichorrhexis nodosa	☐	a
Monilethrix	☐	b
Tinea capitis	☐	c
Fragilitas crinium	☐	d

Q6   Dandruff is a condition of the scalp usually caused by fungal infection.   True or False

Q7   Which of the following tests are carried out *during* technical services?   Multi-selection

Skin test	☐	1
Strand test	☐	2
Curl test	☐	3
Incompatibility test	☐	4
Porosity test	☐	5
Test cutting	☐	6

Q8   The lower layers of the skin are called the ....   Fill in the blank

Q9   Which face shape suits most hairstyles and lengths?   Multi-choice

Square	☐	a
Oblong	☐	b
Oval	☐	c
Triangular	☐	d

Q10   During consultation and hair analysis, a contra-indication will not allow the planned service to be carried out.   True or False

Colour depth and tone

This tonal lightened effect is created by colouring horizontal sections, gradually changing from darker underneath to lightest on the surface.

Step-by-step guidance

1 The profile section is taken from crown to nape area

2 A vertical section is taken down the centre of the back. The hair is pulled out at 90° from the back of the head using a pivot section. Then point cut a square line parallel to sections

3 Use the back section as a guide and follow it through to the sides taking vertical sections

4 Find the natural parting and direct hair forward at approximately 45° at a low elevation

5 Blow-dry the hair with a Denman brush. Personalise haircut by point cutting the perimeter

6 When the hair is dry point cut the fringe to desired length

Gabriella

Essensuals: Sacha Mascolo-Tarbuck

Shape and form

The volumised, tousled effect is wonderfully balanced and in proportion to the model's natural image and features.

Applied techniques

The techniques applied in this finished effect combine clubbing, graduation and texturising, particularly pointing and chipping in. The voluminous crown and top areas have been initially clubbed and blended into graduated layering at the nape and sides. Perimeter outlines have been softened using texturising techniques. Pointing has been used in the perimeter shape and chipping in provides lift in the internal style structure.

Apparent texture

The feel that radiates from the image is due to the contrast of the areas of smooth and chunky hair. The resultant effect is created by the application of product and cutting.

Movement and direction

The naturally 'bodied' hair has been given gentle movement throughout the shape.

Colour

Texturising colour has been achieved by pre-colouring before cutting and layering alternating chocolate brown with chestnut throughout the top.

Step-by-step guidance

1 A wide profile section is taken from the recession area to behind the crown

2 Vertical sections are taken from the crown to the nape. Then the hair is directed up at 90° and deep point cut vertically. Use this as your guide and work to high point of the ear

3 Side areas overdirected back to your guide behind the ear

4 The horizontal section pattern is taken through the top and point cut to follow the head shape

5 The hair is overdirected back and point cut

6 The front is overdirected back to the last section behind the ear. Finally personalise the front to suit

Irene

Shape and form

The fullness of the shape counterbalances the lines of the features of the head, particularly enhancing the focal point of the eyes within this romantic image.

Lines and angles

The lines of the chin and face merge with the movement, line and direction of the hair shape.

Colour depth and tone

The lightened tresses fully complement the line and direction of the hairstyle. The colour chosen for the low-lighting technique blends subtly with the darker hair and fair skin complexion. The range of cooler tones blends well together.

Condition

The 'fluffiness' of the hair is diminished by a final application of wax.

Step-by-step guidance

1 Blow-dry the hair straight and divide with a centre parting

2 Disconnect the front area working a diagonal section from the centre parting to the high point of the ear

3 Take a profile line which is a section about an inch wide from front to back. Pull the hair straight up and cut by slicing

4 Pull the hair up at 90° from the top of the head. Then cut a square line by slicing

5 Personalise by channel cutting into the base line and slice cutting the front

Katie

Essensuals: Sacha Mascolo-Tarbuck

Shape and form

This contemporary classic provides a new slant to a familiar 'one length' at the shoulder effect.

Lines and angles

The compounded angles of shorter collar length at the back 'diconnecting' to a reverse graduation across the shoulders and down longer to the front provide an exciting option for longer hair. An asymmetric fringe and side part complete the overall effect.

Dimensions distribution and abundance

The hair at the front sides, i.e. above the ears, must be densely populated to provide a full and complete side section of hair. The fringe and frontal area have been left deliberately long to give a demure look.

Colour depth and tone

This particular effect has been created by panelled colour techniques. The apparent contrast between light and dark hair, although subtle in appearance, has been achieved by using at least three colours within each mesh of hair taken. The ranges within each section vary from lighter at the ends to darker nearer the root. The effect is an illusion of light chestnut on a dark toffee base.

Step-by-step guidance

1 Section the crown to the high point of the ear

2 Make a diagonal forward sectioning pattern bringing all the sections down through the comb. Then cut the line parallel to the section pattern

3 Slice cut from the back to front to blend the disconnection, pulling the hair down to the natural fall

4 Personalise by pulling hair down to natural fall and slicing

5 The fringe is pulled forward and sliced asymmetrically

Cutting and styling

As you become more skilled in styling hair, you must remember that your work still rests on the accurate application of fundamental techniques, as well as on the more advanced ones you are now learning. Level 3 work is a continual process of building on experience. Fashion styling can now be attempted, but as always the following points must be considered:

- client communication
- determining baselines
- cutting tools and effects required
- methodical cutting
- cutting accuracy and checks
- client care
- health and safety

Communication with the client is an essential prerequisite to style cutting. In discussion with the client before any work takes place, you can determine what the client requires and thus what you need to do. You need to understand your client fully and negotiate with her throughout the service.

Be sure to listen to your client's requests. Many mistakes can be avoided at this stage if you achieve a clear understanding of what the client is asking for. The hair cutting style that you choose with your client should take into account each of the following points:

- the face and head shape
- face, head and body features
- what is appropriate to a given dress and occasion
- the quality and quantity of hair
- the client's age
- the hair's growth, position and proportion

These factors are discussed in more detail in Chapter 2.

Cutting baselines

It will be necessary to agree with your client the baselines to be cut. A **baseline** is a cut section of hair which is used as a cutting guide for the following sections of hair. There may be one or more baselines cut: for example, a graduated nape baseline may be cut; another may be cut into the middle of the hair at the back of the head. Other baselines may be cut at the sides and the front of the head. The baselines will determine the perimeter of the hairstyle, or part of the style, and may take different shapes according to the effects required:

- **Symmetric** – the baseline for evenly balanced hair shapes in which the hair is equally divided on both sides of the head. Examples are hairstyles with central partings or with the hair swept backwards or forwards.

Charlie Taylor

Charlie Taylor

Robin Callender at McMillan Hair

Symmetrical hairstyle

Vidal Sassoon

Side perimeter shape

Vidal Sassoon

Back perimeter outline

Robin Callender at McMillan Hair

Asymmetry

- **Asymmetric** – the baseline to be used where the hair is unevenly balanced, for example, where there is a side parting and a larger volume of hair on one side of the head, or where the hair is swept off the face at one side with fullness of volume on the other.
- **Concave** – the baseline may be cut curving inwards or downwards. The nape baseline, for example, may curve downwards.
- **Convex** – baseline may be cut curving upwards and outwards; the nape baseline, for instance, may be cut curving upwards.
- **Straight** – the baseline may be cut straight across, for example, where you wish to produce a hard, square effect.

Cutting tools

The choice of cutting tools is an individual one. It is important to select those that will enable you to achieve the specific effect that you want and to know what is required for the style or design that you are working on.

You must be able to control the cutting tool you select. It must be comfortable to hold and not too large to handle skilfully. The cutting edges must be sharp or the hair will be torn and broken. Loose hair can be used to test the sharpness of scissor edges. If the blades cut cleanly, they are sharp enough; if the hair is bent or dragged during cutting they are unacceptable.

Scissors

Scissors may be used to produce a variety of effects. Many scissors have serrated (saw-like) edges. If the serrations are small and fine, the scissors remove a small amount of hair with each cut. If they are large and coarse, the scissors remove a large amount of hair with each cut. Thinning scissors are designed to produce variation in the lengths in a section of hair; this gives tapered, thinned or texturised effects.

Cutting techniques reduce the length of some of the hairs in the section. The more hair is removed, the more severe the effect of the cutting. The weight of the hair tends to straighten it, so the more you remove, especially towards the point ends of the hair section, the more the hair will tend to curl.

When you are tapering or thinning hair, remember not to remove hair lower (closer to the head) than the middle third of the hair section unless you intend to produce a drastic effect. For most style cutting, tapering and texturising is kept to the point third of the hair section (that is, the third furthest from the head). When thinning, it is usually the middle of the hair section where most hair is removed.

Scissors are also used to produce clubbed effects – blunted ends of the hair sections. This technique retains the full weight of the hair at the ends. Non-serrated or finely serrated blades may be used to achieve clubbed effects. To ensure accuracy, take only small sections of hair each time you club cut, otherwise the cut line produced will be uneven. Although hair may be clubbed when it is either wet or dry, it is easier to control the hair when it is cut wet. Wet cutting is considered to be more hygienic, especially if it is done after cleaning the hair with shampoo.

Cutting using a wide-toothed razor comb

Holding the hair at the correct cutting angle for graduation

Clubbing – inner hair lengths

Razors

Razors have traditionally been used to cut hair. They are mainly used to produce tapered, thinned and textured effects. The modern *hair shaper* is now replacing the traditional razor. This has

Trevor Sorbie

1 Start the cut at the front so the client can see the emerging shape. Neat sectioning is essential

2 The outline produced is softened by the razor

3 Graduate the section by holding at 45° to the head

4 This produces a softly textured result

5 Shape the sides by holding the hair close to the skin

6 which produces this effect

7 The finished effect after finger drying

exchangeable blades which do away with the honing and stropping needed for open razors – the blade is always sharp and able to produce clean cuts. Although razors and hair shapers are mainly used to produce tapered and thinned effects, they can with care be used to produce clubbed effects.

Clippers

Clippers are either hand operated or electric and designed to produce clubbed hair effects. The closeness or shortness of the cut is determined by the size of the cutting blades. With some clippers, the blades are removable and designed to cut close to or further away from the head. Other clipper models have adjustable blades to determine the fineness of cutting.

A closely graduated effect in the nape may be produced using electric clippers or shapers. Alternatively, finely graduating the hair by cutting with scissors over a comb can be just as effective in achieving the style required.

Shaping and texturising

Removing bulk without affecting the length

To achieve this you should taper or thin the hair using scissors, thinning scissors or a razor. Each of the texturising techniques – slicing, chipping, chopping, and so on – removes small amounts of hair bulk without reducing the overall hair length. These techniques should be used with thought and care to achieve the desired individual effects.

Remember: Cutting terms

Texturising	A way of cutting hair to increase movement and texture
Personalising	Introducing particular features to a style to give unique individuality
Point cutting	A way of shattering clubbed ends by removing slices from the ends of held meshes
Chipping	Removal of hair within held mesh at either root, mid-length or ends
Slicing	A technique of removing hair with scissors similar to the action of razoring
Channel cutting	A technique for removing 'laterally' wide but narrow sections of hair from near to the root

Vidal Sassoon

Texturising by point cutting

Philip Cristie at Unity, Aberdeen. Photograph by John Rawson

To remove bulk from long, thick hair, it is generally necessary to cut the hair at the middle third of the hair section. For more drastic thinning, the hair can be removed from nearer the roots. This can be achieved by point tapering, by razoring close to the scalp, or by using thinning scissors. On medium length hair, removal of bulk can be achieved by cutting the hair about the middle section. To achieve bulk removal on short hair, you have to resort to root thinning.

Achieving lift and volume

To achieve lift and volume you need to reduce some of the hair lengths from each hair section. You can then use the shorter hairs as support for the longer hair. This applies particularly when you *chip in* or *point cut* into the hair: the shorter hairs are more easily turned back to support the lengths. Thinning, tapering and texturising techniques can be used for these effects, on both short and medium length hair.

Enhancing movement

For this you need to use tapered, thinned and texturised effects. Removing bulk hair by tapering and thinning encourages the remaining hair to curl more. This enables you to achieve tight, curly effects on long hair and curl or waved effects on medium length and short hair.

Producing non-uniform effects

Here you may use a variety or combination of texturising techniques: your choice will depend on the style effect that you want to produce. You must decide how much hair is to be removed and how much you want to remain. Always remember that the head curves from above to below and from side to side.

Accuracy and checks

To achieve your agreed cut shape and style, you will need to carry out checks before, during and as you finish the cut. Without such care and continuity, unpredictable effects are likely to result.

Before the cut

1 Communicate with your client and interpret her requests.

2 Examine the hair – its type, length, quality, quantity and condition.

3 Explain whether requests can or cannot be carried out.

4 After further discussion, agree with the client exactly what is to be done.

The holding and cutting angle

5   Try to show the hair length to be removed.

6   Discuss the time that will be taken and the price that you will charge.

7   Proceed only when all checks have been made and the client has agreed to your proposals.

8   Ensure that you choose the correct tools and techniques scissors for club cutting, razors for tapering and texturising, castle serrations for texturising, and so on.

During the cut

1   To achieve precision cutting throughout, take care to check each angle at which the hair is taken and held from the head.

2   Before you cut the hair section, be sure that it is at the angle you require.

3   Your baselines and guideline cuts must be accurate as subsequent sections will be cut in relation to them. Think carefully before you make the first cut and again before you follow on.

4   When preparing baselines and guide sections, make sure that you attend to the features of your client's face and head. Use these as guides for accurate directions in the cut lines.

5   Remember always that the first cuts you make often determine the finished shape of the style.

After the cut

1   Check each of the sections of the side, nape, top and front for accuracy and finish.

2   Carefully remove any straggly ends.

3   Push and mould the hair as necessary to see the shape clearly.

4   Satisfy yourself that you have achieved what was agreed.

5   When all loose hair has been removed and the client is prepared and comfortable, continue to blow dry, set and finish the style.

Client care

You must take care at all times when you are working on your client. The client should be comfortable. She should never be apprehensive about what is being done. Give your client your undivided attention. Bear in mind the following points about client care:

Guillaume Vappereau at Guy Kremer

1   Check the client's record card if she has attended the salon before. If this is a new client, make out a new record card.

2   Protect the client adequately with cutting capes and gowns to prevent hair from spoiling clothes or causing irritation.

3   All sharp-edged tools must be carefully used so that they never endanger the client.

4   Talk to your client from time to time, explaining what is happening. Don't just ignore her and leave her to wonder.

5   Aftercare is necessary if your client is to make the most of the cut style you have achieved. Suggest and show how the hair is best arranged and handled.

6   Your client may wish to wash and condition the hair, or use hairsprays or hair cosmetics at home. Be prepared to offer professional guidance.

7   Finally, give your client the opportunity to make the next appointment.

Good practice: Health and safety

It is your responsibility to ensure your client's well-being and safety at all times. First and foremost, cross-infection must be avoided. This requires that you operate hygienically and carefully at all times. All tools and materials must be clean:

● Metal tools should be cleared of all hair and debris. They should be sterilised by being placed in an autoclave for the recommended time, or disinfected by cleaning with 70 per cent alcohol wipes.

● Combs, brushes, plastic section clips and similar implements should be cleared of all hair, then washed and sterilised.

● Towels, gowns, wraps and other coverings must be freshly laundered. Only clean materials should be used on clients. They should then be discarded for washing or cleaning.

● It is important that you follow all the COSHH regulations and meet all other health and safety legislation. See Health and Safety at Work Act 1974 and the Offices, Shops and Railways Act 1974 in Chapter 1.

Self-test section

Quick quiz: a selection of different types of questions to check your knowledge

Q1 Accuracy is achieved by .... and cutting the hair at the correct angle?   Fill in the blank

Q2 A razor should be used on wet hair?   True or False

Q3 Select from the following list those that are *not* texturising techniques: Multi-selection

Club cutting	☐ 1
Graduation	☐ 2
Slice cutting	☐ 3
Layering	☐ 4
Point cutting	☐ 5
Chipping	☐ 6

Q4 Symmetrical shapes produce equally balanced hairstyles.   True or False

Q5 Which of the following is not a cutting term?   Multi-choice

Cross-checking	☐ a
Thinning	☐ b
Free hand	☐ c
Free style	☐ d

Q6 Precision cutting is dependent upon cutting angles and even tension.   True or False

Q7 Which of the following hair growth patterns will affect the way that a fringe lies after it is cut?   Multi-selection

Nape whorl	☐ 1
Double crown	☐ 2
Widow's peak	☐ 3
Low hairline	☐ 4
Cow's lick	☐ 5
High hairline	☐ 6

Q8 A .... is the perimeter shape produced by cutting.   Fill in the blank

Q9 Which of the following cuts would easily describe a disconnection?   Multi-choice

Graduation in a long hair style	☐ a
Reverse graduation in a long hair style	☐ b
A fringe in a shoulder length bob style	☐ c
Texturising in a short cropped style	☐ d

Q10 'Personalising' is the term that refers to any technique which is used to complete a style, tailoring it to the client's specific needs.   True or False

Styling and dressing hair

4

Desmond Murray

What do I need to learn?

You need to know and understand:

- **How health and safety legislation affects you and your clients**
- **The importance of good communication**
- **The physical effects on hair from styling and dressing hair**
- **The ways in which hair can be dressed to create a variety of effects**
- **The benefits of 'prescribed' after care and home maintenance**
- **A range of styling and finishing products, their application, uses and overall benefits to clients**
- **A range of styling equipment**

| **Unit H25**
Style and dress hair to achieve a variety of creative effects | → | **Element H25.1** Maintain effective and safe methods of working when styling hair |
| | → | **Element H25.2** Style and dress hair creatively |

| **Unit H26**
Style and dress long hair | → | **Element H26.1** Maintain effective and safe methods of working when styling hair |
| | → | **Element H26.2** Creatively dress long hair |

What does it mean?

This chapter covers the basic principles of styling and dressing hair. The text later extends to cover long hair skills and techniques.

What do I need to do?

You will need to create a variety of effects resulting from a range of styling techniques and equipment on different lengths of hair.

Other info

Related topics and other useful information:

- **Health and safety legislation**
- **Client consultation**

Science bit!

- **The effects of humidity on the hair**
- **The physical changes in hair when styling**

Key words

- **Dexterity**
- **Pli**

- Longer hair requires larger rollers unless tighter effects are wanted.
- Poorly positioned hair overfalling the sides of the roller will have reduced/impaired movement in the final effect.
- Incorrectly wound hair around the roller will create 'fish hooks' and/or split ends.
- Twisted hair around the roller will distort the final movement of the style.

Barrelspring curl

Pincurling

Pincurling is the technique of winding hair into a series of curls which are pinned in place while drying. The two most common types of curl produced in this way are the *barrel curl* and the *clockspring*.

The barrel curl has an open centre and produces a soft effect. When formed, each loop is the same size as the previous one. It produces an even wave shape and may be used for reverse curling, which forms waves in modern hairstyles. In this, one row of pincurls lies in one direction, the next in the opposite direction. When dry and dressed, this produces a wave shape.

Clockspring curl

The clockspring curl has a closed centre and produces a tight, springy effect. When formed each loop is slightly smaller than the previous one. It produces an uneven wave shape throughout its length. It can be suitable for hair that is difficult to hold in place.

Common pincurl faults

- Tangled hair is difficult to control. Comb well before starting.
- If the base is too large, curling will be difficult.
- If you don't turn your hand far enough it will be difficult to form concentric loops.

Finger waving: first crest

Finger waving

Finger waving is a technique of moulding wet hair into S-shaped movements using the hands, the fingers and a comb. It is sometimes called water waving or water setting. The technique is often used as part of an overall finished style.

Forming the wave

1. Use one finger of one hand to control the hair and to determine the position of the wave. Comb the hair into the first part of the crest and continue along the head.

2. Place the second finger immediately below the crest formed and comb the hair in the opposite direction.

Finger waving: second crest

Finger waving: third crest

3 Form the second crest similarly to complete the final wave shape.

Dressing out

Dressing is the process of applying finish to previously set hair. Setting gives movement to hair in the form of curls or waves. Dressing blends and binds these movements into an overall flowing shape, the style you set out to achieve. It produces an overall form that flows, lightening the head and face and removing dull, flat or odd shapes.

Dressing uses brushing and combing techniques and dressing aids such as hairspray to keep the hair in place. If you have conducted the pli carefully only the minimum of dressing will be required.

Good practice: Finger waves

Points to remember are as follows:

- Finger waving is most successful on medium or fine hair that is about 10cm long. Coarse or lank hair can be difficult.

- Setting lotion, gel, mousse or emulsion will be needed to hold the waves.

- Keep your forearm level with or slightly higher than the wrist, to control the hair and your hand during waving. Hold the comb upright and don't use too much pressure when combing to avoid tearing the scalp.

- Keep the waves the same size and depth. About 3cm (the tips of two fingers) between crests is usually best.

- Pinching or forcing the crests will distort the waves. Correct control and angling will produce the best waves.

- Positioning is important. Comb the hair to make it lie evenly and return it to this position after each wave movement is complete.

- Keep the hair wet (but not dripping) during waving. If you find that it is drying out, dampen it while you work and apply more setting lotion if necessary.

- Dry the completed shape under a hood drier, preventing movement or slip.

- Dressing out should not disturb the waves. The hair is not normally brushed.

Remember

Finger waving

The elbow and arm should be held above the hand when it is placed on the head. Only the index finger should touch the head. This gives the required control and pressure. A comb with both widely and closely spaced teeth is the most suitable.

Brushing

Brushing blends the waves or curls, removes the partings left at the curl bases during rollering and gets rid of any stiffness caused by setting aids.

1 One way of achieving the finished dressing is with a brush and your hand.
2 Apply the brush to the hair ends. Use firm but gentle strokes.
3 Work up the head, starting from the back of the neck.
4 Brush through the waves or curls you have set, gradually moulding the hair into shape.
5 As you brush, pat the hair with your hand to guide the hair into shape. Remember, though, that overdressing and overhandling can ruin the set.

The technique of *double brushing* uses two brushes, applied one after the other in a rolling action.

Backbrushing

Backbrushing is a technique used to give more height and volume to hair. By brushing backwards from the points to the roots, you roughen the cuticle of the hair. Hairs will now tangle slightly and bind together to hold a fuller shape. The amount of hair backbrushed determines the fullness of the finished style.

Tapered hair, with shorter lengths distributed throughout, is more easily pushed back by brushing. Most textures of hair can be backbrushed because it adds bulk. The technique is especially useful with fine hair.

Backcombing

This technique is similar to backbrushing but in this situation a comb rather than a brush is used to turn shorter hairs within a section to provide support and volume. Backcombing is applied deeper towards the scalp than backbrushing and therefore provides a stronger result.

All these styling aspects create the basis for creating a variety of effects. The next part of this chapter looks at how this is applied to long hair dressings.

Backcombing

Creative long hair

Quick 'hair ups'

Much of long hair work is very involved and requires a lot of practice and patience. The secret to maintaining these skills is to ensure that you make it a regular occurrence. It doesn't take long to create simple effects and these form the basis of more intricate work.

Just set and comb out

Shape and form

The balance in this style is maintained by the weight and fullness at the back being counter-balanced by the height and movement at the front.

Movement and direction

The mass of curls and movement transform this finer straight hair into a 'glitzy' ball or cocktail effect.

Step-by-step guidance

Guy Kremer

1 The before look

2 Individual sections of hair are wound around the finger to create loose clockspring curls

3 Straightening irons are used to heat 'press' the curls into shape

4 Grips secure the curls into place whilst all the head is completed

5 A tailcomb combs out the placed curls

6 Use your fingers to gently back tease the curls, creating body and width at the roots

7 Spray the root area to create a durable lasting shape

8 Distribute the weight evenly by pinning hair into shape

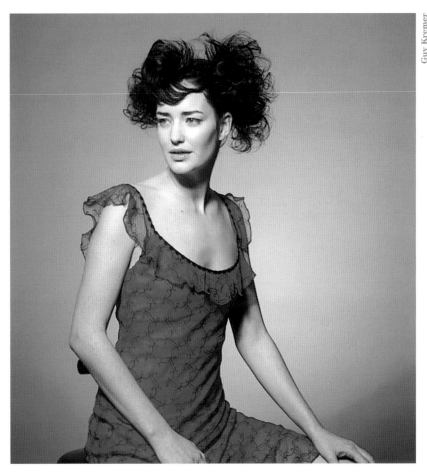

Guy Kremer

9 The total look

Charlie Fawlk at Headquarters

High knot

Shape and form

The position of the high knot centralises the hair weight at the crown, adding height to the overall image.

Lines and angles

The lines of the hair move directly up from the nape and sides and contrast with the lateral movements of the knot. The position of the knot is determined by the cranial structure and facial features.

Movement and direction

The clean line that the hair takes, with its simple movement, emphasises the structure and proportions of the head and neck.

1 Brush and smooth the hair

2 Position the hair bulk centrally at the crown and secure

3 Twist the hair at the root end. Continue to twist and turn to the points, first with one hand and then with the other. Pin invisibly

Step-by-step guidance

Low knot

Shape and form

The position of the low knot counterbalances the sleek hair covering the head shape and centralises the hair weight within the nape.

Lines and angles

A dramatic effect is created by the contrast between the vertical line and the crossing of the horizontal fold.

Movement and direction

The clean line that the hair takes, with its simple movement, emphasises the structure of the head and neck.

1 Brush the hair and hold it at the nape in a low ponytail. Secure it with a band

2 Use your finger as a former for the bottom of the knot

3 Secure the ponytail at one side with grips while holding the tail hair above

4 Wrap the remaining tail directly across and secure on the other side

Step-by-step guidance

Pleat

Shape and form

The position of the pleated hair at the back creates interest and emphasises the facial features.

Lines and angles

The line of the hair is smooth or positioned so that it moves from right to left at the back of the head. It is secured firmly into position. The hairline is made to move back from left to right, overriding the base hair which is firmly anchored by grips and pins.

Movement and direction

The curves of the pleat soften the harshness of the contrasting directions within the hair.

Step-by-step guidance

Patrick Cameron

1 Backcomb hair and mist with hairspray

2 Smooth using a bristle brush and insert a row of grips up centre back of head

3 Divide off lower section of hair from lobe of ear. Position hand vertically as shown to keep flat

4 Smooth with bristle brush then twist hair around thumb using an upward movement so the ends of the twist are placed following the line of grips. Pin grips vertically down seam of roll

5 Continue moulding hair into the pleated section as before, tucking and pinning as you go

6 To finish top area, brush around and join top ends to those of the two sections and swirl round to finish

Plaiting

Plaiting is a method of intertwining three or more strands of hair to create a variety of woven hairstyles. When this work is undertaken by the professional stylist for specific occasions, it is often accompanied by ornamentation. Fresh flowers and coloured ribbons are popular. The numerous options for plaited effects are determined by the following factors:

- number of stems (or plaits) used
- positioning of the plait or plaits across or around the head
- way in which the plaits are made (under or over)

Three-stem plait

Patrick Cameron

Three-stem plait

The three-stem plait is easily achieved and demonstrates the basic principle of plaiting hair:

1 Divide the hair to be plaited into three equal sections.
2 Hold the hair with both hands, using your fingers to separate the sections.
3 Starting from either the left or the right, place the outside section over the centre one. Repeat this from the other side.
4 Continue placing the outside sections of hair over the centre ones until you reach the ends of the stems.
5 Secure the free ends with ribbon or thread.

Three-stem plait – head-hugging style

1 Brush the hair to remove all tangles.
2 With the hair tilted backwards, divide the foremost hair into three equal sections.
3 Starting from either the left or the right, cross an outside stem over the centre stem. Repeat this action with the opposite outer stem.
4 Section a fourth stem (less in thickness than the initial three stems) and incorporate this with an outside stem.
5 Cross this thickened stem over the centre and repeat this step with the opposite outer stem.
6 Continue this sequence of adding hair to the *outer* stem, before crossing it over the centre.
7 When there is no more hair to be added, continue plaiting down to the ends and secure them.

Step-by-step guidance

Head-hugging plait

1 Sectioning the hair

2 Plaiting the sections in with the main stem

3 Plaiting down to the ends   **4** The completed plait

Four-stem plaits

1 Brush the hair to remove any tangles.

2 Divide the hair to be plaited into four equal stems.

3 Begin to plait by crossing the left-hand centre stem over the right-hand centre stem.

4 Now cross the outside right stem over the stem next to it.

5 Then cross the outside left stem *under* the next one.

6 Repeat steps 3–5 until you reach the hair ends.

Six-stem plaits

1 Brush the hair to remove the tangles.

2 Divide the hair into six equal stems.

3 Pass the outside right stem over the next two stems.

4 From the left, pass the outside stem *under* two stems and *over* one.

5 Repeat this until you reach the hair ends.

Other plaits

- Using *different starting positions* – start plaiting at the side of the head and take the hair around the hairline to produce a halo effect. Or start the plait at the nape, working *up* the centre of the back and towards the front of the head. Secure the tucked ends with grips to shorten long hair.

- *Under-plaiting* – instead of crossing strands over the centre, cross them under the centre. This will produce a plait that sits along the head contour.

- *Cornrowing* – divide the hair into small parallel sections and plait it to the scalp. Secure the end of each individual plait with cotton thread. To enhance the effect, decorate the hair with small beads.

Weaving

Hair weaving is a process of interlacing strands of hair to produce a wide variety of effects. A small area of woven hair can be very effective by itself, or used to highlight a particular part of a style. Hair weaving is also used to place and hold lengths of hair. At its simplest, hair weaving may be used to hold long hair back from the face. This may be done by taking strands of hair from each side, sweeping them over the hair lengths and intertwining them at the back.

More intricate is the *basket weave* which uses a combination of plaiting, twisting and placing to form many shapes and patterns. It is important to wet or gel the hair before starting to weave. Weave tightly or loosely according to the effect you are aiming for. The hair may be woven as follows:

1 Use six meshes of hair, three in the left hand and three in the right.
2 Start with the furthest right-hand mesh. Pass this *over* the inner two meshes.
3 From the left, pass the outside mesh *under* the next two and *over* one.
4 Continue to the ends of the hair.
5 Tuck in the hair ends and secure them in position.

Practise on colleagues or models and experiment with different woven shapes before you attempt to weave hair for clients.

Added hair postiche

The addition of hair in the form of postiche – natural or synthetic false hair – has been a feature in many dressings throughout the ages. Postiche has been used to disguise physical injuries and scars, thinning hair and baldness. In dressings it is intended to enhance the overall style and may take various forms. Here are some examples:

pincurls are small pieces which you can add to different parts of the dressing. **Ringlets** are larger than pincurls but made and used similarly.

marteaux are flat, folded pieces of weft attached to the hair by sewn loops or combs. These pieces are useful in adding a wave or waves.

switches are lengths of weft, spiral-wound or twisted, coiled or plaited in a variety of ways.

torsades are ornamental twists made from marteaux and switches to form pieces of coiled hair.

swathes, which may also be made from marteaux and switches, are worn encircling the head. They are useful in securing long hair.

chignons are rolls or knots worn between the crown and the nape. They are useful in producing additional height, fullness and shape.

cape wiglets consist of a long length of hair which fits the top of the head and drapes down to the neck. They are used to convert a short head of hair into a longer looking style. A simple decorative band holds the piece in position.

There are other varieties of postiche, including diamond-mesh foundations, frontal pieces, transformations, scalpettes and full wigs. Each of these has specific uses and may be used as decorative added hair.

Attaching a hairpiece

Sam Cairney at Headquarters

1 Brush the hair to remove any tangles

2 Position the hair centrally at the crown

3 An interlocked base of grips encircles the band on the hair

4 Remove the band and spread the hair evenly to provide a secure base

5 The hairpiece is ready to attach

6 Position the base of the hairpiece centrally over the crown and grip into position

Care and cleaning

Hairpieces, whether made from real or synthetic hair, must be carefully treated if they are to give good service. To remain hygienic, regular cleaning must be carried out. The more often a hairpiece is worn, the more often it will require cleaning. A wig that is constantly worn should be cleaned at least fortnightly, if not weekly. Care must be taken to avoid damaging the foundation of the hairpiece. Here are some general points about handling postiche:

- Avoid using sharp combs and brushes which can damage the foundation. Use only the correct dressing techniques.

- Many different synthetic fibres are used in postiche. Follow the manufacturer's instructions for each piece. Synthetic hair may be washed with shampoos.
- Modern synthetic fibres may be set and blow dried. Some may even take heated rollers and tonging. If the temperature is too great, however, the curl or wave may be lost.
- Use only those cleaners recommended for the particular hairpiece.
- Real hair postiche must not be cleaned with shampoo or rinsed with water. This might result in tangling and loosening of the hair and could shrink and distort the foundation base.

Cleaning synthetic fibre postiche

1 Add shampoo to a bowl of tepid water.
2 Gently move the postiche in the foamy water.
3 Rinse it in cool, clean water.
4 Repeat steps 1–3 if the postiche is still dirty. Rinse clear at the end.
5 The hairpiece can now be styled. Remember that too much brushing or combing can loosen fibres.

Cleaning real hair postiche

1 Do not use shampoo and water. Use recommended cleaners only and follow the instructions for their use. Use the cleaners in well-ventilated rooms – the fumes may be irritating.
2 Comb the postiche carefully before cleaning it.
3 Pour the cleaner into a bowl. Place the postiche in the cleaner, ensuring that the hair is covered.
4 Gently move the hairpiece in the cleaner for a minute or two; then lift it out and allow it to drain from the roots to the points.
5 Repeat steps 3 and 4 if necessary.
6 Remove any excess liquid, gently shaking the hairpiece, and allow the remaining liquid to evaporate, preferably in the open air.
7 When dry, styling may be carried out. If using water or setting lotions, keep these away from the foundation so as not to damage it. An unclean piece of postiche can be dangerous and irritating to wear. Be sure to clean it regularly.

Self-test section

Quick quiz: A selection of different types of questions to check your knowledge

Q1   Self cling rollers are commonly known as .... rollers.   Fill in the blank

Q2   Humidity in the atmosphere will help to retain set hairstyles.   True or False

Q3   Which of the following dressings are traditionally, long 'hair up' styles?   Multi-selection

Plaits	☐	1
Knots	☐	2
Weaves	☐	3
Rolls	☐	4
Braids	☐	5
Pleats	☐	6

Q4   The keratin bonds of stretched hair are said to be in the beta state.   True or False

Q5   Which chemical bonds within the hair are *not* affected during setting?   Multi-choice

Hydrogen bonds	☐	a
Disulphide bonds	☐	b
Salt bonds	☐	c
Oxygen bonds	☐	d

Q6   Heated rollers are a quick way of setting wet or dry hair into style?   True or False

Q7   Hair set on rollers produces which of the following results and effects?   Multi-selection

Increased body at the roots	☐	1
No body at the roots	☐	2
No movement at the ends	☐	3
Straighter effects	☐	4
Wavy effects	☐	5
Same as blow dried effects	☐	6

Q8   The common name for a centrally positioned, vertically folded effect, worn on the back of the head, on long hair is a ....   Fill in the blank

Q9   Which item of equipment would smooth and flatten frizzy, unruly hair best?   Multi-choice

Curling tongs	☐	a
Ceramic straighteners	☐	b
Crimping irons	☐	c
Blow dryer	☐	d

Q10   'Hair ups' are easier to perform on hair that has just been washed, conditioned and dried off.   True or False

Colouring

Chris Moody, Optime

What do I need to learn?

You need to know and understand:

- **How health and safety legislation affects you and your clients**

- **The importance of good communication**

- **Colouring science and a range of colouring processes and products**

- **The range of tests that need to be conducted**

- **The benefits of sound advice followed up by prescribed home maintenance**

- **A range of tools and equipment and their uses**

5

Unit H30 Colour hair using a variety of techniques	**Element H30.1** Maintain effective and safe methods of working when colouring hair
	Element H30.2 Prepare for colouring
	Element H30.3 Create a variety of colouring techniques
	Element H30.4 Resolve basic colouring problems

Unit H28 Provide colour correction services	**Element H28.1** Maintain effective and safe methods of working when correcting hair colour
	Element H28.2 Determine the problem
	Element H28.3 Plan and agree a course of action to correct colour
	Element H28.4 Correct colour

What does it mean?

This chapter covers the fundamental aspects of colour theory and practice. The text later extends to cover the advanced principles, skills and methods of colour correction.

What do I need to do?

- **You should always make sure that a comprehensive preliminary assessment is undertaken so that a correct plan of action can safely be implemented.**

- **Be able to carry out a range of different colour techniques and applications.**

Other info

Related topics and other useful information:

- **Health and safety legislation**
- **Client consultation**

Science bit!

- **Principles of colour and colour correction**
- **Types of colour**
- **Incompatible chemistry**
- **Hydrogen peroxide and product chemistry**

Key words

- **Colour correction**
- **Discolouration**
- **Pre-pigmentation**

Started it ✓	I know and understand the principles of positive communication ✓	I can carry out colour consultation and understand the colour selection process ✓	I always recognise the critical influencing factors when I analyse the client's hair ✓
I know and understand the science in respect to colour and colour correction ✓	I know how to carry out a variety of full head and partial colouring techniques on a variety of hair lengths ✓	I always carry out working practices according to the salon's health and safety policy ✓	I've covered most of it! ✓
I always carry out tests prior to any new colouring treatment ✓	I know when and to whom to refer clients in situations where external assistance is required ✓	I know how to recognise and implement colour correction procedures on a variety of hair lengths ✓	I know how to advise, promote and sell other services and products to clients ✓
I know and respect the clients rights: data protection EO, discrimination, consumer legislation ✓	Done it all! ✓		**CHECKER BOARD** ✓

Introduction

This chapter combines two of the most complex but exciting optional units of Level 3. These colouring units are comprised of eight elements:

H30   Colour hair using a variety of techniques
    H30.1   Maintain effective and safe methods of working when colouring hair
    H30.2   Prepare for colouring
    H30.3   Create a variety of colouring techniques
    H30.4   Resolve basic colouring problems

H28   Provide colour correction services
    H28.1   Maintain effective and safe methods of working when correcting hair colour
    H28.2   Determine the problem
    H28.3   Plan and agree a course of action to correct colour
    H28.4   Correct colour

Colouring is arguably the most exciting and often the most difficult aspect of contemporary hairdressing. The increasing demands and expectations of clients have made colouring and in particular the application of special colour effects the 'must have' of hairdressing. Our clients are getting more informed about hair styling, hair condition and the benefits of product usage. But colouring for them has a compulsory 'magnetic' but still elusive draw. Techniques and products are developing all the time and the possibilities are boundless so *dare* to create a little magic.

Remembering the essential design elements of:

- shape and form
- lines and angles
- applied techniques
- apparent texture
- movement and direction
- dimensions, distribution and abundance
- colour depth and tone

Some can be applied in the following colour step by steps courtesy of Toni & Guy Essensuals.

Antea

Lines and angles

The colouring technique used for this model accentuates the perimeter shape by increasing contrast by darkening the shattered edges. Without the colour, the textured edges would be lost against the skin tones.

Applied techniques

Tonal lightening techniques have been used in order to provide a graduated colour effect.

Colour depth and tone

Prior to colouring the hair was natural base 7, medium blonde with previously lightened highlights within the lengths.

Step-by-step guidance

1 Working with a centre parting, a herringbone section was taken either side of the parting

2 Apply the surface colour on the underneath. Color Touch Long-lasting Semi-permanent 7/73 Sienna + 7/47 Tera Rosa with Color Touch Crème Lotion

3 Using foil, slices are alternated through the herringbone section. Koleston Perfect 12/17 Special Soft Velvet with 12 per cent Welloxon Perfect, alternated with Blondor Coco with 6 per cent Welloxon Perfect. The ends were 'smudged' randomly with Color Touch which was used to create a two-tone effect

4 When half the herringbone section is completed, sections are pivoted on the crown area

Essensuals: Sacha Mascolo-Tarbuck

5 Completed section pattern. The top is block coloured to achieve different tonal effects

The finished effect

Gabriella

Essensuals: Sacha Mascolo-Tarbuck

Shape and form

The colouring technique used for this model augments this popular hairstyle by defining the upper surface and body in this multi-textural effect.

Applied techniques

Texturising colour has been used in order to maximise this soft and subtle effect.

Colour depth and tone

Prior to colouring the hair was natural base 6, dark blonde with previously semi-permanent colour.

Step-by-step guidance

1 A diamond section is taken on the top of the head and split into four triangles

2 Under colour is applied Koleston Perfect 4/6 Rich Damson + Sherry Brown with 6 per cent Welloxon Perfect

3 Colour wraps are applied then slices are taken from each section. Koleston Perfect 6/6 Sherry Brown with 6 per cent Welloxon Perfect is applied, then Blondor Coco with 6 per cent Welloxon Perfect is applied to the ends

4 Another layer of colour wraps. The next slices are taken and Koleston Perfect 6/6 Sherry Brown is applied. Slices are alternated, one with Blondor Coco on the ends, one without

Katie

Essensuals: Sacha Mascolo-Tarbuck

Shape and form

The colouring technique uses this one-length style to the best advantage by graduating the colour throughout the lengths.

Applied techniques

Panelling has been used to provide subtle multi-toned effects.

Colour depth and tone

Prior to colouring the hair was natural base 6, dark blonde with no previous colour.

Step-by-step guidance

1 The halo section pattern was taken then zig-zagged to enable the colour to blend. Below this section four panels are taken

2 The remaining hair below these sections is coloured with Color Touch Long-lasting Semi-permanent 6/37 Indian Bronze with Color Touch Crème Lotion

3 Working on each panel, slices are taken using wraps. Each slice was alternated with three colours to create panels of colour. Color Touch 6/37 Indian Bronze with Crème Lotion, Koleston Perfect 88/43 Vibrant Celtic Copper with 9 per cent + Blondor Coco with 6 per cent Welloxon Perfect

4 Each slice colour was placed in different positions to create different panels. With the panels completed Color Touch 6/37 Indian Bronze was applied to the halo section at the top

Irene

Essensuals: Sacha Mascolo-Tarbuck

Shape and form

The colouring technique used in this style produces a natural effect that can only be compared to sun-lightened 'holiday' hair.

Applied techniques

Hidden lightening has been used to provide this soft, subtle popular effect.

Colour depth and tone

Prior to colouring the hair was natural base 7, medium blonde with previous highlights within the ends.

Step-by-step guidance

1 A triangle section is taken on the top of the head with the point facing towards the front. Underneath a small triangle and a rectangle section are taken. This will be the focal point of the haircut

2 Working first on the rectangular section, woven highlights are worked through. Colours are alternated, Koleston Perfect 12/16 Special Soft Ash with 12 per cent Welloxon Perfect + 9/93 Soft Cendre with 12 per cent Welloxon Perfect

3 After the rectangular sections are completed, work through the smaller triangle. Repeated both sides

4 Colour is applied to the back and the top triangle. Color Touch Long-lasting Semi-permanent 6/35 Rich Bronze with Color Touch Crème Lotion

5 Completed application: the underneath at the front will be the focal point of the colour

Colour principles

The colour spectrum from visible light

Seeing colour

When you look at an object, what you are actually seeing is light reflected from it. White light is really a mixture of many colours, which is why sunlight *refracted* through falling rain can produce a rainbow. This *splitting* of white light creates what we see as seven different colours: red, orange, yellow, green, blue, indigo and violet.

A white object *reflects* most of the white light that falls upon it. A black object *absorbs* most of the light falling on it. A red object reflects the red light and absorbs everything else.

Hair colour depends chiefly on the pigments in the hair, which absorb some of the light and reflect the rest. The colour that we see is also affected by the light in which it is seen and (to a lesser extent) by the colours of clothes worn with it.

- White light from halogen bulbs and full daylight will show the hair's natural colour.
- Yellowish light emitted from standard electric lightbulbs adds warmth to hair colour but neutralises blue ash or ashen effects.
- Bluish/green light from fluorescent tubes reduces the warmth of red/gold tones in hair.

Mixing colours

The colours of the pigments in paints arise from three *primary colours* – red, blue and yellow. Pairs of these give the *secondary colours* – violet, green and orange. The various other colours are made from different proportions of the primary colours: i.e. red and blue mixed together create violet; yellow and blue create green; yellow and red create orange. White and black can be added to vary the tone of the colour.

The primary colours in *light* are different – red, green and blue. These are the three colours used in video cameras, computer screens and television. The secondary colours are yellow, cyan and magenta.

Hair colour (pigmentation)

The natural colour of hair is determined by the colour of pigments within the hair's cortex. These are formed when the hair is in its germinating stage of growth. Hair colour pigments – **melanin** – are deposited into the hair shaft at the region of the papilla and germinal matrix. The pigments responsible for black and brown hair are called **eumelanin**. Those responsible for red and yellow hair are called **pheomelanin**. There are in fact others but these are the main pigments. The hair colour you actually see is affected by the amount and proportion of the pigments present, by the light in which the hair is seen and to a certain extent by the colours of the clothes and make-up worn.

London Hair Academy at the Aveda Institute

With age or after periods of stress, the production of natural pigments may be reduced. The hairs already on the head will not be affected but the new ones will. As hairs fall out and are replaced, the proportion that have the original pigmentation diminishes and the hair's overall colour changes. It may become lighter. If no pigment is produced at all, then the new hairs will be white.

The proportion of white hairs among the naturally coloured ones causes the hair to *appear* grey. Greyness is often referred to as a percentage: for example, '50 per cent grey' means that half of the hairs on the head are white and the rest are pigmented. It is not uncommon for young people to exhibit some grey hairs. This does not necessarily mean that they will go grey or completely white at an early age.

Depth and tone

These two key factors help us to describe the hair's colour.

We refer to hair colour in the following terms:

depth = how light or dark it is

tone = the colouration or hue, i.e. ashen, golden, mahogany, etc.

These terms are easier to understand if we tabulate them in the following way.

Remember

Compound henna

Compound henna is not pure vegetable henna. It is mixed with other element oxides and is therefore incompatible with modern colouring and perming materials.

Depth	Very light			
	Light			
	Medium			
	Dark			
	Very dark			
Tone	Copper	Gold	Natural	Ash

Active learning

Handling clients

As a group exercise work through your salon's shade chart and for each shade note down its shade name, number or code, then whether it is a warm or cool tone. Save the tabled information in your portfolio for future reference. How many warm shades were there? How many cool shades were there? How many were neither warm or cool? Did you find any surprising results?

Key skills: Communication

2.1 Take part in discussions

2.2 Produce written materials

2.3 Use images

Taking this principle further, the International Colour Chart (ICC) offers a way of defining hair colours systematically (although charts may vary between manufacturers). Shades of colour are divided and numbered, with black (1) at one end of the scale and lightest blonde (10) at the other. Tones of other colours (/1 /9 or also stated as .1 .9) are combined with these, producing a huge variety of colours. Charts are usually arranged with shades in rows down the side and tones in columns across the top. To use them, first identify the shade of your client's hair. That row of the chart then shows the colours you could produce with that hair. For example, if your client has medium blonde hair (depth 7) and you tint with a red tone (.4), the result should be a rich copper blonde (7.4). The possibilities are almost endless, as these examples indicate:

- to produce ash shades, add blue
- to produce matt shades, add green
- to produce gold shades, add yellow
- to produce warm shades, add red
- to produce purple or violet shades, add mixtures of red and blue

The International Colour Chart System is therefore a table of colours.

	Natural .0 or /0	Ash .1 or /1	Soft ash .2 or /2	Gold .3 or /3	Red .4 or /4	Mahogany .5 or /5	Violet .6 or /6
10	Lightest blonde 10						
9	Very light blonde 9	Very light ash blonde 9.1					
8	Light blonde 8			Light golden brown 8.3			
7	Medium blonde 7	Medium ash blonde 7.1			*Paprika* 7.44		
6	Dark blonde 6			Dark golden brown 6.3	*Acapulco* 6.46		*Berry* 6.62
5	Light brown 5		Truffle 5.2		Russet 5.4	*Burnt Toffee* 7.52	
4	Brown 4			Medium golden brown 4.3			
3	Dark brown 3						
2							
L'Oréal Majirel							

Trevor Sorbie

Incompatibles

Always check with your client what they have been using on their hair previously. Often men will use a simple lotion to stain over greying hair. Many of these types of dye are metallic salt based and are therefore incompatible with modern colouring and perming products.

In the table we see how the L'Oréal shades are positioned within the colour table. The three shades Acapulco, Burnt Toffee and Berry are defined in italic as these colours identify additional colour properties. These shades are denoted, as are many others, with having a second number after the decimal point: i.e. 6.46.

Shade: Acapulco	Depth	Primary tone	Secondary tone
	6	.4	6

The primary tone denotes the range that the shade is in, whereas the secondary tone indicates additional colouration within the shade. This provides lots of extra colouring permutations. Sometimes colour manufacturers want to increase a shade's intensity and vibrancy. This is achieved by adding *double* the tone to the particular shade.

Shade: Paprika	Depth	Primary tone	Secondary tone
	7	.4	4

Hair colourants

Goldwell

Young Artistic Team, Ishoka

Temporary colourants

Temporary colourants are available in the form of lotions, creams, mousses, gels, lacquers, sprays, crayons, paints and glitterdust. On hair in good condition these do not penetrate the hair cuticle, nor do they directly affect the natural hair colour. They simply remain on the hair until washed off.

Temporary colourants are ideal for a client who has not had colour before as they are readily removed if not liked. They have subtle colouring effects, particularly on grey or greying hair. Hair condition, shine and control are enhanced. If used on badly damaged or very porous hair, the temporary colourant may quickly be absorbed into the cortex, producing uneven, patchy results.

Semi-permanent colourants

Semi-permanent colourants are made in a variety of forms – some ready-mixed for immediate use, others needing to be mixed and prepared as necessary before use. Always check the manufacturer's instructions to ensure that you know which type of colourant you are going to use.

Semi-permanent colourants contain pigments which are deposited in the hair cuticle and outer cortex. The colour gradually lifts each time the hair is shampooed. Some colourants will last through six washes, others longer. These colourants are not intended to cover large percentages of white hair – for instance, black used on white hair would not produce a pleasing result. Choose colours carefully.

Note that some permanent colourants may be diluted for use as semi-permanents. However, these products may contain skin sensitisers so skin tests must be performed before use in this way.

Longer lasting colourants

Now that frequent use shampoos have become popular, some semi-permanent colourants are soon removed. A new generation of longer lasting colourants has been introduced which is more practical and economical. These colourants allow for a greater coverage of white hair and last for up to 12 washes.

Good practice: Health and safety

Dyes or tints may contain irritants that can cause a skin reaction. Always carry out a skin test before using them.

Always follow manufacturer instructions for the use of peroxide products. Check with your salon's COSHH risk assessment for the correct salon policy in handling these products.

> ### Remember
>
> #### Using colours
>
> If you are in any doubt about shades, always use the lighter one as it is easier to add more depth to hair than it is to remove unwanted colour from hair.

Quasi-permanent colourants

These colourants are nearly permanent. They last for a longer period of time than semi-permanent colourants but not as long as the true permanent colourants. When using them, follow the manufacturer's instructions strictly. (Always carry out a skin test.)

Permanent colourants

Permanent colourants are made in a wide variety of shades and tones. They can cover white and natural coloured hair to produce a range of natural, fashion and fantasy shades.

Hydrogen peroxide is mixed with permanent colourants. This oxidises the hair's natural pigments and joins the small molecules of synthetic pigment together, a process called *polymerisation*. The hair will then retain the colour permanently in the cortex. Hair in poor condition, however, will not hold the colour and colouring could result in patchy areas and colour fading.

The use of modern permanent colourants can lighten or darken the natural hair colour, or both together in one process. This is achieved by varying the percentage strength of hydrogen peroxide.

Colour choice

Your choice of colour is crucial. Take time to make it carefully. A hurried choice may give disastrous results! A number of questions need to be answered before the final choice of colour is made.

What does the client require?

Clients look to colour as a solution for many things. Many clients requesting a permanent colour are seeking to disguise their greying hair. A client who wants something to tone a few grey hairs may be successfully assisted with temporary, semi-permanent or longer lasting colourants. However, if the client is really longing simply to be young again it is difficult to help much with any type of colour, though it may well be possible to help her to look a little more youthful.

Most colour work undertaken within the salon has been stimulated by fashion. The majority of this work now falls into the partial colouring techniques. The multi-toning permutations present a boundless choice of options, carried out by an ever-growing range of techniques and applications. With the decline in full head tinting (probably much to do with the variety and choice of home colouring products) these partial, varietal, colouring options remain a 'professionals only' option for the client.

> ### Remember: Health and safety
>
> Before using any permanent or semi-permanent colourants, you must always perform a skin (sensitivity) test. If there is any reaction, you cannot carry out the tinting. To do so could result in an allergic reaction and a possible personal injury claim.

Bleaching and lightening

Bleaching is a process of making the hair colour lighter. The colour pigment eumelanin is the first to be acted upon. This affects the black and brown colouring. More difficult to alter is pheomelanin, which gives red and yellow colouring. Just how light you can bleach hair is determined by the proportions of the colour pigments present in the hair. As bleaching proceeds, the hair becomes lighter and lighter. The hair changes colour:

Black-brown	red-brown	orange-yellow	light yellow	very light yellow

Pigment range

To check how light you can bleach the hair, take a cutting of the client's hair and apply bleach to it. By careful timing and processing you should be able to find out exactly how much the hair can take and what colour you can bleach it to. Remember that if the hair contains a lot of red/yellow pigment it must not be lightened too much – the hair's breaking point will quickly be reached.

The chemistry of bleaching

Powder bleach contains ammonium/potassium persulphate and sodium/magnesium silicate. These chemicals bleach the hair by oxidation: i.e. oxygen is added to the chemical pigments. Various types of bleach will do this and the most common is *hydrogen peroxide* (H_2O_2)

Hydrogen peroxide is available in cream, foam and liquid forms. It acts in stages. First the bleaching agent causes the hair to swell: the cuticle begins to lift. The bleach can then penetrate to the hair cortex where the liberated oxygen acts on the pigment, lightening the hair.

Longer times or stronger bleaches may be required for hair of different colours. Just how long is required and what strength of bleach must be used can be determined using a test cutting.

Activating the bleach

Hydrogen peroxide is very reactive – it readily produces oxygen – so it needs to be stabilised if its effectiveness is to be maintained. This is done by adding chemicals such as sulphuric or phosphoric acids when the bleach is manufactured.

To activate the stabilised hydrogen peroxide, you first need to neutralise the **stabilisers**. This is done by adding ammonium hydroxide, sodium acetate or ammonium carbonate: you mix these bleach products together. Remember to read and follow the manufacturer's instructions carefully when using bleach products.

Chris Moody, Optime

Chris Moody, Optime

Chris Moody, Optime

Chris Moody, Optime

Good practice: Calculating hydrogen peroxide strengths

1. Suppose you start with 30% hydrogen peroxide but want 6%
   6/30 = 1/5 which means that in 5 parts, 1 part should be hydrogen peroxide and therefore 4 parts should be water

2. To dilute 30% hydrogen peroxide to 18%
   18/30 = 3/5 which means 3 parts hydrogen peroxide to 2 parts water

3. To dilute 30% hydrogen peroxide to 12%
   12/30 = 2/5 which means 2 parts hydrogen peroxide to 3 parts water

4. To dilute 30% hydrogen peroxide to 9%
   9/30 = 3/10 which means 3 parts hydrogen peroxide to 7 parts water

5. To dilute 30% hydrogen peroxide to 3%
   3/30 = 1/10 which means 1 part hydrogen peroxide to 9 parts water

A *peroxometer* can be used to check hydrogen peroxide strengths.

Overbleaching

Too much bleaching will destroy the hair's structure. Even if the hair doesn't actually break, it can become spongy, porous or patchy in colour. Further chemical processing – colouring, toning, perming or general hair management – is then very difficult. When wet, overbleached hair stretches like chewing gum and the effects of blow styling or setting cannot last. If hair ever reaches this state, it needs to be treated very gently and conditioned. All harsh processes must be avoided.

Some causes of overbleaching

- The hydrogen peroxide solution was too strong. Processing was too long. Hair sections overlapped.
- Bleach was repeatedly combed through previously bleached hair.
- The hair was in too poor a condition at the outset and very porous.
- The hair had been overexposed to sun, wind, sea or chlorinated water.

Choice of bleach

Explore fully the range of bleach products available. Make sure that you are confident about their use and effects. For each client, carefully consider which bleaching process and type of bleach would be correct. Determine which techniques will be helpful. Here are some guidelines in a table.

Bleaching service required	What you need to check for	Technique/application	Bleach type
Full head (on virgin hair)	**Test results** ● (skin tests etc.) **Natural hair depth** ● Bleaches will lift 5 levels quite happily on hair with brown/ ash pigments. However, strong red content will be difficult to remove ● Hair beyond base 5 will not lift safely beyond base 9. Suggest other colouring options **Hair length** ● Lengths up to 10cm lighten evenly, provided manufacturer's instructions are followed ● Lengths over 15cm are not recommended as evenness of colour will be difficult to guarantee **Hair texture** ● Finer hair needs extra care and lower hydrogen peroxide strengths, i.e. 6% ● Medium and coarser hair presents fewer technical problems **Hair condition** ● Only consider hair in good condition for bleaching. (Bleaching removes moisture content during the process, hair that is porous or containing low moisture levels has insufficient durability for bleaching) ● Bleach mixture must be applied to mid-lengths and ends first. A plastic cap should envelope the contents and can be developed with gentle heat until ready	Bleach mixture must be applied to mid-lengths and ends first. A plastic cap should envelop the contents and can be developed with gentle heat until ready When the bleached hair has lightened, 2 to 3 levels of lift the root application can be applied: ● Always follow manufacturer's instructions	Only emulsion bleach is suggested for application to the scalp. These are used with 6% hydrogen peroxide and sachet controllers to handle levels of lift

Bleaching service required	*What you need to check for*	*Technique/application*	*Bleach type*
Full head (on previously coloured)	● Not recommended		
Root application (pre-lightened ends)	**Existing client** ● **Yes**, check previous records and current hair condition and carry out service ● **No, new client**, go through all the checks in the full head application table **and** find out the previous treatment history.	Roots only without overlapping previous lightened ends ● Always follow manufacturer's instructions	Only emulsion bleach is suggested for application to the scalp
Highlights (fine even meshes on virgin hair) **Note** The success of highlights on coloured hair is very poor in comparison. This work is often undertaken in salons, but ends seldom lighten effectively, whilst the roots lighten very quickly. (Colour should be removed with a synthetic colour remover; see decolour)	**Test results** (skin tests etc.) **Natural hair depth** ● Bleaches will lift 5 levels quite happily on hair with brown/ash pigments. However, strong red content will be difficult to remove and require stronger developer and /or additional heat ● Hair beyond base 5 will not lift safely beyond base 9. Suggest other bleaching technique **Hair length** ● Hair length will have an impact on evenness of colour. However a *small* tolerance is acceptable and 'visually' indistinguishable on longer hair lengths **Hair texture** ● Finer hair needs extra care and lower hydrogen peroxide strengths, i.e. 6% ● Medium and coarser hair presents fewer technical problems but generally takes longer **Hair condition** ● Only consider hair in good condition for bleaching (bleaching removes moisture content during the process, hair that is porous or containing low moisture levels has insufficient durability for bleaching)	● Plastic self-grip meshes (e.g. Easi-meche L'Oréal™) ● Foil meshes ● Colour wraps	High Lift Powder Bleach with suitable hydrogen peroxide developer at 6% 9% or for highest lift 12% (providing no product is allowed to contact the skin/scalp)

Bleaching service required	What you need to check for	Technique/ application	Bleach type
Slices, blocks and slab bleaching (on virgin hair)	**Test results** (skin tests etc.)	● Plastic self-grip meshes (eg Easi-meche L'Oréal™)	High Lift Powder Bleach with suitable Hydrogen Peroxide developer at 6%–9% or for highest lift 12% (providing no product is allowed to contact the skin/scalp)
	Natural hair depth	● Foil meshes	
	● Bleaches will lift 5 levels quite happily on hair with brown/ash pigments. However, strong red content will be difficult to remove	● Colour wraps	
	● Hair beyond base 5 will not lift safely beyond base 9. Suggest other colouring options		
	Hair length		
	● Lengths up to 10cm will lighten evenly provided manufacturer's instructions are followed		
	● Lengths up to 15cm are not recommended, as evenness of colour will be difficult to guarantee. However, if the techniques used will allow for bleaching of mid-lengths and ends first, then the problem may be overcome		
	Hair texture		
	● Finer hair needs extra care and lower hydrogen peroxide strengths, i.e. 6%		
	● Medium and coarser hair present fewer technical problems		
	Hair condition		
	● Only consider hair in good condition for bleaching (bleaching removes moisture content during the process, hair that is porous or containing low moisture levels has insufficient durability for bleaching)		

Colour variants

There are many ways of bleaching and toning your client's hair apart from a whole-head bleach process or the usual regrowth application. The hair can be:

- **highlighted** – colour can be applied or lightened in contrasting streaks or areas.

- **lowlighted** – colour can be applied or lightened in streaks or areas, matched more closely to the general colour.

- **tipped, frosted, striped or varicoloured** – names given to various degrees and techniques of lightening or toning parts of the hair.

- **shaded without lightening** – for instance, adding darker or warmer shades to naturally fair hair or burgundy/plum shades to brown hair.

There are endless variations – small blocks of lightened or toned hair, a few streaks or stripes, lightly tipped parts to highlight a style line, and so on. Often the more natural, softer blending tones are the most pleasing, but contrasting tones can be very effective. Check the instructions from your colour manufacturer and take account of their specialist recommendations.

You need to be clear exactly how much and which parts of the hair you are going to lighten. The style worn should help to determine the parts to be bleached. Your proposals should of course be fully discussed and agreed with your client.

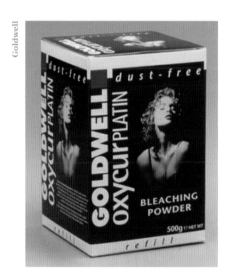

Goldwell

> ### Remember
>
> Always measure product quantities carefully. The manufacturer's instructions provide clear guidelines on mixing products so that successful results are guaranteed.

Essensuals: Sacha Mascolo-Tarbuck

Colouring with foil

Methods of bleaching and colouring

To achieve the variety of effects possible there are several ways in which you can make the bleach or colour application. Always follow the manufacturer's instructions on how to use products. Examples are:

dappling – a popular means of using bleach or colour to produce varied effects.

aluminium foil – this can be ideal for firmly wrapping bleached or coloured parcels of hair. Different coloured foils can be used to identify different areas and colours used.

highlight caps – basic 'lighting' resources, which can be used to achieve advanced effects such as multi-lighting, spot lighting or vari-toning.

colour wraps – these make it easier to process slices, sections or parcels of bleached or coloured hair safely.

Mahogany

1 Colour wraps

2 Positioning the hair

3 Completed back panel

In choosing a process, remember to bear in mind that the bleach must make contact with all of the hair if it is to work properly at all. Often bleaching products are 'thicker' in their consistency when mixed with developer and this makes them a little more difficult to use. The main reason for this is application control. The thicker consistency enables accurate application without running or dripping onto the scalp, towels and gowns.

1 Section and pin

2 Forming the curl

3 Pinning in position

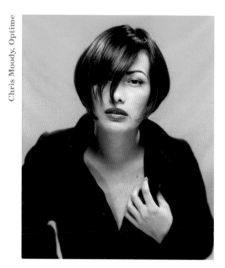

Chris Moody, Optime

Toning

Toning is the process of adding colour to previously bleached or lightened hair. A variety of pastel shades such as silver, beige and rose are used to produce subtle effects. Different types of toners are available; read the instructions provided by the manufacturers to find out what is possible.

The lightest toners can be used only on the lightest bleached hair. If the hair is too dark it will absorb the toner colour. Adding colour to colour produces a slightly darker shade of the previous colour.

Bleach toners contain no hydrogen peroxide and rely upon the porosity of the hair to absorb the coloured pigments. They are liquid or gels in consistency and easy to apply.

Colour correction

Colour correction is proving to be the largest growing market in hair colouring services. This is due to a number of step changes in the overall colouring market:

- more people are having colouring services
- more people are experimenting with home colouring products
- our clients expect more, therefore pushing the boundaries of safe, guaranteed practices to the limits

There are far more people having colour now than ever before. This growing market is looking for change. When these clients arrive in the salon they may want:

- modification of what they have had before
- something totally new
- their dark roots lightened to match the overprocessed lightened ends, which are the result of set after set of highlighting treatments.

These increasing salon colouring services will inevitably result in colour correction sooner rather than later. It is therefore an essential part of Level 3 work.

People experiment at home. Colour after colour is applied with the attitude that it is easy and anyway it saves a fortune. We all know what happens in the end. The biggest problem for hairdressers is getting an honest history of what has taken place, when and with what. We can't complain. It is good business (for those who can sort it out).

The last reason is much to do with the way that we work. Highlights/lowlights are a very attractive option for professional colouring. However they do create some serious long-term problems if they are not carried out with the long term in mind from the outset. That might sound strange, but it is true. It is to do with the success of the service really. Highlights are *addictive*, that is to say that when a new client is introduced to this form of colouring they are compelled by the colour technique's benefits to keep them up. They are a great way for:

- cleverly and subtly covering grey hair
- introducing clients to colour
- personalising colour to individuals
- advertising your colouring prowess
- expressing the hairstyle's attributes

Active learning: Monitoring colour correction

Over a two-month period monitor how many clients come in for colouring services. From this list how many had:

- simple root (retouch) application
- full head colour
- highlights
- highlights and lowlights
- colour correction as part of the colouring service

From your findings what patterns occurred and can you give any reasons for the numerical data?

Key skills: Communication

2.1 Collect and record data

2.2 Tackle problems

2.3 Interpret and present data

Charlie Taylor

Charles Worthington

Neville Daniel

However, hair grows and it is the regrowth that creates the problem – well initially. As the client's hair grows she becomes more conscious of the demarcation between the coloured hair and the natural roots. At the point where the hair has grown 2.5cm a natural parting will show 5cm of regrowth, a further colouring application is necessary. But will it be satisfactory to just highlight/lowlight the roots? In most cases not, particularly if several colours have been introduced to the hair. Even if the hair was only lightened, general shampooing, drying and weathering will have modified the colour on the ends to the extent where newly introduced colour at the root will have little effect. So what do you do? In most situations, faced with the pressure of replicating what you did last time, you redo the service. This reintroduces colour to hair that has already been processed, even if it is merely intended to be taken through to the ends for the last few minutes. Now you have hair that will continue to change in porosity and condition creating a more difficult task for the future, that is until you and your client agree to sort out the problem with colour correction.

Reintroducing colour (tone) into bleached hair

As more clients are willing to experiment with colour at home and want to change the appearance of their hair more frequently, the colour correction service is a growing market within the salon. When recolouring bleached hair back to its original or a darker colour, you need to consider the condition of the hair – how porous it might be and in particular whether there is sufficient colour pigment left in the hair for it to retain new pigment. Think back to how permanent colours work within the hair: i.e. synthetic para dyes work within the cortex of the hair, bonding into the hair's structure where the natural pigments are; conversely, bleaching products simply remove all natural pigment from the hair and weaken the hair's internal structure.

So if the hair's internal structure has been impaired then there will be less chance for reintroduced pigments to bond. This fundamental aspect, if ignored, will have a major impact upon the visual effect of the hair. However, this problem can be resolved by **pre-pigmentation**: During bleaching all (or most) of the natural pigments are removed. When these pigments are *dissolved* they create colourless, air-filled spaces, a bit like the inside of a natural sponge. These gaps are not uniform in shape and when synthetic pigments are put back into the hair not all will fit in the spaces they occupy. Hence, some will come away during washing, leaving a very uneven and unattractive result.

So to avoid *green hair* and to ensure that recolouring is successful, it is usual to pre-pigment (colour fill) the hair. This is done by applying red or warm shades to the hair before the final shade is applied. If this is not done the hair may fade, become patchy or appear greenish.

Remember: Colour wheel principles

Green tones are neutralised by the opposite colour, red tones.

Applying depth/tone into previously bleached hair (pale yellow blonde base 10)

Target depth	Amount of bleached lengths (cm)	Pre-pigment shade and development	Secondary processing and development
7–9	7.5 (approx. 3")	Use a golden/red /04 or /34 shade of same depth (7, 8 or 9) mixed with water. Apply from visible roots to ends. 12–15 mins without heat	After washing, conditioning and drying. Apply target depth 7, 8 or 9 and, if required, tonal ranges /3 or /34 or /03. from visible roots to ends with 3% (10 vol.). Develop without heat for 20 mins
7–9	over 7.5 (3"+)	Use a golden/red /04 or /34 shade of same depth (7, 8 or 9) mixed with water. Apply to mid-lengths and ends for 10 mins then apply to remaining light hair for a further 10–15 mins, without heat	After washing, conditioning and drying. Apply target depth 7, 8 or 9 and, if required, tonal ranges /3 or /34 or /03 mixed with 3% hydrogen peroxide on mid-lengths and ends first. Allow to develop for 10 mins. Then apply to remaining hair for further 10–15 mins
5–6	7.5 (approx. 3")	Use a red/copper of depth (8.43 or 7.43) mixed with water. Apply from visible roots to ends. 15 mins without heat	After washing, conditioning and drying. Apply target depth 5 or 6 and, if required, tonal ranges /3 or /34 /03 or /4 from visible roots to ends with 3% (10 vol.) Develop without heat for 20 mins
5–6	over 7.5 (3"+)	Use a red/copper of depth (8.43 or 7.43) mixed with water. Apply to mid-lengths and ends for 10 mins then apply to remaining hair for a further 10–15 mins without heat	After washing, conditioning and drying. Apply target depth 5 or 6 and, if required, tonal ranges /3, /34, /03 or /4 mixed with 3% hydrogen peroxide on mid-lengths and ends first. Allow to develop for 10 mins. Then apply to remaining hair for further 10–15 mins
4	7.5 (approx. 3")	Use 7.44 mixed with water. Apply from roots to ends with water for 15 mins. After washing and conditioning dry the hair to check that tone is strong enough to receive secondary colour. If not repeat again	After washing, conditioning and drying. Apply base 4 mixed with 3% roots to ends. Allow to develop for 10–15 mins
4	over 7.5 (3"+)	Not recommended	

1 colours used within this table refer to L'Oréal Majirel shade chart
2 ashen tones, violet browns and violet reds should not be applied to pre-pigmented hair

Removal of synthetic hair dye

Synthetic (para dyes) permanent hair colour can only be removed with a decolour treatment. All of the main colour manufacturers produce at least one. The decolouring process is also known as *colour stripping* and *colour reducing* and these products are quite different to bleaching products.

If a client's hair has previously been *permanently* coloured and the client wishes for the colour to be removed or changed in order to go to a lighter shade then only a colour remover (decolour) may be used. The chemical formulation of a colour reducer is very different from powder and emulsion bleach. Hence the colour reducer is specially developed to seek out and remove (dissolve) only the synthetic pigments within the hair.

Process preparation

Always make sure that you protect your client before undertaking any permanent colouring operation. The removal of hair colour becomes more problematic in proportion to length of hair, i.e the longer the hair, the more difficult the task and the easier it is for spillages to occur. Clients waiting for chemical processes to take place will often have to wait seated for long periods of time. Make sure that they are regularly attended to. Do not just check for development. Check also for clothing protection placement of towels and capes as well as poorly secured hair and product drips.

Belavance Colour by Labothene International, Germany

Mahogany

Removal of permanent, synthetic hair dyes

Client expectation/target colour

What is the purpose for removing the permanent hair dye?

- to recolour back to natural depth and tone
- to recolour to a lighter shade
- to remove unwanted/discoloured tonal effects from the hair

Treatment history

If you have no previous history available for the client and you want to undertake the technical operation, you must do a skin test and take a test cutting for incompatible chemicals and ability to achieve target shades *before* conducting any chemical process.

Condition

What are the existing hair condition attributes: elasticity; porosity; strength? Will these limit the effectiveness of the treatment?

Hair length

The longer the hair, the more difficulty will be encountered in stabilising the evenness of the lightening.

Natural hair colour

Do you know what the natural hair colour is?

1 If the natural hair colour is darker than the resultant, permanent hair colour, can the target colour be achieved without removing previous colour?
2 If the natural hair colour is lighter than the resultant permanent colour, how many levels of lift are required and is this feasible? (Reducing synthetic hair dye above four levels of lift is not recommended.)

Uneven, permanent hair colour

Where worn lengths have produced an uneven colour effect, the darker bands/areas must be lightened to match the other lighter areas first.

Work method

Always follow the manufacturer's instructions when mixing and applying the product. Start on the darkest areas first, then on to lighter areas. It is normally not necessary to apply to mid-lengths and ends first as worn hair colour tends to lighten on the ends anyway.

Often the consistency of colour reducers makes it more difficult to work with on pre-coloured hair, so make sure that the product is applied evenly.

Development

Slow development is easier to control, so develop without thermal acceleration. Ensure adequate air circulation, do not paste hair flat, lift sections and separate the hair to assist an even lifting process.

Removal of product

Always follow manufacturer's instructions and remove the product with suitable shampoo and tepid water. After conditioning, dry the hair before further processing.

Reapplying to natural depth

Removal of synthetic hair colour is usually only a part of a larger technical operation. More likely than not it will be the client's wish to return to her natural colour. Clients who merely want to change their hair colour to a different new shade would not normally have to go through the process of colour reduction first.

So the reapplication of base shade follows the removal of the synthetic tones. However, hair that has undergone the reduction process does now respond to the application of new colour in a different way. The new state of the hair referred to is called *double processed hair*. This degree of treatment will make the hair respond to reintroduced colour more readily. Therefore the porosity levels

Mahogany

Clynol

are increased, which means that the hair becomes more absorbent. In these situations there are certain *unwritten rules* that should be observed:

1   Do a colour test on the hair first mixed only with water.
2   Try using a liquid-based, quasi-permanent colour (e.g. diacolour) as these are easier to apply evenly and more quickly.
3   Choose a colour one shade lighter than the expected target shade to avoid *colour grab*.
4   Check development every few minutes (scrape colour off the hair and rub between fingers to see the colour development clearly).

Banded hair colour

Sometimes colour correction is undertaken to counteract partial colouring defects. These types of technical problems can seem quite daunting, particularly when we are used to applying colour in either a 'blanket' operation or by sectioning and covering in foil, etc. These problems can be overcome and usually require a change of mindset in their execution. There is something particularly difficult in tackling this type of situation though.

Horizontally banded hair colour will occur from one of the following:

● poor home product application
● poor home product reapplication and subsequent colouring
● poor salon product application
● excessive heat/'hot spots' occurring during development
● uneven porosity of the hair (possibly from *masking* where conditioning treatments have bonded to different sites upon the surface of the hair unevenly)

Horizontally banded hair colour usually appears on long hair at or near one length. If the hair is to be restyled or layered, it is worth cutting and drying first to see if the problem still exists. If decolouring is still necessary in these areas, it would be advisable to apply the product by the following methods:

1   Use a thicker consistency. This will allow you to *spot colour* applying freehand to the central areas of 'patchiness'.
2   Apply with the natural fall of the hair so that any natural light shadowing can easily be seen.
3   Later during development extend the product to the edges of the gradated patches.
4   Remove occasionally with warm water, then dry smoothly to see when the development is complete.
5   Reapply to those areas requiring further development.
6   Finally remove at the backwash with suitable shampoo and condition the hair with an anti-oxidising treatment.

Normally when colour is applied to hair people tend to liken the process to painting. Not true. Imagine painting emulsion on a dining-room wall. We paint the wall white and the saturation of the paint covers where we apply the brush. On finishing the wall, say we want to change an area in the middle and we paint a blue horizontal stripe. Wherever we apply the brush, the saturation of the paint again will provide cover and change it to blue.

Banded hair colour can often have a tendency to a type of gradation of colour and is particularly noticeable at the *patchy* edges. Part of the effect can be the result of how light reflects off the hair's surface, so when dealing with this situation look at the hair in different lighting backgrounds (ideally, natural daylight, white halogen light and out of bright lighting in more normal lit interiors).

Gradated colour

Gradated colour or gradation of colour is where the hue changes with the levels of saturation: i.e. black and white mixed together create grey; depending on how much white or black is added, the colour either deepens or lightens, moving from shade to shade *seamlessly*.

This merging of colour occurs in hair naturally after tinting and is difficult to remedy. It occurs partly by colour fade, i.e. natural wear and tear and weathering. However, this subtle colour fading is far more easy to tackle than the gradated banding that occurs after incorrect colouring. Imagine what happens when a dark colour, say base 5, is applied to natural hair base 7. As the hair grows, the regrowth becomes more obvious. Initially, this appears as a solid line of demarcation. But hair doesn't all grow at the same rate, and this becomes more apparent the further away from the roots the hair grows. The inconsistent growth *blurs* the edge of demarcation, creating a gradated effect. In this scenario the recolouring is simple, just retouch with base 5. However, if the hair was to be colour stripped then the complexity is increased because of the uneven *edge* of colour to be removed.

Discoloured highlights/lowlights and partial applications

Historically, we used the term discoloured hair as a description for hair that has resulted from the presence of incompatible chemicals: e.g. organic chemistry (carbon, hydrogen and oxygen) and metallic salts (silver nitrate). As these are now few and far between, the term has been applied in a different context and its presence is visible as a routine occurrence.

Partial colouring techniques are extremely popular and remain firmly as the 'professional only' route to achieving exciting colour effects. So therefore with an increasing higher expectation by clients for partial colouring techniques it is no surprise to find that much of the colour correction work undertaken within the salon is a result of previous highlighting and/or lowlighting services. Problems will tend to occur in the following instances:

- on longer hair over a period of time following several subsequent treatments
- on hair that involves two or more newly introduced colours on an uneven background colour
- poorly executed application or removal of product/s
- overporous hair
- lifestyle – hair subjected to excessive sunlight, UV and chlorinated swimming pools

Longer hair

Longer hair that has had several highlighting and/or lowlighting services is the most frequent reason for discoloured hair. Let's look at a typical example: a regular client has shoulder length hair of base 6 (i.e. dark blonde). The client has her first colouring service which involves two colours (a) a bleach with 9% (b) a beige midtone to harmonise the final effect. After 6–8 weeks with regular washing and blowdrying the midtones fade off. Some pigments are washed away and some are absorbed into the more porous lightened hair, discolouring the original highlights.

At the 12-week stage the client returns for a *'T' section* root application (recolouring of the roots at the parting and sides). What do you do? You are unable to do a reapplication of the midtone just at the roots as the ends have faded off. Similarly you may not be able to locate the initial bleached highlights. Most stylists in this situation will end up recolouring the hair with both colours again just within the 'T' section but roots to ends.

The client is happy once again. However, a longer term problem will start to develop. Much of the surface hair is now double processed (i.e. it has had two applications of the same chemicals). Double processed hair is more porous and this impaired condition leaves the client's hair in a state less able to retain colour pigments. So again a 'fade off' occurs. This problem is compounded by the fact that the ends will now be predominantly lighter. The new roots will be darker and the hair in between will be lighter than the roots, but not as light as the ends.

This colour state has now created an uneven background colour. A gradation from dark at the roots to light at the ends. Before any further partial colouring takes place this must be taken into consideration. At the point where this client wishes once again to have the same colours applied, a colour correction of the discoloured background hair will have to be undertaken.

This is done at the same time as the highlighting service. When the meshes of coloured hair are secured in their packets/foils, the

Remember

Colour stability

The stability of a synthetic colour within the hair is directly affected by the condition of the hair. The better the condition, the more able the hair to retain the pigments. Conversely, the poorer the condition, the less able the hair to retain the pigments.

remainder hair is coloured back to the natural shade. However this may exacerbate the problem further. If this newly introduced colour leaches out into the lightened hair, all of the hair will be discoloured and the problem is compounded further.

Newly introduced colours

A similar problem occurs when newly introduced colours are applied to an uneven background. If the unevenness of the background colour is not corrected during the service, the impact of the newly applied colour will be greatly devalued.

The hardest choice to make in this type of colour correction is whether to colour back the uneven background colour first or to attempt the correction at the same time as the application of the new colours. If the hair needs pre-pigmentation you would be better advised to complete the task in two separate phases:

1   Pre-pigment and then colour back the hair to natural base.
2   Carry out the partial colouring technique.

However, remember that hair that has been coloured back will be more porous and less able to sustain further colouring operations. This is particularly problematic if you intend to lighten portions of the hair (it just won't work satisfactorily!).

If you intend to lighten as well reintroduce colour to the background, you are better off conducting the process in a single phase: i.e. colour back the remaining hair that is not part of the partial colouring effect.

Poorly executed application/removal

As partial colour techniques become more involved, the complexity of processes and procedures also increases. This is all too apparent in poorly executed removal of product. When two or more colours are applied in the same operation, particular care must be taken in how they are removed. For example, let's take a client who has lightened highlights with vibrant copper lowlights on a reintroduced background of base 6. In this example three separate colour combinations exist: (a) highlight (b) lowlight (c) background. Imagine what would happen in the following scenarios:

● Highlight packets are removed and shampooed at the same time as the lowlight packets!
● Highlight packets are removed and rinsed with the background colour!
● All packets are removed and collectively shampooed at the same time!

Potentially, the effects created by clever techniques and artistic application can be totally wiped out if the individual colour combinations aren't removed one by one.

Overporous hair

The condition of the hair dictates what should and can be done. Never ignore the obvious. As we have already stated, clients want more and this pressure by the client should not override common sense. If you believe that a treatment cannot be undertaken or is unachievable, it is your duty to tell the client your assessment of the situation. By all means get another opinion from a colleague, but if the client insists you must make a decision. Do you:

- ask her to sign a disclaimer as she refuses to listen to reason?
- recommend another competing salon?

Lifestyle

Everyday wear and tear is the main reason for colouring problems and colouring problems often lead to colour correction. Lifestyle has the biggest impact upon hair condition and client expectation. Busy work schedules, social lives and the search for sun all have major impacts. Very few clients, even armed with the right products and equipment, are capable of the continual analysis and assessment needed to combat the external forces that affect the condition of their hair.

For example, how many times have you recommended a shampoo/conditioner to a client, they have gone away and used it, only to come back and say that it was great for a while, but then it didn't seem to have the same effect? So they went back to using their own particular favourite (probably because it smells nicer or is advertised by a celebrity icon). The truth of the matter is that what you recommended actually did its job and from the client's point of view in achieving the desired result it seemed to stop working. Therefore the needs have now changed. This constantly changing situation is difficult to master, particularly when the client arrives in the salon and you in this 'snapshot' of time are expected to guess what will happen if: (a) she goes on an exercise binge and swims every day; (b) spends two weeks in the Caribbean; (c) spills paint on her hair during redecorations at home; (d) gets talked into trying a home colour because a friend found it to be a great winner.

Goldwell

Goldwell

And finally...

Colour correction is becoming more frequent within the salon. However, it is still quite some way from becoming a routine service. On the contrary, it is work that is specially tailored to suit the needs of the individual client and therefore it is different every time, in every case.

Your colour confidence will build upon experience. The more that you are involved with the service, the better prepared you will be in undertaking this essential work. The main thing is knowing and understanding the situation in hand. You must conduct a thorough consultation to find out exactly what has taken place and over what period of time. Planning a course of corrective action is imperative before anything else. Unless you understand what you are seeing, you cannot hope to stumble on the correct course of action. Remember, there will be times when what you see before you doesn't make sense. In other words what you see and believe to have taken place is clearly missing some vital information. This could happen for a number of reasons, but is more likely to be a result of embarrassment on your client's part either for things she has done but doesn't wish to admit, or quite simply by accident.

In order for you to get as much 'honest' information as possible, don't make an issue of the situation. You will get a lot more help if you don't apportion blame or look for someone to be the scapegoat. If this is a new client, you have a unique opportunity to forge a professional relationship that is built on respect which should last and last.

The corrective service doesn't end there either. The condition of the client's hair will always be impaired in some way following double processing. You need the client to help you in maintaining the colour's fastness and the hair's condition during routine daily handling between salon visits.

Diagnosing a course of action is one thing, but it should also be followed by *prescription*. Selecting and advising the right products is almost as important as doing the job in the first place. The misuse or wrongly used products will quickly negate the value of the completed work. You only need to make the client aware of what could go wrong in order for her to take your sound advice in keeping up the regimen.

Problem	*Possible causes*	*Action*
Uneven colour	Poor application Section too large Incorrect mixing	Spot-bleach recolour Strip colour and recolour if necessary
Dark ends	Ends underbleached Toners too dark Toner overprocessed Dark tint remains	Rebleach Remove using lighteners After removal, time accurately. Remove and tone
Too yellow	Underbleached base too dark Wrong toner used Wrong bleach	Rebleach Try stronger bleach Use violet toner Use other than oil bleach
Too red	Underbleached Too much alkali Wrong toner used	Rebleach Use different bleach Use green matt or olive
Dark roots or patches	Poor application Toner too dark	Rebleach evenly Remove using lightener
Roots not coloured	Underbleached Undertimed Toner too dilute Unclean or coated	Rebleach Rebleach Reapply Clean and reapply
Colour fade	Overporous Harsh treatment Overexposure	Condition Advise on hair care
Hair breakage	Overprocessed Incompatibilites present Harsh treatment Sleeping in rollers Tied-back long hair	Recondition remaining hair Retest to make sure Provide hair care advice
Discolouration	Underprocessed Excessive exposure Home treatment	Colour match or develop further
Green tones	Incompatibles Blue used on yellow Too blue ash used	Test hair Use warm or red shades Use violet
Too orange	Underprocessed Pigment lacking	Apply blue ash Add blue
Too yellow	Underprocessed	Add violet and/or bleach further

Problem	Possible causes	Action
Hair tangled	Overbleached Raised cuticle/overporous	Use antioxidants/treatment reconditioners
Colour not taking	Overporous Chemicals masking the hair Colour bounce/red pigment grabbing at roots	Precondition and pre-fill hair Use deep cleanser to remove build-up Recolour with brown as pigments (not deposited into hair correctly)
Colour build-up	Overporous Excessive over-application	Recondition and pre-pigment Consider colour removal

Self-test section

Quick quiz: a selection of different types of questions to check your knowledge.

Q1   A .... test will identify a client's sensitivity to colour products.   Fill in the blank

Q2   A quasi-permanent colour lasts longer than semi-permanent colour.   True or False

Q3   Which of the following products are likely to be incompatible?   Multi-selection

Permanent colour containing PPD	☐	1
Retail permanent colour containing PPD	☐	2
Vegetable henna	☐	3
Compound henna	☐	4
Single-step applications for covering grey, e.g. 'Just for men'	☐	5
Single-step toners for application to bleached hair	☐	6

Q4   Bleaches and high lift colours are the same.   True or False

Q5   Which of the following tests do not apply to colouring services?   Multi-choice

Skin test	☐	a
Incompatibility test	☐	b
Porosity test	☐	c
Curl test	☐	d

Q6   Permanent colours alter the pigmentation of hair within the cuticle.   True or False

Q7   Which of the following colour products do not require the addition of hydrogen peroxide as a developer?   Multi-selection

Powder bleach	☐	1
Semi-permanent colour	☐	2
Quasi-permanent colour	☐	3
Temporary colour	☐	4
Vegetable henna	☐	5
High lift colour	☐	6

Q8   Green tones within hair are neutralised by adding .... tones.   Fill in the blank

Q9   Hair lightened from natural base 7 should be capable of maximum lift to: Multi-choice

Base 10	☐	a
Pale yellow	☐	b
Yellow	☐	c
Yellow / orange	☐	d

Q10   Lightened hair that appears too yellow can be neutralised by adding mauve.   True or False

Perming

6

Chris Moody, Optime

What do I need to learn?

You need to know and understand:

- **How health and safety legislation affects you and your clients**

- **The importance of good communication**

- **Perm science and the range of perming processes and products**

- **The range of tests that need to be conducted**

- **The benefits of sound advice followed up by prescribed home maintenance**

- **A range of tools and equipment and their uses**

Unit H29
Perm hair using a variety of techniques

Element H29.1 Maintain effective and safe methods of working when perming hair

Element H29.2 Prepare for perming

Element H29.3 Create a variety of permed effects

What does it mean?

This chapter covers the fundamental aspects of perming theory and practice. The text later extends to cover more advanced skills and techniques.

What do I need to do?

- **You will need to create a range of effects resulting from a variety of winding techniques on different lengths of hair.**
- **These effects should take account of client requirements, pre- and post-perm tests and physical limiting factors.**

Other info

Related topics and other useful information:
- **Health and safety legislation**
- **Client consultation**

Science bit!

- **The effects of chemically processing and modifying the hair's structure**
- **Perming and neutralising solutions**
- **pH values of perming products and how that affects hair (acid and alkaline solutions)**
- **The effects of pre- and post-perm treatments**

Key words

- pH values
- contra-indications
- alpha and beta keratin
- acid and alkaline solutions
- post-damping, pre-damping

Started it ✓	I know and understand the principles of positive communication ✓	I know when and how to conduct tests on the hair for perming ✓	I always recognise contra-indications when I analyse the client's hair ✓
I am familiar with a range of perming equipment and winding techniques and know when to apply them ✓	I know how to negotiate, reaching a mutually beneficial conclusion ✓	I always carry out working practices according to the salon's policy ✓	I've covered most of it! ✓
I understand the science of perming and know the effects of heat and chemicals upon the hair ✓	I know when and to whom to refer clients in situations where external assistance is required ✓	I understand the necessity of personal hygiene and presentation ✓	I know how to advise, promote and sell other services and products to clients ✓
I know and respect the client's rights: data protection EO, discrimination, consumer legislation ✓	Done it all! ✓		**CHECKER BOARD** ✔

Introduction

This chapter covers one of the most difficult optional units of Level 3. This perming unit comprises:

H29   Perm hair using a variety of techniques

     H29.1   Maintain effective and safe methods of working when perming hair

     H29.2   Prepare for perming

     H29.3   Create a variety of permed effects

Perming and colouring are arguably the most complex aspects of contemporary hairdressing. The combination of client's expectations, reality and ability to maintain their hair carefully and competently between salon visits is crucial. These factors have made perming a very problematic technical procedure. As we strive to obtain softer, kinder, longer lasting results on longer length hair, a division, based upon technical ability, experience and confidence, now exists between professional hairdressers and it is still growing. These stylists now fall into the following groups: the technicians that *can*, hairdressers that *can but won't*, and others who *cannot*.

Like many other hairdressing services, condition is the main consideration, i.e. the condition before starting and the condition when the job is finished. *Moisture is the key*. If the hair retains its natural *moisture* levels after perming, the signs of healthy hair are obvious: shine, easy 'combability' and great flexibility. Together these features indicate a style that is easily managed. Lose these qualities and the hair will be dull, lifeless, tangled and difficult to manage. So after giving away the big secret, let's see how you get everything else right too.

Perming principles

Cross-section of hair

Perming is the term given to the physical and chemical processing of hair, changing it into waves or curls. Perming, also known as permanent waving, can be achieved by a variety methods, some using heat, or by cold wave lotions and a variety of winding techniques. Unlike the movement and curl produced by blow-drying and setting, the curls produced by perming are permanent. The hair does not straighten out later when dampened. However, hair continues to grow and the new hair retains its natural tendency. So the waves and curls produced by perming gradually get further and further away from the scalp as the hair grows. To keep the same style the hair will at some point need to be permed again.

Because perming really does make a permanent change to the hair, you cannot easily correct mistakes (as you can with blow-styling, for example). The process also involves various chemicals. It is therefore important that you make sure you understand what you are doing.

How perming works: changing the keratin

Before going ahead with this section, refer to 'The chemical properties of hair' in Chapter 2 (p. 56).

Of the cross-links between the polypeptide chains of hair keratin, the strongest are the *disulphide bridges* that give hair its strength. Each disulphide bridge is a chemical bond linking two sulphur atoms, one in each of two polypeptide chains lying alongside each other. Each sulphur atom forms part of an amino acid unit called *cysteine*; the pair of linked units is called *cystine*.

During cold perming some of these bridges are chemically broken, converting each cystine into two cysteine units. The breaking of the bridges makes the hair softer and more pliable, allowing it to be moved into a new position of wave or curl. Only about 20 per cent of the disulphide bridges need to be broken during a perm. If too many are broken, the hair will be damaged. You need to keep a check on the progress of the perm and stop it at the right time. You do this by rinsing away the perm lotion and neutralising the hair. During neutralising, pairs of cysteine units join up again to form new cystine groups. The new cross-links thus formed hold the permed hair firmly into its new shape.

Changing the bonds

The hair is first wound onto some kind of former such as a *curler* or *rod*. Then you apply perm lotion to the hair, which makes it swell. The lotion flows under the cuticle and into the cortex. Here it reacts with the keratin, breaking some of the cross-links within and between the polypeptide chains. This softens the hair, allowing it to take up the shape of the former: You then rinse away the perm lotion, neutralise the hair and allow it to harden in its new, curlier shape.

This process is often described in chemical terms. The first part – softening the hair by breaking some of the cross-links – is a process of *reduction*. The disulphide bridges are split by the addition of hydrogen from the perm lotion. (The chemical in the perm lotion that supplies the hydrogen is called a *reducing agent*.) The keratin is now stretched: it is beta-keratin.

The last part of the process – hardening the hair by making new cross-links – is an **oxidation** reaction. New disulphide bridges form and the hydrogen that was added is lost again. The hydrogen reacts with the oxygen in the neutraliser, forming water. (The chemical in the neutraliser that supplies the oxygen is called an *oxidising agent* or *oxidant*.) The keratin is now in a new unstretched form: it is alpha-keratin again.

Reducing agents

In the past, most cold perming lotions were alkaline, but these tend to roughen the cuticle. Newer lotions are acidic instead and these are becoming popular. Some perm lotions contain ammonium

Disulphide bridges

Reduction: breaking existing disuiphide bridges

Oxidation: forming new disulphide bridges

thioglycollate. This is environmentally damaging and new perm solutions use other chemicals.

Oxidising agents

Hydrogen peroxide is the most common oxidant. Others include sodium perborate, sodium percarbonate, sodium bromate and potassium bromate.

Acidity and alkalinity: the pH scale

The pH scale measures **acidity** or **alkalinity**. It ranges from pH 1 to pH 14. Acids have pH values from 1–6, whereas alkalis have values ranging from pH 8–14. Substances that are neither acid or alkaline, i.e. neutral, have a pH value of 7. The higher the pH number, the more alkaline is the substance; the lower the pH number, the more acid the substance.

The normal pH of the skin's surface is 5–6, referred to as the skin's acid mantle. This acidity is due in part to the sebum, the natural oil produced by the skin. The pH can be measured using *pH papers*, *universal indicator papers*. *Litmus papers* will indicate whether something is acid, alkaline or neutral. If hairs are placed in alkaline solution they swell and the cuticle lifts. In slightly acid solutions the hair *clenches* and the cuticle is smooth. However, stronger acidic or alkaline solutions will impair the hair's structure, causing it to break down.

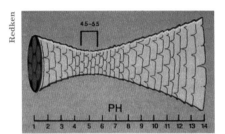

How pH affects the hair

The pH scale

Preparing and planning the perm: the client

For the client a perm is a major step. She will have to live with the result for several months. She may not be familiar with the range of perms available. She will need you to explain what is involved in each and help her decide which is the most suitable.

- There are several cold perms designed to curl straight hair.
- Acid perms are popular because their effects are gentle. Strongly alkaline perms can be too harsh: new forms are being developed.
- Not all perms contain ammonium thioglycollate: 'non-thio' perms tend to be gentler in their action.

Discuss your client's requirements. Find out what she is expecting from a perm and determine whether this is the best solution.

1   Consider the style and cut, together with your client's age and lifestyle.

2   Examine the hair and scalp closely. If there are signs of inflammation, disease or cut or grazed skin, *do not* carry out a perm. If there is excessive grease or a coating of chemicals or lacquer, you will need to remove these by washing first. Previously treated hair will need special consideration.

3   Analyse the hair texture. Carry out the necessary tests to select the correct perm lotion.

4   Always read manufacturers' instructions carefully.

5   Determine the types of curl needed to achieve the chosen style.

6   If this is a regular client, refer to her records for details of previous work done on her hair.

7   Advise your client of the time and costs involved. Summarise what has been decided to be sure there is no misunderstanding.

8   Minimise combing and brushing to avoid scratching the scalp before the perm.

Analysis/examination

It is important to make sure you choose the most suitable perm lotion, the correct processing time and the right type of curl for the chosen style. Consider the following factors:

1   **Hair texture** For hair of medium texture, use perm lotion of normal strength. Fine hair curls more easily and requires weaker lotion; coarser hair can often be more difficult to wave and may require a stronger lotion for resistant hair. (This is not true for oriental hair types.)

2   **Hair porosity** The porosity of the hair determines how quickly the perm lotion is absorbed. Porous hair in poor condition is likely to process more quickly than hair with a resistant, smooth cuticle (see pre-perming treatments).

3   **Previous treatment history** Virgin hair – hair that has not previously been treated with chemicals – is likely to be more resistant to perming than hair that has been treated. It will require a stronger lotion and possibly a longer processing time.

4   **Length and density of hair** Long, heavy hair requires more perming than short hair because the hair's weight will pull on the curls. Short, fine hair may become too tightly curled if given the normal processing time.

5   **Style** Does the style you have chosen require firm curls or soft, loose waves? Do you simply wish to add body and bounce?

6   **Size of rod, curler or other former** Larger rods produce larger curls or waves; smaller rods produce tighter curls. Longer hair generally requires larger rods. If you use very small rods in fine, easy-to-perm hair, the hair may frizz; if you use rods that are too large you may not add enough curl. To check make a test curl before you start.

7   **Incompatibility** Perm lotions and other chemicals used on the hair may react with chemicals that have already been used, for example, home-use products. Hair that looks dull may have been treated with such chemicals. Ask your client what products she uses at home and test for incompatibility (see below).

Tests

1 **Elasticity** Stretch a hair between your fingers. If it breaks easily the cortex may be damaged and perming could be harmful.

2 **Porosity** Rub the hair between your fingertips to feel how rough or smooth it is. Rougher hair is likely to be more porous and will therefore process more quickly.

3 **Incompatibility** Protect your hands by wearing gloves. Place a small cutting of hair in a mixture of hydrogen peroxide and ammonium hydroxide. Watch for signs of bubbling, heating or discoloration: these indicate that the hair already contains incompatible chemicals. The hair should not be permed, nor should it be tinted or bleached. Perming treatment might discolour or break the hair and might burn the skin.

4 **Test curl** Wind, process and neutralise one or more small sections of hair. The results will be a guide to the optimum rod size, processing time and strength of lotion to be used. Remember though that the hair will not all be of the same porosity.

5 **Processing** Unwind and then rewind rods during processing to see how the curl is developing. If the salon is very hot or cold this will affect the progress of the perm: heat will accelerate it, cold will slow it down. When you have achieved the S shape you want, stop the perm by rinsing and then normalising the hair.

> ### Remember
>
> Temperature has a major impact on perming. This could be general salon temperature or added heat. In either case remember that processing times will be reduced considerably.

Pre-perming and post-perming treatments

Matching the correct perm lotion to hair type is an essential part of the hair examination. However, many perming solutions come in only a tinted, normal or resistant formula. This alone does not cater for all hair conditions. Dry, porous hair will absorb perming solutions more readily; therefore special attention needs to be given in these situations. Pre-perming treatments are the way to combat these condition defects. Porous hair that is suitable for perming will have an uneven porosity throughout the lengths. Hair that is nearer the root will have a different porosity level to mid-length hair, or that of the ends. Therefore the hair's porosity levels will need to be balanced before the perm lotion is applied. This enables the hair to absorb perm lotion at the same rate, evening out the development process and ensuring that the perm doesn't over-process in certain areas. A pre-perming treatment is applied before winding on damp hair and combed through to the ends. Any excess is removed and the hair is wound as normal.

After perming and neutralising it is also necessary to rebalance the hair's pH value of 5.5. Post-perm treatments do this by removing any traces of residual oxygen from the neutralising process. These treatments are also known as **antioxidants**.

Perming technique

Perming is a straightforward procedure – the more organised you are, the simpler and more successful it will be. Once you have consulted your client and made the necessary tests, you are ready to start.

General preparation

1   Protect your client and her clothes as necessary with a gown and towels.

2   Shampoo the hair to remove grease or dirt that would otherwise block the action of the perm lotion.

3   Towel-dry the hair. (Excess water would dilute the perm lotion, but if the hair is too dry the perm lotion won't spread thoroughly through the hair.)

4   Some perm lotions contain chemicals to treat porosity. If you are going to use a pre-perm lotion, apply it now. Make sure you have read the instructions carefully. Too much pre-perm lotion may block the action of the perm itself.

5   Prepare your trolley. You will need:
   - rods, curlers or formers of the chosen sizes
   - end papers, for use while winding
   - a tailcomb and clips, for sectioning and dividing
   - cotton wool strips to protect your client
   - gloves to protect your hands
   - perm lotion and a suitable normaliser/neutraliser (read the instructions carefully)
   - water spray to keep the hair moist (hence reduces the 'quenching' action of the perming lotion upon the hair)
   - A plastic cap to 'envelope' the hair and retain moist heat during processing

6   Check your client's skin and clothes are adequately protected.

General sectioning

Standard technique

The first part of the process is to divide the hair into sections that will be easy to manage and wind. Done properly, sectioning makes the rest of the process simpler and quicker. If it's not done well though, you will have to resection the hair during the perm and this may spoil the overall result.

Cold perm sectioning

1   Following shampooing and towel-drying, comb the hair to remove any tangles.

2   Make sure you have the tools you will need, including a curler to check the section size.

3 Now divide the hair into six sections, as follows, using clips to secure the hair as you work:

- divide the hair at or near the crown into a horizontal mesh, no wider than a perm rod, secure the top hair out of the way

- divide the back hair into a vertical, yet parallel section down into the nape, secure in sectioning clip(s)

- divide the front hair approximately above both mid-eyebrows, to create a central parallel section meeting the first division at the crown, secure in sectioning clip(s)

- divide the sides into two equally wide sections, one continuing down into the nape and the other terminating above the ears

- divide the opposite side likewise to give two equal width sections

Winding techniques

Basic winding

Winding is the process of placing sectioned hair onto rods, curlers or formers. There are various winding techniques, designed to produce different effects, but the method is basically the same in each case. In modern cold perming systems you need to wind the hair firmly and evenly, but without stretching the hair or leaving it in tension (see also 'Fashion and alternative winding techniques' p. 187).

Method

1 Divide off a section of hair of a length and thickness to match the curler being used.

Winding: taking a hair section

2 Comb the hair firmly, directly away from the head. Keep the hair together, so that it doesn't slip.

3 Place the hair points at the centre of the curler. Make sure the hair isn't bunched at one side and loose at the other, or twisted.

4 Hold the hair directly away from the head. If you let the hair slope downwards, the curler won't sit centrally on the base section: hair will overlap and the curler will rest on the skin.

5 Before winding, make sure the curler is at an angle suited to the part of the head against which it will rest when wound.

6 Hold the hair points with the finger and thumb of one hand. The thumb should be uppermost.

7 Direct the hair points round and under the curler. Turn your wrist to achieve this. The aim is to lock the points under the curler and against the main body of hair. If they don't lock, they may become buckled or fish-hooked. Don't turn the thumb too far round or the hair will be pushed away from the curler and won't lock the points.

Winding the section onto the curler

8 After making the first turn of the curler, pass it to the other hand to make the next turn. The hands need to be in complete control: uncontrolled movement or rocking from side to side may cause the ends to slip, the hair to bunch, or the firmness to slacken.

Winding: securing the curler

9 After two or three turns the points will be securely locked. Wind the curler down to the head in a steady and even pressure, keeping the curler horizontal. (If it slips, wobbles or bunches the curl result will be uneven.)

10 At the end the curler should be in the centre of the section. If it isn't it will need to be rewound.

11 Secure the curler. Don't let the rubber band pinch or press the hair as it may cause damage.

Winding: depth of section

Winding: width of section

Acid and alkaline perming solutions

The systems we currently use to perm hair rely on alkaline or acid based solutions. Their benefits and suitability for use are listed here.

Alkaline

- Effective on strong, coarse, resistant hair which is difficult to wave.
- Alkaline lotion, up to pH 9, is suitable for different hair textures.
- The lotion swells the hair, lifts the cuticle and penetrates to the cortex.
- Less winding tension is required.
- Suitable for all winding techniques.
- The test curl forms a stronger, sharper shape.
- The hair must be normalised or neutralised.
- The higher the pH and the stronger the lotions, the more potential there is for damage.
- No additional heat is required.

Acid

- Suitable for fine, delicate, porous and previously chemically processed hair.
- Shrinks hair and smoothes cuticle.

- Some require additional heat to be applied: climazone, rollerball, accelerator or infra-red dryer.
- Make sure that the reagents are activated by mixing the solutions correctly: check with the manufacturer's instructions.
- The test curl forms a softer, looser shape – a crisp, snappy test curl could result in overprocessing.
- Needs a longer processing time than alkaline perms.
- Pre-damp or post-damp – more often post-damp.

Active learning: Experimenting with curl effects

Over a period of a month, save the longer length waste clippings from the salon floor. Collect and trim them into meshes, fixed together with sticky plastic tape. Make them the same width as your ranges of perming rods so that you can conduct the following perm tests:

1 Produce a variety of different curl effects (varying diameter curls and movement effects).

2 Test the hair to destruction by over-processing with strong lotions, excess timing and heat so that you know what would happen in a worst case scenario.

Keep and record the findings in your portfolio for future reference.

Key skills: Communication

2.1 Take part in discussions

2.2 Produce written materials

Processing and development

Perm lotion may be applied before winding (pre-damping) or when winding is complete (post-damping). Follow the manufacturer's instructions. Post-damping is perhaps more convenient. You can wind the hair without wearing gloves and the time taken in winding doesn't affect the overall processing time.

Applying the perm lotion

Most perm lotions come in an applicator bottle, ready to use. Others may need to be applied from a bowl, using cotton wool, a sponge or a brush. Read the instructions carefully before applying.

1 Underlying hair is usually more resistant to perming. Apply lotion to these areas first.
2 Keep lotion away from the scalp. Apply it to the section, about 12mm from the roots.
3 Don't overload the applicator and apply the lotion gently. You will be less likely then to splash your client.
4 If you do splash the skin, quickly rinse the lotion away with water.

Processing time

Processing begins as soon as the perm lotion is in contact with the hair. The time needed for processing is critical. Processing time is affected by the hair texture and condition, the salon temperature and whether heat is applied, the size and number of curlers used and the type of winding used.

- **Hair texture and condition** Fine hair processes more quickly than coarse hair and dry hair than greasy hair. Hair that has been processed previously will perm faster than virgin hair.
- **Temperature** A warm salon cuts down processing time; in a cold salon it will take longer. Even a draught will affect the time required. Usually the heat from the head itself is enough to activate cold perming systems. Wrap your client's head with plastic tissue or a cap to keep in the heat. Don't wrap the hair in towels: these would absorb the lotion and slow down the processing. Some perm lotions require additional heat from lamps or dryers. Don't apply heat unless the manufacturer's instructions tell you to. You might damage both the hair and the scalp. Don't apply heat unless the hair is wrapped; the heat could evaporate the lotion, or speed up the processing too much.
- **Curlers** Processing will be quicker with a lot of small sections on small curlers than with large sections on large curlers. (The large sections will also give looser results.)
- **Winding** The type of winding used and the tension applied also affect processing time. A firmer winding processes faster than a slack winding. Indeed, if the winding is too slack it will not process at all. Hair wound too tightly may break close to the scalp. The optimum is a firm winding without tension.

Testing curls during processing

As processing time is so critical, you need to use a timer. You also
need to check the perm at intervals to see how it's progressing. If
you used the pre-damping technique, check the first and last curlers
that you wound. If you applied the lotion after winding, check
curlers from the front, sides, crown and nape.

1 Unwind the hair from a curler. Is the S shape produced correct
for the size of curler used?
2 If the curl is too loose, rewind the hair and allow more
processing time. (But if the test curl is too loose because the
curler was too large, extra processing time will damage the hair
and won't make the curl tighter.)
3 If the curl is correct, stop the processing by rinsing.

Rinsing and neutralising

When processing is complete, leave the curlers in place while you
rinse away the perm lotion. Use tepid water (not hot). Direct the
spray head onto and between the rollers for several minutes to make
sure all the lotion is removed. Long hair will require more rinsing
than shorter hair.

After rinsing, blot the hair with towels and cotton wool to remove
excess water. The hair is now ready for neutralising.

Neutralising

Neutralising is the process of returning hair to its normal condition
after perming. The word is a little misleading: chemically speaking,
a 'neutral' condition is neither acidic nor alkaline (pH 7.0). In fact,
healthy hair is slightly acidic.

How neutralising works

As described above, perm lotion acts on the keratin in the hair. The
strongest bonds between the polypeptides are the disulphide
bridges. Perm lotion breaks some of these, allowing the keratin to
take up a new shape. This is how new curls can form.

What neutralising does is to make new disulphide bridges. If you
didn't neutralise, the hair would be weak and likely to break and
the new curls would soon fall out. Neutralising is an oxidation
process – a process that uses oxidising agents such as hydrogen
peroxide, sodium bromate and sodium perborate.

Preparation

1 Gather together the materials you will need.
2 Make sure there is a washbasin free, preferably one where the
client can put his or her head back to use it. (This makes it
easier for you to keep chemicals away from the client's eyes.)

L'Oreal

Neutralising: first rinse

L'Oreal

Neutralising: towel-drying the hair

Good practice: Equipment care

Always wash, dry and talc perming rods immediately after use. This will avoid the corrosive action of perming products perishing the rubber fasteners and will remove any traces of acidity or alkalinity from the equipment.

First rinsing

1 As soon as the perm is complete, move your client immediately to the washbasin. Make sure she is comfortable. Offer her hand towels or tissues in case any liquid trickles over her face.

2 Carefully remove the cap or other head covering. The hair is soft and weak at this stage, so don't put unnecessary tension on it. Leave the curlers in place.

3 Run the water. You need an even supply of warm water. The water must be neither hot nor cold. Check the pressure and temperature against the back of your hand. Remember that your client's head may be sensitive after the perming process.

4 Rinse the hair thoroughly with the warm water. This may take about five minutes. It is this rinsing that stops the perm process – until you rinse away the lotion, the hair will still be processing. Direct the water away from the eyes and face. Make sure you rinse *all* the hair, including the nape curlers. If a curler slips out, gently wind the hair back onto it immediately.

Applying neutraliser

1 Raise your client to a comfortable sitting position.

2 Blot the hair thoroughly using a towel or tissues. It may help if you pack the curlers with cotton wool.

3 When no surplus water remains, apply the neutraliser. Follow the manufacturer's instructions. These may tell you to pour the neutraliser through the hair, apply it with a brush or sponge, or use the spiked applicator bottle. Some foam neutralisers need to be pushed briskly into the hair. Make sure that neutraliser comes into contact with all of the hair.

4. When all the hair has been covered, time the process according to the instructions. The usual time is five to ten minutes. You may wrap the hair in a towel or leave it open to the air – follow the instructions.

5 Gently and carefully remove the curlers. Don't pull or stretch the hair. It may still be soft, especially towards the ends.

5 Apply the neutraliser to the hair again, covering all the hair. Arrange the hair so that the neutraliser does not run over the face. Leave for the time recommended, perhaps another five to ten minutes.

Second rinsing

1 Run the water, again checking temperature and pressure.

2 Rinse the hair thoroughly to remove the neutraliser.

3 You can now treat the hair with an after-perm aid or conditioner. Use the one recommended by the manufacturer of the perm and neutraliser to be sure that the chemicals are compatible.

Successful neutralising

At the end of the neutralising process, you will have returned the hair to a normal, stable state.

Neutralising: first application

Removing curlers

Second application of neutraliser

- The reduction and oxidation processes will have been completed
- Finishing aids or conditioners (antioxidants) may need to be applied to counteract the oxidants used.
- The hair will now be slightly weaker – fewer bonds will have formed than were broken by the perm. Special conditioners may be needed. If the cuticle is lifting or roughened, this too may be countered with conditioners.
- Record any hair or perm faults on the client's record. Correct faults as appropriate.
- Under-neutralising – not leaving neutraliser on for long enough – results in a slack curl or waves.
- Over-oxidising – leaving the neutraliser on too long or using oxidants that are too strong – results in weak hair and poor curl.

The hair should be ready for shaping, blow-drying or setting.

After perming

Check the results of perming:

- Has the scalp been irritated by the perm lotion?
- Is the hair in good condition?
- Is the curl even?

Dry the hair into style. Depending on the effect you want, you may now use finger drying, hood drying or blow-drying, treat the hair gently. If you handle it too firmly the perm may relax again.

Advise the client on how to manage the perm at home. The hair should not be shampooed for a day or two. The manufacturer's information should be passed on to the client.

Clean all tools thoroughly so they are ready for the next operation. Complete the client record, noting type of perm, strength of the lotion, processing time, curler sizes and winding technique. Record any problems you have had. This information will be useful if the hair is permed again.

Zullo and Pack, Nottingham. Photograph by John Rawson

Roberta Kneller at Bobs Hair Company. Photograph by John Rawson

Fashion and alternative winding techniques

Basic sectioning and winding techniques create lateral waves and curl that are in the horizontal plane to the head: this is not the only curl placement option.

Spiral (vertical) curl movement

Selecting the size and position of the curls

The spiral curl is dependent on the length of the client's hair. If the hair is less than 10cm long it will be difficult, and perhaps impossible, to form spiral shapes of any size. Hair longer than 10cm will permit reasonable spiral formations: longer hair will enable fuller, thicker and longer curls to be shaped.

The position that these spiral curls take and the overall effect they produce must be discussed with your clients: you must ensure that they understand what is being done. Because the handling and maintenance of this type of perm is quite different to traditional methods, it is important that they know how to maintain the effects before they leave the salon.

Spiral curls may be formed all over the head, length permitting, or they may be formed and positioned to make a cascade in the nape. Alternatively, bunches of spiral curls may be positioned asymmetrically. The degree of the spiral curl shape and the effect finally produced is for you and your client to determine jointly at the outset.

1 Spiral rods

2 Position on the head

3 The curl expected with a small rod (left) and with a large rod (right)

Starting the wind

The spiral wind can be started at the root end of the hair or from the hair points. If you use a curl former that is of the same thickness overall, the curl you produce will be even throughout. If you use a former that tapers or is concave, the results will be uneven.

For the resultant curl to be even, springy and smooth, your winding must be firm without undue tension, wrapped cleanly over the former and secured without indenting or marking the wound hair.

If you apply uneven tension to your winding, the spiral formation will be inconsistent – the loops and turns will not follow on and there may be gaps in the shape.

Securing the wind

When you secure the hair formers, be careful not to cut into the wound hair. Breakage could result if you did. Follow the recommendations of the makers of the curl former that you are using. You must also ensure that the formers are secured firmly: if they are loose, the hair may drop or unwind.

Monitoring the perm process

Once you have completed your winding and secured the formers, you must monitor the perm process. If the perm lotion is applied to the hair before winding – a technique called pre-damping – the winding must be carried out without delay. Alternatively, the lotion can be applied after the winding is complete – post-damping. Perm processing is always timed from the moment the lotion is applied.

A completed spiral wind

You will need to check the development of the perm process. You can achieve this by taking a test curl. By gently unwinding the hair part-way you can check the development of the S shape. If the shape is loose then further development may be required. If the shape is well formed, begin normalising straightaway: the perm is said to have 'taken'.

As well as monitoring the timing carefully you must check the following:

- ensure your client's comfort
- keep excess lotion off the skin to avoid skin irritation
- remove damp cotton wool (used to protect the skin) when it has absorbed the lotion or scalp 'burns' will occur
- continually reassure the client so that she never feels she has been forgotten
- use a timer which makes an audible noise when the time has elapsed

Normalising

When the perm has taken, you must stop the perming process quickly. This is an important stage. If you are supervising a junior hairdresser, be sure to double-check with her that she is monitoring whether the perm has taken and is ready to normalise the hair. Normalising should include the following stages:

1 Rinse the wound hair thoroughly with warm water to remove the perm lotion. Make sure the water is not too hot or there may be a sudden tightening of the perm.

2 Blot the curlers or formers to remove surplus water, using tissues or towels. (If this is not done the normaliser may become diluted and the perm is likely to drop.) When monitoring others, ensure that this has been done thoroughly.

3 Apply the normaliser as recommended by the manufacturer. Care must be taken that it covers all of the wound hair. Ensure that the curlers in the nape and around the ears are not missed.

4 When you have completed the normaliser application, start the timing. The time the normaliser should remain on the hair varies with the type and make of perm used: make sure that you know the recommended time for the normaliser you are using.

5 When the first application of the normaliser has been on the hair for its allotted time, the curlers may be removed. This must be done with care as the hair may still be soft. Harsh handling could weaken the perm.

6 You may now apply the second stage of normalising. This too must be carefully timed. Again, check that the normaliser has covered all the hair.

7 Now rinse the hair well to remove all traces of normaliser. At this stage the hair may be conditioned and made ready for setting for blow styling.

Problems

Below are some problems that you may encounter when producing permanent spiral curls:

- **The root end is straight** You can avoid this by securing the former firmly at the root end of the hair. The helical loops of hair will be too loose if they are not firmly wound and in close contact with the former.
- **Hair flicks out** Ensure that the hair is not twisted when you form the spiral curl. After each turn, the hair should be repositioned. If you allow the hair to twist, an irregular spiral will be formed: this could cause the hair to stick out from the head. It is difficult to remedy this afterwards.

Philip Bell, Ishoka

Remember

Health and safety

Take care not to splash your client's face while rinsing. Even dilute perm lotion can irritate the skin.

Young Artistic Team, Ishoka

- **The spiral curl is too loose** Provided that the hair condition permits it, the hair may be reprocessed. You must take special care if you do this as the hair will be far more receptive to the perm lotion and could easily become over-processed.

Perming hair of different lengths

Short lengths of hair (less than 10cm) are not suitable for permanent spiral curls because it is impossible to form the helical shape on the curl former.

Medium hair lengths (10–15cm) do allow spiral formations. These are likely to be short and narrow.

Longer lengths of hair (15cm and longer) are the most suitable. Here there is sufficient hair to produce a variety of full, long, springy shapes. Greater lengths allow the hair to be placed onto the former more easily and a wider variety of curl formers may be used.

Direction and degree of movement

The direction of perm movement is determined by the angle that you wind and position the curlers or rods. If a forward direction of the fringe area is required, the wound curlers must be positioned accordingly.

The degree of perm movement is the 'tightness' or 'looseness' of the wave or curl. This is determined by:

- size of curlers, rods or formers used
- time for which the hair is processed
- amount of tension used
- hair texture and its condition
- perm lotion strength
- type of winding used

Directional winding

The hair is wound in the direction in which it is to be finally worn. This technique is suitable for enhancing well-cut shapes. The hair can be wound in any direction required and the technique is ideal for shorter hairstyles.

Staggered winding or brick winding

The wound curlers are placed in a pattern resembling brickwork. By staggering the partings of the curlers, you avoid obvious gaps in the hair. It is suitable for short hairstyles.

Weave winding

The normal size section is divided into two and then the hair is woven. A large curler is used to wind the upper subsection and a smaller one is used for the lower subsection. This produces two

Pincurl

Double wind

Directional wind

Stack wind

Weave wind

Winding and the finished effects

different curl sizes, giving volume without tight curls. Alternatively, one subsection is wound and the other left unwound. With short hair this produces spiky effects.

Double winding

This technique consists of winding a section of hair halfway down on a large curler, then placing a smaller curler underneath and winding both curlers down to the head. This produces a varied curl effect.

Piggyback winding

This is winding using a small and a large curler. The normal size section is wound from the middle onto a large curler, down to the head. The ends are then wound from the points onto a smaller curler, which is placed on top of the large curler. This produces softly waved roots and curly points. Alternatively this technique can be used to produce root movement only by not winding the point ends.

Stack winding

This is used where fullness of long hair is required, with little curl movement on top – it is ideal for bobbed hair lengths. The sections are wound close to the head in the lower parts; the upper sections are part wound only at the points. This allows the curlers to stack one upon another.

Other types of perm which give volume support

- **Root perms** – perming the lower root ends of the hair. The hair is wound at the root ends only: the point ends are left out and not processed. This allows the hair to produce fullness and volume. Reperming must be kept strictly to the regrown root ends.
- **Body perms** – the root and middle hair lengths can be processed to give added body to the hair.
- **Pin perms, roller perms, semi- or demi-perms** – these involve the application of a weaker form of perm lotion, which lasts for six to eight weeks. Reprocessing can take place through the hair lengths after this time has elapsed. These are not intended to be permanent, but to produce body fullness.

Other types of perming equipment

Foam rollers and formers

1 Take a small rectangular section of hair.
2 Secure the hair points in an end paper.
3 Wind the hair around the foam roller.
4 Secure the roller in position by bending over the ends.
5 Repeat steps 1–4 to complete the entire head.

Hair extensions

7

Hair by Jackie McShannon, Photograph by Anders

What do I need to learn?

You need to know and understand:

- **The range of products and equipment used in hair extension work**
- **The techniques of safe application and removal of extension products**
- **The blending, handling and mixing of colours and fibres**
- **How to shape and finish styles incorporating hair extensions**

Unit H23 Add hair extensions to create a variety of looks	→	**Element H23.1** Maintain effective and safe methods of working when adding hair extensions
	→	**Element H23.2** Plan and prepare to add hair extensions
	→	**Element H23.3** Add hair extensions
	→	**Element H23.4** Cut and finish hair extensions
	→	**Element H23.5** Remove hair extensions

What does it mean?

This chapter covers the technical aspects of consultation, planning, preparation, application, and removal of real and synthetic hair extensions.

What do I need to do?

- **Make sure that you conduct a comprehensive client consultation so that a correct plan of action can safely take place**
- **Be able to prepare materials appropriately and according to service requirement**
- **Be able to safely apply, shape, style and remove both real and synthetic hair extensions**

Other info

Related topics and other useful information:

- **Client consultation**
- **Health and safety**

Science bit!

Key words

- **Contra-indications**
- **Synthetic fibre extensions**
- **Real hair extensions**

Started it ✓	I know and understand the principles of a hair extension consultation ✓	I always recognise the contra-indications for hair extension services during consultation ✓	I recognise the differences between the different hair extension types ✓
I can identify the range of different tools and products required for this service ✓	I know how to select the correct proportions of extension hair colours to enable me to mix it to match the client's natural hair colour ✓	I recognise and understand that there are several different extension application techniques ✓	I understand the natural hair sectioning to take before applying extensions ✓
I understand the planning of a hair extension lifestyle ✓	I know where to place extensions in a client's hairstyle ✓	I can identify the range of cutting techniques used for cutting extension hairstyles ✓	I know how to advise a client to style a hair extension hairstyle ✓
I know what aftercare products to advise clients to use on their extension hairstyles ✓	I know how to apply and remove one of the hair extension applications ✓	Done it all! ✓	**CHECKER BOARD** ✔

Introduction

This chapter covers the increasingly popular and exciting optional unit of hair extensions. At Level 3 this comprises the following five elements:

H23   Add hair extensions to create a variety of looks
- H23.1   Maintain effective and safe methods of working when adding hair extensions
- H23.2   Plan and prepare to add hair extensions
- H23.3   Add hair extensions
- H23.4   Cut and finish hair with extensions
- H23.5   Remove hair extensions

Hair extensions are now accepted as a routine hairdressing service. What was once a specialism for just a few has grown so much in popularity that it is now a core service for the comprehensive salon that endeavours to provide a host of service options for its clientele. This chapter provides the essential knowledge for the application, styling and maintenance of both real hair and synthetic fibre hair extensions.

Hair extensions consultation

Conducting a thorough hair extension consultation before a stylist or client embarks on a hair extension hairstyle is one of the most important parts of the hair extension service as there are many issues to cover and explain. Armed with this knowledge both parties can conclude the suitability of this service for each client. A consultation appointment should be booked for the minimum of 30 minutes.

An extension hair stylist should then thoroughly analyse the client's natural hair. The stylist is checking the client's hair condition as the natural hair should be strong and healthy enough to hold an attachment of extension hair in place for a three-month period of time.

The stylist is looking at the first 2–4 inches of the client's natural hair as this area is where an extension will be secured. The analysis includes establishing whether the client's hair is normal, fine, coarse, dry or greasy. If a client has a greasy hair condition that necessitates shampooing on a daily basis, then a hair extension service is not suitable. The sebum will either break down the bonds securing the extension in place or the sebum will make the natural hair too slippery and the attached extensions will slip down the hair shaft and fall out.

The extension stylist has to establish whether the client's natural hair is strong enough to withstand extension hair attached at the root area and whether the mid-lengths and ends of the client's hair will withstand the friction and wear and tear of added extension hair for up to three months. If the client's natural hair is delicate or broken then it will not be strong enough to wear a hair extension hairstyle.

Contra-indications for hair extensions

The following are the contra-indications (issues that adversely affect a service being performed) of wearing a hair extension hairstyle that have to be taken into account during a hair extension consultation:

Remember

The stylist has to satisfy himself that a client's fine hair will be strong enough to hold a secured extension in place for up to three months.

Remember

The porosity of the client's natural hair has to be analysed from root to point, checking whether the client's hair is normal, dry, chemically treated or bleached.

Good practice: Consultation considerations

- The first question that should be asked is what hair extension hairstyle is to be achieved – length, thickness, volume, body, colour, decoration or texture?
- It is vital to establish what style is to be achieved before embarking upon this service as this will determine which hair extension application technique can be used and whether the client's natural hair length, condition and porosity is suitable for the required hairstyle.
- A client's natural hair should be a minimum of 3 inches long to apply a textured extension hairstyle.
- A client's natural hair should be a minimum of 4 inches long to apply hair additions that create decorative looks, e.g. crystal strands, highlights or flashes of colour.
- A client's natural hair should be a minimum of 5 inches long to create volume and thickening extension hairstyles.
- A client's natural hair should be a minimum of 6 inches long to create a natural-looking lengthened extension hairstyle. When applying a weave or weft extension to ethnic/African Caribbean hair types, the client's natural hair must be long enough to enable the stylist to create a continuous and firm tight corn braid or scalp plait.

- clients suffering hair fall or who are having medication or treatment for hair fall
- clients who suffer from any form of alopecia
- clients with thin or thinning hair
- clients with breakage through the first 2–4 inches of their hair at the root area
- clients taking medication or treatment for cancer
- clients who are pregnant or during the first six months after giving birth
- clients suffering from psoriasis or eczema on the scalp
- clients who suffer skin allergies or excessive skin sensitivities
- clients who have excessively oily hair and scalp

Extension hair choice

After establishing that the client's hair condition, porosity and length are suitable for the requested hair extension hairstyle, the stylist must then choose what extension hair is suitable for the client.

Real human hair, either Asian or European hair (real hair) or synthetic acrylic fibre hair (fibre) can be applied. The choice of extension hair to be used to create the extension hairstyle depends on the client's budget, suitability of the client's natural hair or the choice of application tools and attachment techniques.

Real hair is sold in different lengths from 10–24 inches. Synthetic fibre is sold in various lengths from 35–60 inches.

Remember

The price of the extension hair normally increases as the length of the hair increases.

Remember

Hair extension hairstyles can take from 30 minutes to 10 hours to apply. During the consultation clients should be informed about the length of time needed to apply their hairstyle.

Good practice:

On average a trained extension stylist should take one minute to apply one extension. A lengthened hairstyle needs approximately 150–250 single extensions. The time of each appointment will be dictated by the amount of extensions to be applied and the hairstyle required.

Remember

All hair extension hairstyles are to be removed from the client's natural hair after three months' wear. All removal should be conducted in the salon by a professional trained person as the removal of extensions, if poorly performed, will break and damage the hair.

Establish the length of extension hair needed for the required style to be achieved. Real hair is supplied in several structures, straight, soft wave, deep wave, curly or spiral curled. Synthetic hair is supplied in several structures, straight, soft wave, deep wave. Pre-made dreadlocks, braids and crimped hair can be purchased. During the consultation establish the correct structure suitable for the client extension hairstyle. After establishing the extension hair that is to be used – either real hair or synthetic hair – the extension hair colour must be selected. Using a colour ring or colour shade chart select the base colour, major tone and minor tone required (see colour selecting, mixing and blending section p. 207).

During the consultation, the stylist should educate the client about the home after-care products and procedures that need to be followed throughout the duration of the extension hairstyle (see advice and home care maintenance p. 222). There are two different product ranges and procedures to follow, depending on whether the client is wearing real extension hair or fibre extension hair.

Each hair extension hairstyle needs regular maintenance appointments at the salon. These appointments are every two, four or six weeks depending on the hairstyle, application technique and extension hair used to create the style. During the consultation each client should be informed about the maintenance appointments required for their hairstyle.

Health & Safety

Each person loses 80–100 hairs per day in natural hairfall. Whilst wearing extensions this hairfall cannot fall out and becomes trapped at the root area above the extension attachment. If the extension strand is left in the hair for more than three months, the trapped hair will begin to matt. When the matting occurs it becomes impossible to remove an extension hairstyle without damaging the natural hair.

Good practice: Consultation

- Analysis of the client's natural hair condition, porosity, strength, length and required style.
- Selection of the extension hair type, style, length, colour and structure.
- Advising the client about the correct after-care products, maintenance appointments and removal procedures.
- Quotation of the total price, including application, maintenance appointments, removal service and after-care products.
- Booking the correct time for each appointment and ensuring you have the trained staff available to complete the service.
- Ordering the correct extension hair structure, length and colour for the client.

Price quote

The price of the extension hairstyle is quoted during the consultation. Finally an appointment date and time are booked. It is vital to record the consultation on a record card as this assists the salon reception when booking the appointment time, maintenance appointments and the removal appointment. Additionally the record card assists in ordering the extension hair required and selecting the correct after-care products.

Hair extension products and equipment

The products and equipment required to perform the hair extension service are many and varied, depending on which application technique you choose to work with. The following is a list of products and equipment needed when working with several extension systems.

Hair extension connector tools

Application of hot bonded real hair extensions

Section clips

Silicon strips or pads

Tail comb

Old Hairdressing scissors

Real Extension Hair

Polyamide resin adhesive sticks

A bonding applicator

Silicone Dripmator – a drip tray

A mixing mat

Mane Connection Enhancement System

Remember

Bonding applicator tools must be placed on a flat stable work surface when in operation as the heated resin that drips from this tool will deliver serious burns if accidentally spilled on skin.

Hair Direct

Heat sealer or heat clamp

---

1 **Professional heat clamp**. Heat clamps are designed to attach and seal fibre extensions. They will not attach real hair extensions. This tool has two heated tips that melt fibre hair at a specific temperature. This tool heats from 140°C to 220°C. When the fibre has melted it creates a hard heat seal bond that holds a fibre extension in place at the root area or seals the end of a fibre extension when the stylist has created a braid or dreadlocks (see below).

2 **Professional bonding applicator**. This tool accommodates polymer resin adhesive sticks that are inserted into the tool. This tool heats to a temperature of 180°C. The resin is then dispensed from a nozzle of the applicator, enabling the stylist to deposit the resin on to real hair or fibre hair and then attach an extension in place by creating a polymer resin bond (see above).

3 **Heated pre-bonded extension applicator**. This tool has one or two heated tips that reach a temperature of 100°–140°C. This

tool melts pre-bonded extensions, which are extension strands with a wax, protein or keratin polymer resin already applied to the end of a piece of extension hair. Pre-bonded applicators melt the resin on to the natural hair, creating a bond that attaches the extension in place. Pre-bonded applicators will attach pre-bonded fibre hair and pre-bonded real hair.

4   **Needle and thread**. A curved mattress needle can be used to sew weaves or wefts on to ethnic/African Caribbean hair. The weave is sewn on to a scalp plait or corn braid. The thread used is designed to sew weaves on to hair. It is a silk thread that can be purchased in a variety of colours.

Health & Safety

- Perform a skin test before using cold fusion liquids as some of these products can cause allergic reactions.

- Read the manufacturer's instructions contained with these tools and products before using them.

Hair extension connector products

1   **Liquid, cold fusion adhesives**. These products vary greatly from gum to rubber or latex-based liquids. They are applied from bottles that have brushes attached to the lids, similar to the application of a nail varnish. Cold fusion liquids will attach fibre hair and real hair in place by painting the liquids on to the real hair and extension hair, then placing the two hair types together. These products are not heated.

2   **Polymer resin adhesive sticks**. This is a resin stick inserted into a bonding applicator that is melted and then dispensed from the applicator. Designed to create extension bonds on individual fibre or real extension hair.

3   **Synthetic acrylic fibre hair**. This extension hair is made from acrylic and designed to be used for extension hairstyles. The fibre is manufactured in a variety of deniers (thickness or fineness). The deniers are designed to look and feel as similar to natural hair as possible with an acrylic. Fibre hair is manufactured in specific colours that once produced cannot be altered. The fibre comes in a variety of structures – straight soft wave, deep wave, braids and dreadlocks and crinkled structures that mimic straightened ethnic/African Caribbean hair textures. Fibre structure can be changed using heat from a hot hairdryer or heated rollers. Fibre hair will be damaged or melted when excessive heat is applied to it.

Fibre can be purchased in lengths from 35–160 inches, and comes in more than 100 colours ranging from natural colours to neon fantasy colours. Fibre is packaged in 100-gram bales or packets or it is sewn into weaves/wefts. The weaves/wefts are sold in 4oz packets.

Remember

Do not use heated electrical hairdressing tools on fibre hair, e.g. tongs or straighteners, as this will melt the fibre and cause irreparable damage.

Remember

Neon-coloured fibre hair will glow under ultra-violet lights.

4 **Real human extension hair.**

- *Asian hair*

  Asian real hair comes mainly from China or India. This hair is cleansed in a caustic soda solution to remove infestation. It is then rinsed and dried, bleached and tinted to match manufacturer's colour shade charts. When wavy or curly structures are required, the Asian hair is permed. After the above chemical treatments have been performed the cuticle layer of the Asian hair is damaged and must be treated as chemically damaged hair when applied into natural hair. Asian hair is coarse in structure and very strong, which is why it is used for extensions, wigs, toupées and hair pieces. Asian hair comes in a variety of lengths from 10–24 inches. It is normally packaged in 4oz packets or sewn into weaves/wefts. The weaves/wefts are sold in 4oz packets.

- *European hair*

  This hair comes mainly from the eastern bloc countries such as Russia. It is tinted to match extension colour shade charts. If a wave or curl structure is required it is permed. European hair is finer than Asian hair and should be treated as chemically damaged when applied into natural hair. It comes in a variety of natural colours and fantasy colours plus several lengths from 10 to 24 inches. It comes in 1oz packets and is sometimes sewn into weaves/wefts in 1oz packets. European virgin hair has had no chemical treatment. It comes in only natural colours and structures. This hair comes in lengths from 10 to 24 inches. It is very rare and very expensive. It comes in 1oz packets and is sometimes sewn into weaves/wefts in 1oz packets.

5 **Pre-bonded extensions**. These are strands of fibre or real hair with wax, protein or keratin resin applied at the root end of an extension at the manufacturers. These are applied using a heated pre-bonded tool. These extensions come in a range of structures and a variety of colours and lengths. Pre-bonded extensions come in packets of 5, 10, 20 or 25 strands.

6 **Silicone pads**. These are small pieces of heat-resistant silicone sheet measuring 2cm by 4cm. They are used during the application of bonded extensions. The silicone pads protect stylists' fingers from the intense heat of resin bonds and are used to roll resin into bonds at the root area of the natural hair attaching extensions in place.

7 **Scalp protectors or scalp shields**. These are circular plastic discs 4cm in diameter. They are placed at the root area of an extension. They are secured on to the natural hair before attaching an extension in place. Scalp protectors have a small hole in the centre where natural hair feeds through. This strand of natural hair will have the extension attached. Scalp protectors prevent loose strands of natural hair becoming trapped in an extension bond and keep the natural hair sections clean and neat.

8 **Soft bristle brush**. This is a brush that has a padded face and soft bristles which protrude from the padded base. Soft bristle brushes should be used when blending, mixing and brushing extension hair.

Remember

Real hair prepared for hair extensions is root point correct. The roots and tips are aligned together or tangling of this loose hair will occur

Remember

Real hair that is not prepared on weaves or wefts comes loose. This loose hair is tied in 1oz or 4oz bundles called *bulk* hair.

Hair Direct

Remember

Do not place fibre hair in a mixing mat as it will tangle if drawn through the interlocking teeth.

Health & Safety

Stylists should wear protective rubber gloves when using removal solutions to protect their hands. Always use these products in well-ventilated areas. Do not smoke or have naked flames near these products as some of them are highly inflammable.

9 **Mixing mats**. Mixing mats are designed to hold real hair root point correctly and they assist in the blending of real hair colours. They are used to hold real hair safely whilst applying extensions. They are two square mats, 6 × 6 inches. Each mat has small wire teeth or pins protruding from one side. These teeth are slightly bent. They are bent backwards (away from you) on the bottom mat and forwards (towards you) on the top mat. The two mats are then placed together so that the teeth can interlock, trapping the real hair in between. The real hair is then drawn out of the mats in small pieces the size of an extension. This hair then has a resin bond dispensed on the root end of the real hair ready to be attached to the natural hair as an extension.

10 **Removal tool**. This tool is similar to a small pair of pliers. It crushes and breaks extension seals and resin bonds during the removal of extension.

11 **Removal solutions**. These are acetone, alcohol, oil or spirit based solutions that are recommended by the extension product companies to break down the resins, acrylics, rubber, latex and wax bonds which attach extensions in place.

12 **Resin drip tray**. A metal dish or silicone mat the size of an ashtray is placed underneath the nozzle of a bonding applicator to catch dripping resin.

13 **Client after-care products**

● *clarifying shampoo* – shampoo designed to remove sebum, oil, wax, styling products and pollutants from the extension hair and natural hair. This shampoo must be oil and silicone free.

● *light conditioner* – a conditioner specifically designed for fibre hair and natural hair. It is manufactured by extension product companies and designed to coat the fibre hair, forming a surface barrier and protecting the fibre from any heat or friction damage caused by brushing and styling. It is a light conditioner for the natural hair.

● *daily maintenance spray* – a spray mist that is applied to the mid-lengths and ends of the fibre. It untangles the fibre and protects the fibre from heated appliances used for styling. The spray is manufactured by extension product companies. The daily maintenance spray must be used before brushing fibre and before any heated styling tools are used to style the fibre.

● *reconstructive conditioner* – a conditioner that works within the hair shaft designed to strengthen and rebuild hair. Reconstructive conditioners are manufactured by extension product companies specifically for real hair.

● *pH balanced rinse* – an acid balanced rinse that has the same pH as hair and skin (4.5–5.5). This product is diluted in water: 1 part rinse to 10 parts water. It is used after shampooing and conditioning and applied through the mid-lengths and ends of the hair. The acid balanced rinse is designed to close the cuticle layers of the real hair, therefore reducing tangles and matting that can occur when the real hair is wet. A pH balanced rinse is manufactured by extension product companies specifically for real hair.

Hair Direct

14 **Colour ring or swatch**

15 **Cutting comb, pin tail or tail comb**

16 **Hairdryer or air styler**

17 **Flat sectioning clips**

18 **Hairdressing scissors, pair of thinning scissors, razor and razor blades**

19 **Selection** of round brushes or blow drying brushes

20 **Flat stable work surface** on which to place heated bonded tools and a hairdressing trolley

Remember

Do not use your best pair of hairdressing scissors as extension hair will blunt scissors.

Selecting and blending extensions and colours together

Creating extension hairstyles requires learning new skills over and above the stylist's existing hairdressing knowledge. Selecting, mixing and blending fibre hair and real hair is an additional skill that requires a new understanding of selecting colours. When applying a natural-looking extension hairstyle it is important to create extension hair which is the same colour as the natural hair. If there is seen to be even a fractional difference in colour the extension hairstyle will look false. Therefore selecting, mixing and blending colours is a vital new skill for a stylist to learn with this service.

Handling and controlling extension hair can be awkward at first but with practice and proper practical training these new skills can be mastered. Find below the broad principals of selecting, blending and mixing extension hair to match a client's natural hair colour.

Remember

It is very rare to find extension hair that matches natural hair exactly. Often a second or third colour will have to be selected and mixed into the base colour to get an exact match of natural colour. Natural hair is not one colour but made up of several colours. Extension hair must mimic this natural phenomenon.

Selecting extension hair colours to match to the natural hair colour

Take a hair extension colour ring or shade chart. Place the colour ring swatches of hair colour against the client's natural hair. Select the extension hair colour that is the nearest colour to the client's own hair colour. This is the *base colour* or *first colour*. Use the colour ring to identify the *second colour* that is the nearest colour to the client's own hair colour. This is the major tone or second colour. Use the colour ring and look closely for the *third colour* that matches the hue (glint) of the client's natural hair colour. This is the minor tone or third colour.

Remember

- Fibre extension hair is packaged in 100g bales.
- Real extension hair is packed in 4oz bulk or weaves/wefts.

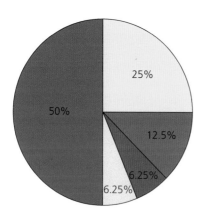

Remember

Do not attempt to brush real hair colours together in order to blend the colours as most of the real hair will stay in your brush or fall on the floor.

You have now selected the base colour, major tone and minor tone of the natural hair. Blending the extension colours in their correct proportions to match natural is a very visual technique. However, find below a formula to follow that will assist you in calculating the correct proportions of colour to mix in order to make an exact colour match.

Colour formula for mixing extensions

Colour mix formula

Adding 25% (25g or 1oz) of a second colour to the base colour will lighten or darken the base colour.

Adding 12.5% (12.5g) of a second colour to the base colour will give a strong tone.

Adding 6% (6g) of a second colour to the base colour will give a hue or glint of colour.

Adding equal amounts (25g + 25g) of two different extension hair colours together will change the base colour.

Blending extensions together

Remove the selected base colour of extension hair from its packaging, then divide 25 per cent, 12.5 per cent or 6.25 per cent of the second colour and third colour from the packing (using the formula above). After selecting the quantities of extension hair, place the colours together. Ensure the ends of the extension hair are together. When blending fibre hair colours together, hold the fibre hair in the centre. Lightly spray fibre with a daily conditioning spray. Use a soft bristle brush to blend the fibre hair colours together. Start brushing from the ends of the fibre, working towards the centre.

When blending real hair colours together, always place real hair in a mixing mat with the root ends together.

Place the first colour or base colour onto the mixing mat. Then place the second colour and third colour on top of the base colour. Place the lid of the mixing mat on top of the selected colours. As you draw the real hair out of the mixing mat during application the colours will mix together.

Remember: Special note

Do not place the root of the human hair at the tip end of the human hair. It is vital that real hair is always placed root point correct – this means roots together and tips together. If the real hair is mixed with root and tips laying in opposite directions then the hair will severely matt, locking together as tightly as velcro. When real hair is in this state it is virtually impossible to separate or untangle.

Attaching prebonded hair extensions

Natural hair extensions bought from the supplier arrive prepared by the manufacturer. They are available in a variety of strand colours, sizes and types – finer strands are for use around hairlines and partings, thicker strands are for use in other areas. You can also choose between straight, wavy and curly hair types. The wefts of hair are 'gummed' together with a polymer resin, so no colour blending is required. They are ready to attach to the hair.

Although the procedures for natural hair extensions may seem similar to those for synthetic hair extensions, in reality the processes are quite different. The polymer resin is activated by a device which emits ultra-high-frequency sound waves: once activated it moulds around the section of hair and creates a strong permanent bond.

Natural hair extensions can be styled by blow-drying, tonging or using heated rollers. It is possible to use semi-permanent or temporary colours, but perming and tinting are not recommended.

Attaching processed hair extensions

1 Prepare the high-frequency equipment according to the manufacturer's instructions.
2 Prepare the other tools – the plastic strand shield, brushes, combs, clips, and whatever else you will need.

Great Lengths

3 For hair extensions over the whole head, section the head into five working areas.

4 Leave a 7mm section of hair out around the hairline.

5 Start at the nape area. Take a band of hair above the hairline. Secure the remainder out of the way with clips.

6 Starting in the centre of this band, take a section of hair 5mm × 5mm and again clip the remainder out of the way.

7 Slide on the plastic protection shield and push it near to the scalp area.

8 Place the polymer-bonded end of the extension into the centre of the hair section, approximately 12mm from the scalp and forming a V-shaped wedge of hair around the bond. An even distribution of natural hair should surround the bonded end of the hair extension, to prevent uneven tension or breakage.

9 Place the grooved tip of the high-frequency device below the hair section.

10 Wait for the polymer to bubble before rolling it smoothly between your index finger and thumb. (Bubbling will occur in just a few seconds.)

11 Check that the bottom end of the bond is adequately sealed.

12 Continue the process, repeating steps 1–11 until the complete row is finished.

13 Continue working up the back of the head until the section is complete.

14 After all the extensions have been applied, cut and dress the hair into the desired style.

Planning and placement

So many extension hairstyles can be created with this service using fibre hair and real hair. Once the principles of the planning and placement of the extensions are understood, virtually any style can be created.

Sectioning of client's natural hair

This diagram shows the sectioning of the client's natural hair and the areas where extensions can be placed. Hair extensions are applied in the interior of the natural hairstyle. They are placed 1–2cm behind the hairline, parting and crown area. The natural hair is sectioned into six areas.

- **Area 1** is the nape section. Take a section using a tail comb from the top of the ear to the top of the ear across the occipital bone.
- **Area 2** is at the back section of the head above the occipital bone up to the crown. Take a section using a tail comb from the top of the ear to the top of the ear over the top of the head and through the crown area.

Synthetic, acrylic fibre extension hair

The home care products required for fibres are:

1 **A clarifying shampoo**. This is a shampoo designed to remove sebum, oil, wax, styling products and pollutants from the extension hair and natural hair. This shampoo must be oil and silicone free.

2 **A light conditioner**. This is a conditioner specifically designed for fibre hair and natural hair. It is normally manufactured by extension product companies and designed to coat the fibre hair, forming a surface barrier and protecting the fibre from any heat or friction damage caused by brushing and styling the fibre. It is a light conditioner which sits on the surface of the natural hair.

3 **A daily maintenance spray**. This is a spray mist that is applied to the mid-lengths and ends of the fibre. It untangles the fibre and protects it from heated appliances used for styling. The spray is only manufactured by extension product companies. The daily maintenance spray must be used before brushing fibre and before any heated styling tools are used to style the fibre.

4 **A soft bristle brush**. This is a brush that has a padded face and soft bristles that protrude from the padded base. Soft bristle brushes should be used when blending, mixing and brushing hair.

Real extension hair

The home-care products required for real hairs are:

1 **A clarifying shampoo**. This is a shampoo that is designed to remove sebum, oil, wax, styling products and pollutants from the extension hair and natural hair. This shampoo must be oil and silicone free.

2 **A reconstructive conditioner**. This is a conditioner that works within the hair shaft, designed to strengthen and rebuild hair. Reconstructive conditioners are manufactured by extension product companies specifically for real hair. Real hair has gone through several chemical processes before application, making it porous and chemically damaged. Reconstructive conditioners should be used to assist in maintaining the strength, shine and manageability. Light conditioners are not recommended for real hair as these products would build up on the real hair, making it dull, lifeless and heavy.

3 **A pH balanced rinse**. This is an acid balanced rinse that has the same pH as hair and skin (4.5–5.5). This product is diluted in water 1 part pH rinse to 10 parts water. This product is used after shampooing and conditioning and is applied through the mid-lengths and ends of the hair. The acid balanced rinse is designed to close the cuticle layers of the real hair, therefore reducing tangles and matting that can occur when the real hair is wet. This rinse can be used as a daily product contained in a water spray and applied to damp down real hair before restyling. A pH-balanced rinse is manufactured by extension product companies specifically for real hair.

4 **A soft bristle brush**. Soft bristle brushes should be used when brushing real hair extension hairstyles.

Remember

Oil and silicone based shampoos can break down the bonds attaching extensions in place. They can also build up on the hair shaft, causing the extension to slip out of the hair.

Remember

Conditioner must not be applied to the root area of the client's hair or directly onto the bonds that attach the extensions in place. If applied to the roots or bonds it will leave a deposit on the natural hair causing the extension to fall out and it can break the bonds down.

Remember

Do not use brushes that have balls on the end of the bristle as this can rip and tear fibre and damage the bonds holding the extensions in place.

Good practice:

All home-care products and tools must be recommended to the client by the stylist who has created the extension hairstyle. Products used on extensions that are not recommended by a stylist could damage or make extensions fall out.

Home care advice for extension hairstyles

This is a step-by-step procedure to be followed consecutively by clients when cleansing conditioning and styling extension hairstyles.

1 Shampoo extension hairstyles at least twice a week, reducing natural oil build up at the root area.
2 Before shampooing brush gently with a soft bristle brush. Begin brushing at the ends of the hair in downward strokes until you reach the root area. Then brush from the root through to the tips.
3 Using your fingers ensure all the extensions are separated at the root area.
4 Whilst shampooing real hair the head should be in an upright position. Standing in the shower is an ideal position. The hair and water should flow in a vertical downward direction. The water temperature should be warm.
5 Use a clarifying shampoo recommended by your stylist specifically for your hair extension hair. Using your fingertips, stroke the shampoo gently into the hair from the roots to the tips. *Do not massage or rub the extensions when wet.*
6 Apply a recommended conditioner to the mid-lengths and ends of the extension hair. Then rinse thoroughly.
7 After shampooing and conditioning, wrap a towel around the hair and pat gently to remove excess water. Wrap hair in a towel and leave for 20 minutes for the towel to absorb all the moisture from the extensions and natural hair.
8 Separate the extensions at the root area with your fingers before drying.
9 Dry the extensions with a warm hairdryer using a diffuser if required.
10 After drying the root area brush gently from the ends towards the root area in a downward direction. Always hold the hair extensions at the roots whilst brushing to avoid placing unnecessary tension on the bonds and root area.
11 Long or lengthened hair extensions must be plaited and secured with a covered band on the ends before going to bed at night. Do not go to bed with damp or wet extensions as matting and tangling will occur.

Styling extension hair styles dos and don'ts

- Always use brushes and styling products that are recommended by your stylist.
- Use hairdryers and heated rollers on the fibre hair. Heat will straighten or curl fibre extensions. Once heated and cooled down the fibre will retain this texture until more heat is applied to recurl or straighten. Water will not alter the movement of fibre extensions. Do not use curling tongs, curling brushes, straighteners or crimpers directly on the fibre.
- Use hairdryers and heated rollers on real hair. Electric curling tongs, straighteners and hot brushes may be used on Asian or European hair extensions.

> **Remember**
>
> Do not allow natural oils to build up at the scalp area as this can break down the bonds and then the extensions slip out.

> **Remember**
>
> Hair extension hairstyles must be dried immediately at the root and bonded area. Do not brush or comb extensions when they are still wet as the bonds can break down and fall out.

> **Remember**
>
> Do not apply excess tension on the root area by tying tight ponytails.

- Always avoid the bonded areas with these heated tools as direct heat will soften the bonds.
- Do not backcomb the hair extensions as this will cause irreparable tangling.
- Do not use styling products that contain oils, wax, silicone or excessive alcohol as these will break down the extension bonds.

Removing hair extensions

Health & Safety

Some removal solutions can irritate the skin or dissolve nail polish and nail extensions – ensure you wear rubber gloves.

Health & Safety

Some removal solutions are highly flammable so make sure you work in a well-ventilated area. Ensure there is no smoking and no naked flames while the solution is being used.

This is an example of one of the main techniques to remove hair extensions:

Step-by-step guidance

Mane Connection Enhancement System

A You need a removal tool, removal solution (if applicable), pad of cottonwool and rubber gloves. If you are removing real hair extensions have a mixing mat available.

B Dip your removal tool in the removal solution, placing a pad of cottonwool underneath the resin bond. Then apply a drop of removal solution onto the resin bond that attaches the extension in place.

C Crush the resin bond with the removal tool and the bond will begin to crumble.

D Holding the end of the extension slide the extension out of the natural hair.

There may be some residue of resin left in the client's natural hair. Brushing the natural hair, and shampooing and conditioning will easily remove this.

Self-test section

Quick quiz: a selection of different types of questions to check your knowledge.

Q1   The condition of the client's hair near the .... is   Fill in the blank
particularly important when considering a hair extension service.

Q2   Clients who have to wash their hair on a daily basis are suited to hair   True or False
extension services.

Q3   Which of the following are contra-indications for hair extensions?   Multi-selection

Psoriasis	☐	1
Dandruff	☐	2
Alopecia	☐	3
Excessive oily scalp	☐	4
Warts	☐	5
Gel, mousse or hair wax	☐	6

Q4   Synthetic fibre and acrylic fibre are the same thing.   True or False

Q5   A full head of extensions would on average amount to: Multi-choice

75–125 single extensions	☐	a
150–250 single extensions	☐	b
300–500 single extensions	☐	c
500–1000 single extensions	☐	d

Q6   The cost of real hair extensions is proportional to the length.   True or False

Q7   Which of the following are *not* connector products for hair extensions?   Multi-selection

Heated pre-bonded extension applicator	☐	1
Cold fusion adhesive	☐	2
Polymer resin adhesive sticks	☐	3
Mixing mats	☐	4
Acetone	☐	5
Spirit based solutions	☐	6

Q8   In making colour choices the main or first colour is known   Fill in the blank
as .... colour.

Q9   Which of the following is not recommended as home-care maintenance   Multi-choice
for real hair extensions?

Washing the hair with a clarifying shampoo	☐	a
Refreshing the hair with a daily maintenance spray	☐	b
Applying conditioners to the root area	☐	c
Drying the hair with a warm drier	☐	d

Q10   You should always hold the hair extensions at the roots whilst brushing. True or False

Finance and resources

Saks: Covent Garden

What do I need to learn?

You need to know and understand:

- **How legislation affects the way that business operations are conducted with clients**
- **The importance of good communication techniques**
- **The principles of effective stock control**
- **Effective and efficient ways to handle salon resources**

8

Unit G10 Support customer service improvements	**Element G10.1** Use feedback to identify potential customer service improvements
	Element G10.2 Contribute to the implementation of changes in customer service
	Element G10.3 Assist with the evaluation of changes in customer service

| Unit G11 Contribute to the financial effectiveness of the business | **Element G11.1** Contribute to the effective use and monitoring of resources |
| | **Element G11.2** Meet productivity and development targets |

What does it mean?

This chapter will explain how you can help your manager/employer to maximise the salon's resources and how customer service operations and personal output can be improved.

What do I need to do?

- **You need to ensure that your input at work makes the best use of the salon's stock, equipment and time available.**
- **You can also support the salon by helping to improve customer services and achieve personal targets.**

Other info

Related topics and other useful information:

- **Health and safety legislation (see p. 19)**
- **Consumer and retail legislation**
- **Data Protection Act**
- **Working time directives**
- **Equal opportunities**
- **Disability discrimination**

Science bit!

Key words

- **Effectiveness**
- **Productivity**
- **Resources**
- **SMART**

Started it	I know and understand the principles of positive communication	I can communicate positively and professionally with the clients	I always use stock items effectively, minimising wastage
✓	✓	✓	✓
I am knowledgeable in the services, treatments and products that the salon offers	I know how to monitor the salon's resources	I always carry out working practices according to the salon's policy	I've covered most of it!
✓	✓	✓	✓
I always explain technical terms eliminating ambiguity and false beliefs	I know when and to whom to refer clients in situations where external assistance is required	I can achieve personal targets in line with salon expectation	I know how to advise, promote and sell other services and products to clients
✓	✓	✓	✓
I know and respect the client's rights: data protection EO, discrimination, consumer legislation	Done it all!		**CHECKER BOARD** ✓
✓	✓		

Introduction

This chapter combines two optional units and covers the following five elements:

G10   Support customer service improvements

    G10.1   Use feedback to identify potential customer service improvements

    G10.2   Contribute to the implementation of changes in customer service

    G10.3   Assist with the evaluation of changes in customer service

G11   Contribute to the financial effectiveness of the business

    G11.1   Contribute to the effective use and monitoring of resources

    G11.2   Meet productivity and development targets

This chapter looks at the monitoring and effective use of salon resources, meeting targets and customer service issues. You can be effective at work in a number of ways. It's not just about selling, it's more to do with how you work by minimising waste, working together as a team and taking particular note of customers' requests and expectations. Collectively, this will help the business operate more smoothly, running like a machine.

We could describe business as operating a bit like a car. If it is left alone, switched off, it will generate nothing. It may have all the component parts, but collectively they will not be able to create any output and therefore will not go anywhere. However, when the engine is started, the vehicle can move off, gather speed and a journey begins: that is providing the driver knows how to drive and where he is going. In this analogy we could look at the aspects that relate to the car and to business. The essential parts are:

engine – this is the hub of the vehicle that generates power by converting the input of petrol, diesel or gas into an energy which will ultimately provide momentum. This complex machine is made up of many components and these can be likened to the working team: a group of people that only collectively, by working together in harmony, can generate the business output.

radiator/cooling system – the engine may be fine when it is first started. However, disaster is only around the corner unless the engine cooling system is working. The engine generates a lot of energy that converts into heat. If the cooling system isn't working or there isn't any water in it the engine seizes up. This is similar to the systems that control and harness the business. How would a salon operate if there wasn't a telephone, an appointment system, electricity and water?

gauges and speedometer – the bigger the car, the more sophisticated are the gauges. Without being told the temperature of the engine, how much fuel we have and how fast we are going, we would soon be in trouble. This information provides a way of monitoring all of the essential systems, giving us up-to-the-minute details, ensuring that we can keep up progress and stay on the right side of the law.

As a group activity, discuss the various methods of communication that your salon uses and find out what advantages and/or disadvantages each method presents. Record the details of your findings.

Key skills: Communication

2.1 Take part in discussions

2.2 Produce written materials

bodywork and styling – this is what catches people's eye. The shiny, unblemished, body of the car is the image that the salon portrays. It can shout quality, luxury, prestige and status without even being tried out. Conversely, a dirty, dented and slightly battered exterior conveys something else.

interior – the car's upholstery and fitted interior are like the salon's interior. The quality of fittings, colour scheme and materials used are all what the clients get to see and experience when or if they come in.

driver – the *qualified* person in control that manages to harness the power, enabling the vehicle to be taken from A to B, steering carefully to avoid obstacles, controlling the speed and observing the conditions outside at all times.

Therefore in this chapter we consider the factors that contribute to the effectiveness of the business and the way we provide customer care. Being effective in our work is essential. The way in which we use salon resources and maintain productivity has a direct impact on the viability of the business. We can look at these two aspects in closer detail:

- resources
- productivity

The resources are the key aspects that are available to the business. The way they are utilised and controlled enables the business to function properly and refers to the salon staff, salon materials, equipment and time.

Human resources

Hairdressing is a *labour intensive* service industry. It relies solely on the profits generated from the sales of services and treatments to clients. The people that work within a hairdressing salon are therefore an essential part of the business. Many people are involved in the process. The receptionist meets and greets the clients. She handles bookings over the telephone, operates the till and assists in the selling of retail products. The stylists tend to their clients, providing them with services and treatments. The junior staff are in training and adding to the skill base of the salon. They also tend to the clients by providing customer services. The manager delegates the tasks, collects information and makes decisions in order for the business to function. The cleaners ensure that all areas are fit for their purpose and hygienically safe. They are all part of one team and work together collectively in order to make the business work.

The way that the team is orchestrated, i.e. managed, really counts. Each and every member of staff has a duty to perform and personal targets to achieve. So, in order for a business to succeed, it has to make best use of its human resources, engaging people in their work and applying their different skills to achieve one common aim. Assuming that the business has a sufficient and available work force, the manager would be planning staff cover, setting individual goals and monitoring their achievements.

Changing patterns in our working and leisure time now require hairdressing businesses to be more flexible. This will ensure that both the needs of clients and the salon dovetail together. This flexibility will mean that:

- a mix of both full-time and part-time staff could be used
- more staff will generally be required towards the end of the week
- there needs to be a rota for days off when salons open six or seven days a week
- there needs to be a balance of junior and senior staff
- salons could be open at times other than just 9 am to 5.30 pm

 Active learning: Customer service

With the help of your receptionist you can conduct a simple survey to find out when salon customers want to come in. Create a simple graph displaying the days of the month along the bottom axis and a range of times (say 8.00 am–8.00 pm) along the vertical axis.

When customers call the salon, mark each point on the graph to show *when* they want to come in as opposed to what is available. Each plotting point could be colour coded to refer to different staff members. Run the exercise over a complete calendar month to see what happens.

- Are there any specific days that people would like?
- Are there any specific times that people would like?
- Do the findings of the survey highlight any discrepancies with the present work system?

Key skills: Application of number

2.1 Collect and record data

2.2 Tackle problems

Maintaining productivity

Low productivity is the result of poor service, lack of training and ineffective use of materials and time. The guaranteed outcome of this is easy to forecast. It also signifies a failure of management. If people are not given the time, skills and materials in the first place, they can not achieve anyway.

Good productivity is the result of achievement, so it is easy to see that in order to achieve there must be clear objectives. Targets should be clearly understood and attainable. Virtually all salons work on the basis that stylists earn a basic salary with commission incentive scheme. Commission is payable as a bonus on top of wages when individual or group targets have been achieved.

Targets

We may not like the thought of targets, but we all need them. We all like the benefits that come with achievement: credit and praise, higher self-esteem, increased confidence, an ability to please others and, last but not least, rewards. All these are positive outcomes for doing what is expected of us. They are the food on which we all thrive. Collectively, well-defined targets forge a unity within a working team that acts as a motivator for everyone involved.

Targets should be an incentive though. In order for people to respond to the challenge, the targets should be realistic, achievable and tailored to the individual. Unrealistic targets, which from the outset are perceived as unrealistic and unachievable, will have a very negative impact. The result will be a reduction in the bond of the working team and demotivation in the struggling individual.

Targets are not just about selling though. The targets that you will encounter at work can also be relevant to personal learning.

SMART productivity

For a hairdressing business to be successful, the salon owner has to take an overall view of productivity. As we have established the business to be mainly labour intensive, there needs to be a continuous analysis of *personal performance* which can only be measured against a *target* figure.

First, the salon owner has to set an overall salon target. This figure can then be divided between departments of stylists, technical and retail. Each person in each department then has a personal target which they understand and agree with. The personal target can be worked out as follows:

target = service price × number of clients

For example, if stylist Kerry charges £25 for a cut and blow dry and can take ten clients a day, her daily takings for this service would be £250 and her weekly takings would be £1250 (based upon a five-day week). This may be adjusted to allow for different daily performances. We cannot ensure consistent bookings, although through analysis we can establish high and low points. In addition to the styling takings we would also expect some retail sales, so the overall personal target would include this. Target setting should follow the SMART principle and should be:

- **S**pecific – clearly defined
- **M**easurable – quantifiable in some way
- **A**greed – between both parties
- **R**ealistic – able to be achieved
- **T**imed – for the duration of a fixed time period

Targets may be confidential between the manager and employee, in which case salon procedures relating to confidentiality must be observed. Personal reviews or appraisals provide an opportunity for management to establish an employee's performance level, to compare it against her target and to discuss ways of improving productivity. Most hairdressing businesses work on an incentive payment scheme. This can have a major impact on the overall salary rates. The salon owner needs to establish fixed costs and variable costs and the wage percentage needs to be established in order for the necessary profit margins to be maintained. From the overall wage portion of income, an individual target is set for each stylist.

Good practice: Staff incentives #1

Cars, cash, hot air balloon flights, holidays abroad, time out – all of these have been used to spur staff towards new peaks of achievement and some still are, alongside ever more popular perks like private healthcare, childcare, life assurance and pensions.

All incentives closely follow the economy. Cars may rate tops for young employees, but performance-related pay, medical insurance and share options are by far the preferred choice of older staff.

Within hairdressing, as elsewhere, incentives are developed by trial and error and depend largely on what's affordable.

What do you offer?

Image Setters, Gloucestershire: 'We really concentrate on incentives. One which worked a treat was a holiday cruise to Spain, or £100 cash. Most took the holiday. It gave them something to work for and takings went up in all four of our salons.'

Jane Roberts, Northamptonshire: 'We concentrate on quality employment, but do operate incentives spasmodically, including membership of a live music club and bar, percentages off treatments and retail, the occasional skiing holiday or weekend in Paris and vouchers for M&S and Selfridges. Most of the staff have been with us now for more than ten years.'

HQ, Surrey: 'Our schemes include a £100 cash bonus for anyone who hits their sales target six times during a 12-week period, paid for courses with Vidal Sassoon in London and also the opportunity to work on photographic shoots.'

The Cut Club, Yorkshire: 'We've given stylists one free product for every five sold, plus a pair of scissors and a hairdryer for the one who achieved the most sales. It's worked quite well.'

Hairaware, Hampshire: 'We give 10 per cent commission on retail sales, commission on client treatments and let staff have products at cost.'

Problem: Laziness, client-grabbing free-for-alls, demoralisation, high staff turnover.

Solution: Give each person a defined career structure with clear targets and skills/personal development training. Then reward each one with an incentive payment based on a monthly review of basic pay and the amount earned for the salon. Set up a profit-linked bonus scheme for senior staff, including managers, art directors and head technicians.

Outcome: Successful and ongoing.

So why bother?

Money is the greatest motivator, according to American business beliefs, so why not use it as the prime 'carrot'? The best reason is that cash just doesn't guarantee results.

Confederation of British Industry surveys show that more and more personnel think their performance should determine their pay rise. As far as the company owners are concerned, well-implemented incentives have a positive impact on key areas – turnover, profitability, client service, staff recruitment and retention. Proven results include higher earnings, improved loyalty and commitment, more efficient teamwork, personal development, increased skill levels and less absenteeism and sickness.

It's really about developing people's confidence and creating an environment of encouragement, but this has to be translated in the right way. Individuals should not only be allowed to make mistakes, but also given praise and recognition. There should be both financial targets and learning targets. Training is a major incentive – with relevant rewards. People need to be competitive in a healthy, non-destructive way. It's important that everybody understands each other's roles and is willing to help. This takes time to develop. Much of it is about communication. Regular meetings act as incentives because people *feel* involved.

Evaluating results

The benefits must suit individuals and prove worthwhile. Typical amounts spent vary from 3 to 5 per cent of turnover on training budgets, to 30 per cent salary equivalent on total packages. Measuring the return is notoriously difficult since incentives can have a ripple effect. But healthcare benefits (check-ups, dental treatments, counselling) are also tangibly cost effective.

Working together

Always remember that your work colleagues also need your help to meet their targets. Sharing the workload is working as a team and can be achieved by:

- providing support
- anticipating the needs of others
- maintaining harmony
- communicating effectively

In some salons, you might see some staff busy attending to their clients while others hang about around reception, flicking through magazines or disappearing off to the staffroom for a coffee. Teamwork is about making an active contribution, seeking to assist others even if only by passing up rollers. It is good for staff morale and presents a good image to the clients. In short, make yourself useful and contribute to the team effort by assisting your fellow workers.

Anticipating the needs of others follows on from providing support. Clean and prepare the work areas ready for use, locate and prepare products as and when they are required. This will help the smooth operation of the salon. Co-operate with your colleagues. Make a positive contribution to your team by assisting them to provide a well-managed and co-ordinated quality service. Be self-motivated and keep yourself busy. Don't wait to be asked to do things. Maintain harmony and try to minimise possible conflicts. Most good working relationships develop easily. However, others may need to be worked at. Whatever your personal feelings about your fellow work associates, the clients must never sense a bad atmosphere within the salon caused by a friction between staff. You will spend a lot of time in the company of people you work with, but you will not always like everyone you meet. At work, in order to maintain teamwork, a mutual respect for others is more important than close friendships. So remember, treat others with respect and be sensitive and responsive to other's feelings. Show concern and care for others.

Personal development

Managers of people use *performance appraisal* or *progress reviews* to evaluate the effectiveness of the work team. An appraisal is a system whereby you and your manager, in an interview situation, review and evaluate your personal contribution and/or progress over a predetermined period of time, as measured against expected targets or standards.

A similar process would take place at suitable points within a personal programme of training in order to review progress and training effectiveness, measured against specific training objectives.

Measuring effectiveness

To measure progress towards overall work contributions as well as training targets, there need to be clear stated expectations of the performance required. These standards should show:

- what tasks need to be performed
- what training activities will take place
- what standards are expected to be reached
- when assessment should be expected
- when a review of progress towards the agreed targets is to take place

In normal, ongoing work situations, performance appraisal will be based on the following factors:

- results achieved against targets and job requirements
- additional accomplishments and contribution
- contribution made by the individual compared with those of other staff members

The job requirements are outlined in the employee's *job description*. A job description is a written specification of the main purposes and functions expected within a given job. Good job descriptions will include the following:

- job title
- work locations
- responsibility (to whom and for what)
- the job purpose
- main functions (listed)
- standards expected
- any special conditions

Standards expected from the job holder will often include behaviour and appearance. If these have been stated from the outset, the job holder will know what is expected of her.

Job description – Stylist

Location:	Based at salon as advised
Main purpose of job:	To ensure customer care is provided at all times
	To maintain a good standard of technical and client care, ensuring that up-to-date methods and techniques are used following the salon training practices and procedures
Responsible to:	Salon manager
Requirements:	To maintain the company's standards in respect of hairdressing/beauty services

To ensure that all clients receive service of the best possible quality

To advise clients on services and treatments

To advise clients on products and aftercare

To achieve designated performance targets

To participate in self-development or to assist with the development of others

To maintain company policy in respect of:

- personal standards of health/hygiene
- personal standards of appearance/conduct
- operating safety whilst at work
- public promotion
- corporate image

as laid out in employee handbook

To carry out client consultation in accordance with company policy

To maintain company security practices and procedures

To assist your manager in the provision of salon resources

To undertake additional tasks and duties required by your manager from time to time.

The appraisal process

At the beginning of the appraisal period, the manager and employee discuss jointly, develop, and mutually agree the objectives and performance measures for that period. An *action plan* will then be drafted, outlining the expected outcomes.

During the appraisal period, should there be any significant changes in factors such as objectives or performance measures, these will be discussed between the manager and employee and any amendments will be appended to the action plan.

At the end of the appraisal period, the results are discussed by the employee and the manager, and both manager and employee sign the appraisal. A copy is prepared for the employee and the original is kept on file.

An appraisal of performance will contain the following information:

- employee's name
- appraisal period
- appraiser's name and title
- performance objectives
- job title
- work location
- results achieved
- identified areas of strength and weakness
- ongoing action plan
- overall performance grading (optional)

Self-appraisal

In order for you to manage yourself within the job role, you need to identify the areas where you meet the expectations of your job and also the areas where there is room for improvement. Measuring your own strengths and weaknesses against laid-down performance criteria (as found in the NVQ Level 3 standards of competence) is one way of monitoring your own progress. Simply use the performance criteria set out within the standards as a checklist. This will help you to:

- identify areas where further training is required
- identify areas where further practice is needed
- identify areas where competence can be achieved

Time resources

Time is a resource that, although not tangible, is of importance to the financial effectiveness of the business. It affects issues such as pricing structure and staff training. As the financial income of the salon is largely based on client service, the price structure will reflect on the length of time a service takes. For example, a cut and

Company policy should also determine who is responsible for each function:

> **line management** – what are the set down financial procedures for cash transactions? Who is authorised to take money, to process bills, to go to the bank, and to cash up at the end of the day?

Line management for cash transactions

> **training** – who is responsible for the delivery and format of training in relation to taking cash and to processing sales? Remember that the training programme needs to be updated to allow for the introduction of new facilities and systems. When a new facility such as an automatic till is introduced into the salon, the company from which it is leased or purchased will usually provide a session of staff training without further charge, but how will ongoing training be delivered for new members of staff?

The cashpoint

The systems required at the cashpoint need to be created to match the technical resources. The procedures will therefore differ for manual tills, automatic tills and computerised cash desks.

Manual tills

When operating a manual system, a lockable cashbox or drawer is used to store the cash safely. As the name suggests, a manual system relies upon each transaction being recorded by hand. A daily record (a minimum requirement) should itemise each client, with the bill total alongside in the relevant column. This kind of system can be time consuming and is the most likely to incur human error.

Client	Stylist 1	Stylist 2	Sales
Reynolds	£10.00		
Walker	£12.50		
Davies		£10.00	£5.00

Automatic tills

Automatic tills can be programmed for a number of functions. Each person may be given a *department key* which identifies her takings; this code can be used to calculate commission payments. On an

A computerised till

Sharp

automatic till, a *turn key* system can display X and Z totals. When printed out these readings are used to check the amounts registered against the actual amount in the till.

X readings may be used to provide subtotals throughout the day. This is particularly useful in larger companies where it may be helpful to check takings when the cashier or receptionist leaves the till, remove cash, etc. from the till, or for breaks and for lunch. The Z reading is a figure taken at the close of business at the end of day.

Computerised cash desks

Computerised cash desks provide the same facilities as an automatic till but offer many other functions as well. The most important of these functions are the storing and recording of data and the preparation of management reports.

Cashpoint functions

Whichever system is in operation, fundamental procedures are needed to maintain accuracy and efficiency. At all times the person acting as cashier must ensure the client's goodwill.

Float

At the beginning of each working day the cashpoint must be primed with a float – an amount of money which is surplus to the income from daily transactions. The float amount should be determined from experience, according to the average daily cash flow. It should be made up of the small denominations likely to be required for change.

Methods of payment

Payments for sales and services may be made in a number of ways. The salon's house policy will determine what is acceptable.

> **cash** – in the UK cash payments will be in pounds sterling and your salon will probably decline payment in any other currency. Be prepared for unfamiliar coins or notes from other parts of Britain and euros from the EU.

A cheque

A switch card

A traveller's cheque

A gift voucher

cheques – your salon should not accept a cheque unless backed by a *cheque guarantee card*; this will have a limit such as £50, £100 or £250. Company policy may require additional information such as the address of the client and a telephone number. Some salons may choose to waive this requirement with regular clients as a measure of goodwill.

Switch/Connect, Solo cards – these cards act as automatic cheques. The transaction process is the same as for a cheque or credit card, but once processed the account is debited immediately from the client's bank account.

accounts – your salon may provide an account facility for regular clients and a formal arrangement whereby all bills for an individual or family are paid at agreed intervals. It is advisable to ask the client to sign the bill at the time of service. It should be clear to the stylist when the commission will be paid – either at the time of service or at the time of the account payment.

traveller's cheques – are these acceptable to your company? If so, in which currencies? Usually traveller's cheques are taken only if they are in sterling. They should be checked against the bearer's passport for proof of identity.

gift vouchers – vouchers may be sold by the salon for payment against hairdressing and beauty services or retail sales. When the salon is operating as a concession, gift vouchers may be available for purchase from the host company. You in turn will require reimbursement from the source of the voucher. Company policy should outline procedures for issuing and receiving gift vouchers.

Hair Studio

31 High Street
Great Perming   **Tel: Perming 4242**

This voucher entitles

to purchase services and treatments
to the value of £

Signed: Date:

Valid for six months from date of purchase

credit cards – these cards (such as Mastercard and Visa) may be tendered for payment. Upon authorisation from the issuer or their servicing agents, the amount specified is charged to the cardholder. The salon is charged a percentage on all transactions processed.

A charge card

charge cards – these cards (such as American Express) may be tendered for payment in the same way as credit cards. Again, the salon is charged a percentage on all transactions processed.

Card payments

Registered companies may apply to a credit card company to become a *credit card authority*. Upon acceptance of the application, the credit company will issue a transaction machine and the stationery required to make purchase transactions and follow set banking procedures. Credit cards are accepted as a method of payment at the discretion of the salon. When a card has been accepted as the method of payment, a charge will be imposed by the credit company for the use of this facility.

A list of cards that are accepted by the salon for payment should be clearly displayed. Clients usually presume that payment by card will be acceptable; failure to inform them to the contrary can cause an embarrassing situation to arise. Card payments are given a 'ceiling' limit by the card company. Payment will be honoured up to a specific amount but for large amounts prior authorisation by telephone is required. Thorough training needs to be given if staff are to understand these procedures.

Financial records

In order to maintain and analyse the finances of the business, daily records must be completed which will provide weekly, monthly and yearly information. This information can form the basis of development and expansion. The main purpose of these records is to display two things:

1   **Cash receipts** and the proportional amount of value-added tax (VAT).
2   **Varying expenses** paid out – these are usually paid through a petty cash system.

Company policy will determine the layout and systems of records of all daily financial transactions.

Value-added tax (VAT)

VAT is money taken by the business as part of the cost of services and sales and paid to Customs and Excise. VAT is a percentage added to the total, the percentage being set by the government and changed from time to time. VAT registration is required only for companies whose annual turnover exceeds some current threshold imposed by government.

Day sheets

Cash receipts are recorded in the first instance on a day sheet. This breaks down the total amount of *gross* takings into components, services and sales. The VAT is then calculated from the gross amount and deducted to give the *net* amount. (A gross amount is an amount including VAT.) The purpose of the VAT calculation is to know what proportion of the total takings is usable income.

A day sheet

Day					Date		
STYLIST	SALES	BILL NO.	AMOUNT		TOTAL		
				Gross	VAT	Net

	TOTAL	
	EXPENSES	
	TOTAL LESS EXPENSES	
	AMOUNT BANKED	
	PAYING-IN NO.	
	UNDER	
	OVER	

SIGNED ....

Active learning

Adding VAT

Stylist Graham charges £10 (the net amount) for a cut and blow-dry. Assuming VAT is charged at 17.5%

Net amount	£10.00
Add VAT @ 17.5%	£ 1.75
Gross amount	£11.75

Key skills: Application of number

2.2 Tackle problems

Remember

This is not the same as simply deducting 17.5% of the gross figure.

Gross amount deduct 17.5%
£11.75
= £ 2.06 (wrong method)
£ 9.69 (this result is incorrect)

Active learning: Deducting VAT

When the amount taken is the *gross* figure, we need to *deduct* the VAT to find the *net* figure. This calculation is more complicated. In this case we know that the gross amount includes VAT at the current rate. If VAT is charged at 17.5% the gross amount is 117.5% of the net amount.

Gross amount	£11.75
Deduct VAT: divide by 117.5 and multiply by 17.5	–£1.75
Net amount	£10.00

(This is the same as dividing by 47 and multiplying by 7, which you may find simpler.)

Key skills: Application of number

2.2 Tackle problems

The day book

The analysis of each day sheet is transferred into a day book. The day book may include other information as well as records of financial transactions. The basic layout of the book should display the gross amounts taken by each sales and service department, the VAT, and the net takings. This can be totalled weekly, monthly, quarterly, and six-monthly to provide details for precise analysis.

Customer service operations

Hairdressers do exceptionally well in providing good customer service. Their focused work practices have always been directed to the core of a good business strategy, that being customer centred. The reason why this particular occupational sector is not troubled by the 'disease' that most others find hard to implement and ultimately satisfy is because of the way that the industry provides a personal service. Following is a list of factors supporting a strong customer focus within hairdressing, assuming the industry comprises of 34,500 salons of which +90 per cent are small, privately owned 'micro' businesses employing five or less staff:

Remember

Your salon's new clients are somebody's old ones!

- Stylists deliver services on a one-to-one basis with their clients.
- Competition keeps technical standards to 'better than average' levels.
- Clients expect a high level of accountability from their hairdresser.
- Experienced staff develop excellent communication skills with clients.
- Clients are able to develop relationships directly with the people from whom they choose to buy.
- From the numbers of clients that stylists come into contact with, they are able to remember individual likes and dislikes, as well as personal information.

So, good news for hairdressers, but this doesn't mean that you can relax, there's plenty to do. Good customer services are continually developed and improved and it is the rate at which these improvements are made that will give salons a competitive edge in winning new clients.

Remember

On average, it costs 20 times more to find a *new* customer that it does to *retain* an existing one!

Improving customer services

The drivers for improvements to services will occur from these three possible sources:

- trade and industry bodies
- information from clients
- competitor information

The first provides an 'around and about' rough idea to what is happening on a countrywide or national basis. The second option is the most obvious pointer for collecting useful data. The last must be considered too and could be the most important of all.

Trade and industry bodies

Large industry organisations and lead manufacturers play a pivotal role in shaping your salon's customer services. They do not necessarily have any direct link with the day-to-day operations within the salon, but they do have an impact for a number of reasons.

Employer groups, i.e. trade associations, training organisations and sector skills councils, play a strategic role within the industry. They exist by providing a range of beneficial, diverse services to the occupational sector. These services contribute overall to the way in which we work. Their resources in relation to knowledge and collected data about the sector have been sampled, analysed and shaped into policy long before it reaches the salon's doorstep. The training lead body, HABIA, has access to a national network of experts who collectively help to take the industry forward. They do this by shaping the qualification structure and specific training objectives in advance of any demographic, economic and consumer-led expectations: e.g. this book is a new edition that reflects these changes, which is then used by candidates in preparation for meeting new challenges.

Product manufacturers, e.g. L'Oréal, Procter & Gamble, Wella, etc. also play a major role in shaping the services that we do in the salon. Their immense marketing powers influence the consumers buying habits, which in turn cascade down to individual salons. An example of this would be in the home colouring market. In the 1990s manufacturers recognised that demographically a large section of the female market within this country were reaching a certain age bracket. This group or market segment had a number of factors that targeted them for a major push in home colour.

Taking all these influencing factors into consideration, it was obvious that if the salons would not buy sufficient levels of colouring product then it could be marketed and sold direct. Home colour products are now one of the biggest retail ranges, by sales volumes, in the home-care market.

Influencing factors

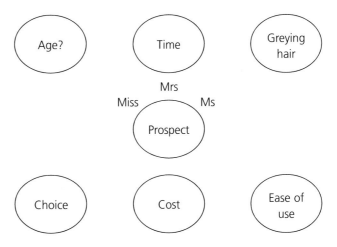

So how does this affect hairdressing services to clients? Because of the external competition created by the manufacturers, salons changed their practices to maximise their position. Salons moved into highlighting, lowlights and partial colour effects in a big way. The salons created new, attractive services by modifying colouring techniques and upshifting the levels of expertise. This boom in colouring techniques is still going on.

The manufacturers have helped the sector in other ways too. National advertising campaigns influence consumers by what they see on TV in magazines and the press. Quite simply, they either sell or create fashion. By employing A-list celebrities in their commercials, they send a strong message to 'wannabes'. This in turn is reflected by the number of clients asking 'Have you seen x on the Elvive advert?' or producing cut-out pictures and saying 'I would like it cut like this'.

Customer feedback

We learn a lot about our services from those people receiving them, or at least we should do. Customer feedback is extremely important. Their likes and dislikes are the first indicators of what works for them and we respond. However, customers expect more. They want to be able to replicate what we do and this has led to the continuing growth in salon retailing. Salons sell a vast number of different items ranging from hair ornaments, silk scarfs, beach bags, towels and equipment, as well as home-care follow-up and treatments.

It doesn't end there. The feedback that we get from our clients should shape what we do in the future. Nothing remains the same. We cannot allow the existing service provision to stay as it is. Continuing business is about improvement, and improvement is born out of continuing development. Unless we accept this fact we will be unable to satisfy our clientbase in the future. 'You can satisfy *some* of the people *most* of the time. You can satisfy *most* of the people *some* of the time. But you can't satisfy *all* of the people *all* of the time!' This saying is a little overused, but serves a purpose. Salons lose customers all the time and this can happen for a number of reasons:

- moving home
- job moves
- friend's influence
- poor service
- boredom

Home moves and job moves are unfortunate for business, but obviously necessary for the clients and their families. This loss of client is a form of *natural wastage* and part of the acceptable percentage that the business has to be prepared for. It is also satisfying when they keep in touch. Most salons will have a few clients who have moved away but can't bear to think of forging new associations with another salon. We love to talk about it too, particularly when others can't understand why they want to travel so far to have their hair styled.

Friends' influence has a powerful yet negative impact on the business. Social groupings have their leaders and followers and this is no good for anyone. When friends pressurise your clients to try their own hairdresser you have a three to one odds of retaining the custom, which is fine if you like gambling:

1   The client likes the new experience and you lose.
2   The client doesn't like the new experience but is too ashamed to return and drifts off. You lose again.
3   The client doesn't like the new experience and can't wait to get back to your safety. You win.

Then again your clients are out there busily recommending your great talents. In this situation you can win again. The power of personal recommendation is immense and should be encouraged. Many salons run *introduce a friend* campaigns. This is a strong business builder so use it.

Poor service – there isn't much too say about this as it is self-explanatory and totally unacceptable (see client complaints p. 83).

Boredom is unfortunately the main reason why salons lose clients. It's very hard to predict when boredom will set in, but if you have a strong rapport with your client you should be able to spot the signs. Typically, it will occur when you fall into the trap of regularly doing the same style over and over again. This may not be your fault either. It is human nature to stick to what you know and it is very damaging. There are only a handful of styles that *truly* suit the client. Shocked? This is based on a number of significant factors and mainly physical proportions, client competence/ability and client lifestyle routines. Embarking on other styling routes is an interesting journey, but you will find that the client will gravitate back to the safe home ground of 'tried and tested' at some point in the future. So when a returning client undergoes the same service as the last time or returns back to the style she has had before, you can 'hammer another nail into the coffin of boredom'. You can combat boredom though in the way in which you handle your client's styling preferences.

Product manufacturers do exactly the same in marketing. '*New and improved!*' means we have modified what you have been happy with before and given it a new slant, in either formulation, packaging or both. In marketing terms this is called 'extended product life'. We can invent a new strategy and call it '*extended client life*'.

Extending product service/life

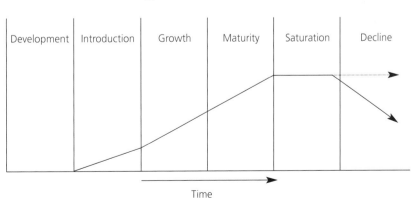

From the diagram we can see the typical graph for a newly introduced product. Taking it through the development phase (this can be similar to planning new services or treatments), we move into the introduction phase where sales start to increase following advertising and promotion. Moving forwards, further sales bring steady growth, which leads to the maturity phase. If continued interest is not stimulated, it is soon followed by a fall-off in sales during saturation. It is at this *boredom* point that the marketers reinvent the product with 'new and improved' in order to achieve an extended life of the sales.

This drop-off in business can be staved off either by introducing new services to your clients or by revival, i.e. reviewing where they are with their present image and ensuring that they are happy with it.

Collecting information from the client

You have a unique opportunity to sample the service that you provide to clients by collecting the information and putting it to good use. This can be done openly or discreetly and is purely a matter of choice. However, if you do keep the collected information on computer etc. you will need to ensure that you do not contravene any personal rights, e.g. the Data Protection Act.

The most popular open form of collecting data would be through a client suggestion box or alternatively via client questionnaire. These are very useful systems but they do need a lot of preparation and planning. If not carefully focused they can create too much information. Suggestion boxes can collect so many diverse comments that these may be difficult to address through the range of available or potential customer services. However, they do point to *real* client feelings and give clear indications and directions towards clients' expectations.

Questionnaires are very useful tools for collecting customer feedback. They do pinpoint customer feelings and provide sufficient data for analysis. This is because well-drafted consumer surveys are designed to 'steer' responses into clear, specific, quantifiable areas. They need a lot of thought in their construction and will often use the multiple choice type of question as a way of channelling the answers. The favoured style of question for eliciting the strength of people's feelings about a specific issue is shown in the figure.

There are many ways of sampling consumer opinion. In the salon it is often easier to talk to the clients as part of the routine

Multiple choice using the Likert scale

Shampooing and conditioning

Q. The newly introduced, complementary head massage has been a useful addition to the backwash service.

☐ Strongly agree

☐ Agree

☐ No opinion

☐ Disagree

☐ Strongly disagree

---

conversation that takes place during visits. If it becomes part of the salon's policy for getting this feedback, a system for collectively discussing and providing this feedback to management needs to be devised. This system should be able to:

- provide fair, unbiased feedback from a wide sample of clients
- welcome contributions from all staff members
- record and 'formalise' the findings of the sampled client feedback
- provide sufficient quantifiable data for future analysis

Competitor information

Knowing your business well is fundamentally crucial to its ongoing success. When a business is started its whole operation and the way in which it is planned to engage with its market are mapped out within a business plan. The climate in which the business operates is constantly changing though. Therefore the originally drafted business plan also needs to change. There are many reasons that necessitate the change, but the main one is competition.

Your salon's market position is constantly being undermined by the increased pressures that your competitors bring to bear. *Your competition wants your customers*. The success of your business is dependent upon increasing:

- service quality and value
- market share
- prices for services and treatments
- levels of staff competence and ability

Therefore, in order to achieve these goals, better understanding and knowledge about your competition are essential. Competitor analysis is big business. There are a growing number of specialist companies offering a wide range of 'undercover' services designed to infiltrate and make comparisons between service quality levels. The types of information that competitors want varies, but the most pointed attacks will elicit your pricing policy and service standards.

You will have seen this at work already. How often does a *bogus client* contact the salon to find out the current costs for particular services or stylist availability? Even if you are sure that another salon is trying you out for size, it would be difficult to decline the information. Pricing policy depends on many things though, so in isolation the information is meaningless. Only when other aspects of service are brought into play can a far more useful customer comparison be made. The pricing of salon services is linked to:

- labour costs
- business fixed costs, i.e. rent, rates, light, heating, insurances
- costs of materials
- expected margins
- target market

Good practice: Competitor comparison

If your competitors know part of this formula, then your salon is vulnerable. The shocking thing is they do!

1   Other businesses know what they should be paying staff.

2   Business costs in relation to salon location are public domain information. Local authorities keep a rateable value listing for all commercial properties. The rates payable for any premises are set at 42 per cent of the market rental. Other costs, e.g. electricity, are common to all.

3   If your competitor knows what products you use, then he knows what he would have to pay for them.

4   From the tariffs you charge, your competitors know which *socio-economic category* you are trying to attract.

The one thing that they have to calculate is the profitability of the service and whether it is something they can match or even beat on price.

So if these factors relate to the total viability of the business, what would happen if the information fell into the wrong hands? The only additional costs that they will incur are those involved in trying to attract your clients through marketing, promotion and advertising. The management guru Michael Porter indicates that there are five forces which act upon any business:

- power of competitors
- power of buyers in the market
- power of suppliers to the business
- threats posed by potential entrants
- threats posed by substitute products

You need to put your services and products to the test, which will mean making like-for-like comparisons between your salon and the competition. The table shows the types of information that you should address.

Much of this information is available through your clients from their feedback and general discussion, but beware the difference between useful data and idle gossip.

The other popular method is mystery shopper, or in this case *mystery client*. This favoured option is an ideal way of making comparisons between you and the competition. If they are using a system on you similar to the one above, then the business is going to be easy to assess. Other useful information includes:

- consumer legislation
- retail legislation
- Data Protection Act 1998
- Working Time Directive 1998
- equal opportunities

Service attributes	*Worse* (–3, –2, –1)	*Same*	*Better* (+1, +2, +3)	*How vital is this attribute (essential, preferred, other)?*
Service availability				
Range of services/treatments				
Ranges of products				
Communication standards				
Presentation/appearance				
Quality of work output				
After-care and advice				
Consultation				
Time allowed				
Refreshments + costs				
Payment options				
Salon image and location				

Consumer Protection Act 1987

This Act follows European directives to protect the buyer from unsafe products. The Act is designed to help safeguard the consumer from products that do not reach reasonable levels of safety.

Consumer Safety Act 1978

There is a requirement to reduce the possible risk to consumers from any product that may be potentially dangerous.

Prices Act 1974

The price of products has to be displayed in order to prevent a false impression to the buyer.

Trades Descriptions Act 1968 and 1972

Products must not be falsely or misleadingly described in relation to their quality, fitness, price or purpose, by advertisements, orally, displays or descriptions. Since 1972 it is also a requirement to label a product clearly, so that the buyer can see where the product was made.

Resale Prices Act 1964 and 1976

The manufacturers can supply a recommended price (MRRP), but the seller is not obliged to sell at the recommended price.

Sale and Supply of Goods Act 1994

The vendor must ensure that the goods they sell are of *satisfactory quality*, i.e. defined as the standard which would be regarded by a reasonable person as satisfactory having taken into account the description of the goods, the price and other relevant circumstances and *reasonably fit*, i.e. ensuring that as a vendor the goods can meet the purpose they are claimed to do.

Data Protection Act 1998

The Data Protection Act 1998 exists to ensure that personal information held on record is not mishandled, mismanaged or used inappropriately. It requires every data controller who is processing personal data to make notification unless they are exempt. *Notification* is the process by which a data controller informs the Commissioner of certain details about the processing of personal data carried out by that data controller. Those details are used by the Commissioner to make an entry describing the processing in a register which is available to the public for inspection. (For more information online go to www.dpr.gov.uk.)

Consumer Protection (Distance Selling) Regulations 2000

These are derived from a European Directive and cover the supply of goods and/or services made between suppliers acting in a commercial capacity and consumers, i.e. an individual acting outside a trade business or profession. The Regulations should be of concern to any individual purchasing goods or services by telephone, using the internet, digital TV or mail order catalogues and conversely be of concern to any suppliers dealing with consumers through these media.

Working Time Directive (1998)

The Working Time Directive (WTR) came into force on 1 October 1998. The Regulations implement the European Working Time Directive and parts of the Young Workers Directive which relate to the working time of adolescent workers (workers above the minimum school leaving age but below 18). The basic rights and protections that the Regulations provide are:

- a limit of an average of 48 hours a week which a worker can be required to work (though workers can choose to work more if they want to)
- a limit of an average of 8 hours work in 24 which nightworkers can be required to work
- a right for night workers to receive free health assessments

- a right to 11 hours rest a day
- a right to a day off each week
- a right to an in-work rest break if the working day is longer than six hours
- a right to four weeks paid leave per year

Equal opportunities (EO)

There are five main Acts of Parliament aiming to eliminate discrimination at work. The main purpose of the legislation is to ensure that people are not discriminated against on the basis of their sex, racial origin or disability, either in terms of pay or by any other means:

- **Sex Discrimination Acts 1975 and 1986 (SDA)** and the **Equal Pay Act 1970 (EPA)** aim to eliminate discrimination on the basis of gender. These Acts receive additional support from European law in the form of the Equal Treatment Directive and Treaty of Rome
- **Race Relations Act 1976 (RRA)** aims to eradicate racial discrimination
- **Disability Discrimination Act 1995 (DDA)** aims to eliminate discrimination against disabled people
- **Trade Union and Labour Relations (Consolidation) Act 1992** makes it unlawful for an employer to treat trade union members less favourably than non-members, and vice versa.

Self-test section

Quick quiz: a selection of different types of questions to check your knowledge.

Q1   Visa and mastercard are both forms of .... card.   Fill in the blank

Q2   A charge card is the same as a debit card.   True or False

Q3   Which of the following card types are debit cards   Multi-selection

Loyalty card	☐	1
Switch card	☐	2
American Express card	☐	3
Mastercard	☐	4
Solo card	☐	5
Affinity card	☐	6

Q4   The VAT within a selling price is calculated by deducting 17.5%.   True or False

Q5   The inclusive VAT figure for an item selling for £10 is?   Multi-choice

0.175	☐	a
1.75	☐	b
1.49	☐	c
8.51	☐	d

Q6   You should always take a contact number when making appointments.   True or False

Q7   Which of the following are examples of ineffective use of resources?   Multi-selection

Explaining services and costs to clients on the telephone	☐	1
Discarding excess product after application	☐	2
Overrunning on appointments	☐	3
Turning the lights off in corridors and staff areas	☐	4
Washing up in the dispensary	☐	5
Ordering stock over the telephone	☐	6

Q8   .... retail products are for maintaining hair between visits.   Fill in the blank

Q9   Which of the following stock procedures is the least important within salons?   Multi-choice

Stock control	☐	a
Monitoring wastage	☐	b
Retail product and display cleaning	☐	c
Stock rotation	☐	d

Q10   A job description is a document containing the employee's terms and conditions of employment.   True or False

Clive Boon at Boons. Photograph by John Rawson

Hair types fall into three main categories: Caucasian, Mongoloid and African-Caribbean.

> **Caucasian (European) hair** is usually loosely waved or straight and can range in colour from light to dark brown. It has a medium, soft texture.

> **Mongoloid (Asian) hair** tends to be straight and lank. Its colour ranges from darkest black to mid-brown. The texture is predominantly coarse so chemical treatments are usually more complex on this type of hair.

> **African-Caribbean hair** is usually tightly kinked or curly. Again, darker hair colouring is more predominant, requiring careful chemical treatment.

Work method

Clive Boon at Boons. Photograph by John Rawson

- Plan the sequence of events which achieve the desired result.
- Always consider safety first.
- Follow manufacturer's instructions.

Methods of creating different style effects vary and there is usually more than one route to achieving the required effect. If you apply your chosen method systematically, it can be repeated if and when required again. You will not be successful if you attempt to achieve style and shape without prior thought and consideration. This kind of haphazard and confused work will usually result in failure. Different and new ways of application can be tried when experimenting on models.

You should ensure that you are comfortable while you work. Minimise stress and strain, keep your hand positions relaxed and make sure your tools are comfortable to hold. Select those that enable you to achieve the specific effect you require.

Methods of application of chemical products are recommended by the manufacturers and these must be followed. They will have tried and tested the best methods before the products are released for sale and public use.

Specialised techniques

Anne McGuigan. Photograph by John Rawson

- Decide which effects you want to create before you start.
- Is there any special equipment needed to achieve the desired effect?

Hair moulding, shaping, finger waving, curling, plaiting, pleating, twisting and weaving can all be used to create special styling effects. Rollers, velcro-rollers, flexible foam-covered rollers, spiral rollers, pins and clips are the tools of hair shaping. You must decide which effects are required before you apply these tools. These are the mechanical aids to hair styling and are additional to the chemical tools and techniques now available.

Roberta Kneller at Bobs Hair Company
Photograph by John Rawson

Cheynes Training

Moulding, forming and shaping

- Shaping and forming – cutting and moulding
- Hair symmetry/asymmetry should balance the final effect

Some types of hair can now be styled in ways which were previously impossible. Unruly hair can now be tamed and difficult hair can achieve realistic shapes. To shape and form hair is to cut and mould – to create. This involves the distribution of portions of hair into fitting outlines and positions. Proportioning the hair means arranging and fitting it to the underlying head and face foundation. The outline shape or silhouette can be viewed from different directions and the balanced symmetry of the hair shape should generally be pleasing and harmonious.

Application of product

- Select the styling product to achieve the desired effect.
- Select the finishing product to achieve the desired effect.

Special and careful consideration needs to be given to hair products. Their contribution to styling makes them an additional hair-crafting tool. As well as the vast range of shampoos and washes, internal and external conditioners, dressings and moisturisers available, you can now create texture, volume and movement by using a variety of gels, sculpting creams, moulding mousses, fixing waves, hair thickeners and other hair controllers. To gain the maximum benefit from these products, it is vital to know how they should be used and applied. Always study the manufacturer's instructions.

Style design

In day-to-day salon work, i.e. commercial hairdressing, hair stylists seldom have the opportunity to let creativity have free rein. (At this point I can hear several people take a sharp intake of breath.) Commercial hairdressing is when your clients believe that you are being creative. The truth is that most of the day-to-day salon work is very routine, dare I say mundane. It is only when creating effects for promotional activities or special events that the creative juices start to flow. So why is that?

Have you ever looked closely and studied great fashion hair images? (I now use the term images instead of photographs.) What is it about images that gives *impact* and appeal? Conversely, what is it about commercial work that seems routine? You could say that it is

Goldwell

make-up or clothes. Is it the lighting, the ambience or location? All these factors contribute to the final effect, but as yet we haven't been looking at the hair!

Balance or imbalance?

- Does balance relate to symmetry?
- Does imbalance relate to asymmetry?
- If balance and symmetry convey harmony, do imbalance and asymmetry convey discord?

The vast majority of commercial work undertaken in salons today leads us, as hairdressers, to ensure that both sides of the haircut are of an even length, that weight is proportionally distributed, that degrees of curl or straightness are maintained throughout the hairstyle. What we are required to do by the majority of clients is to produce a finished effect that may have originated from a picture; that is modified to suit the client and become the perfect example of symmetry. This may be a *nice* style, but does it still have the same impact as the original picture? Why not? (Well, we had to take the fringe shorter so the client could see out, or we needed to calm down the volume so that it would be suitable for work, etc.)

What is often happening with the best fashion images is that we automatically convert an impactive, dynamic, asymmetrical image into a recessive, passive, symmetrical style. If you have never considered this before, start analysing your favourite style images. Going back to the questions *Does balance relate to symmetry?* and *Does imbalance relate to asymmetry?* the truth is that the best images, which are often asymmetrical in appearance, contain a visually excellent artistic balance. The diagrams try to explain

further this unlikely concept. In the first figure we have a 'seesaw' with equal masses on each of the opposing ends. As these masses are of equal weight we arrive at an equilibrium, an apparent balance which is symmetrical and harmonised. In the second figure we have a seesaw which has a weight on one end and another heavier weight

counterbalanced across the pivotal point. We now arrive at another form of equilibrium or balance that is asymmetrical and discordant. Looking at the two figures in turn, which one catches your eye more readily? This is the attention span afforded by your clients when looking through magazines and that brief opportunity that both PR and marketing have in which to sell.

Promoting the salon

Your salon may already organise some form of promotion, for example, a colour or perm incentive. During quiet times, when the salon takings are expected to be at their lowest, offering a discounted price for colouring or a perm may attract new clients to the salon, thereby increasing revenue. However, there are also other forms of promotion that your salon might want to consider, including demonstrations and advertising. In order to promote your services, you need to recognise how they are perceived by prospective clients. To do this you need to consider each service in terms of its features and its benefits:

- **features** are the functions – what the service does
- **benefits** are the results of the functions – what the service achieves.

Wella/James Kimber Salon, Birmingham

For example, suppose you hope to persuade a client to spend £30 on a cut and blow dry. Why should she do so? What are the benefits of the service?

- the **feature** is a precision cut
- The **benefits** are keeping shape and easier home styling – the client must decide whether the payment of £30 is justified by these benefits

Consider a second example: application of a semi-permanent colour. In this case the *feature* is that the colour is not permanent and is applied in a conditioning base. The *benefit* is that it will wash out after six to eight shampoos and meanwhile it will create shine. Knowledge of service and product features enables you to sell your clients the benefits. You thereby create a need and once the client has accepted the need you are in a good position to make the sale.

The first step is therefore to gain a thorough knowledge of each service and product available in the salon and to convert this knowledge into a recognition of the features and benefits in each case. The next step is to inform the potential market by means of promotion. Successful promotion requires careful planning. Time and thought need to be given to each aspect.

Identify the objectives

What do you want the promotion to achieve? Is it to attract new clients, for example, to increase colours or perms, or to increase retail sales? Whatever the objectives, it is most effective always to concentrate the promotion on a *single aim*.

Features and benefits

With your colleagues, select six of the services provided by your salon and jointly consider what the features and benefits to the client are in each case. Make a record of the collective opinions and keep this within your portfolio for future reference.

Key skills: Communication

2.1 Take part in discussions

2.2 Produce written materials

Remember

When running a salon promotion, everyone needs to be informed about the campaign. Make sure before the promotion is rolled out that there are sufficient staff meetings to make everyone aware of the event.

Decide on the type of promotion

There are many possibilities and here are a few:

- offering an introductory discount to new clients
- offering a service with another service, for example, a complementary conditioning treatment with colouring
- introducing a retail product, for example, offering a free retail conditioner for permed hair with each perm treatment
- implementing an incentive scheme for staff who reach sales targets in product sales and treatments
- demonstrating your services through a 'hair show', either at the salon or at a venue chosen to suit the target group.

Prepare promotional activities

It is best to write an outline or plan of your promotion. From that you will be able to identify each area requiring preparation.

Order stock and promotional materials

You may need to have leaflets printed or place an advertisement to inform potential clients. You may need additional materials: for instance, for a perm promotion you will need to order additional perms. Most product houses will provide advice and merchandising support.

Inform staff

Ensure that all staff are fully aware of the promotion. This may require refresher training, for example, in product knowledge. Your presentation to the staff needs to make them enthusiastic. They will then be able to sell the idea to clients.

Active learning: Promotional events

With your colleagues, identify three promotional activities that could be introduced into your salon.

1 Work out the costs involved in respect of people's time, resources and materials.

2 Schedule the event campaign.

3 Present the information to the management.

Key skills: Application of number

2.1 Collect and record data

2.2 Tackle problems

2.3 Interpret and present data

Inform your target group

Select the best medium of communication. You may inform clients verbally. You may try a mail shot, distribute leaflets, display posters or notices, or advertise in local papers or selected magazines. In any written literature, remember to highlight the features and benefits of the service.

Evaluate the outcome

After the promotion, evaluate its success by monitoring your business. If you have been successful, sales will have increased. You may find that promoting a specific service – perming, for example – will generate an increase in salon revenue overall. This is obviously good in itself, but to obtain the true result of the promotion, the increased business should be set against the initial objective. Thus, if the aim of the promotion were to increase the number of perms during February, you would need to know exactly how many clients had perms in that month and how many you would have expected without the promotion.

Record the results

To make full use of the promotion result, you need to keep a permanent record of the facts. This record can then be referred to later. Gradually you will identify strengths and weaknesses and be able to repeat or amend the promotion, depending upon the results.

Date: ....

Promotional Outline: ....

Date .... Leaflets Mailshot (No.)............................
.... Posters (No.)..
.... Advertisement (Type/Place): ....

Leaflets Returned: Week ending: .... No.: ....
Week ending: .... No.: ....
Week ending: .... No.: ....
Week ending: .... No.: ....

New Clients Recorded:

Revenue Increases: Cutting: ....%
Colour: ....%
Perm: ....%
Sales: ....%
Beauty: ....%

Comments: ....
....

Overall Success Rating: ....

Alistair Hughes

A model portfolio spread

it, you could help secure the services of the right PR consultant and you could be working together with that consultant to help achieve both your own and the salon's goals.

Photography and photo sessions

Why do it?

The power of a good photograph is undeniable. It instantly says more about your work and the image you want to project than any free editorial or paid for advertising. However, while fun, photo sessions are not easy. They can be time consuming, expensive and sometimes disappointing if not properly co-ordinated. So how do you go about things? First, ask yourself why the salon would want to invest in an expensive photo session:

- to attract more clients into the salon through coverage in the consumer press?
- to raise your industry profile via the trade press?
- for salon advertising?

Next, study the magazines and newspapers in which you hope to have your salon's work published and check the sort of photographs they use. Individual titles will have a distinctive house style: the type of work published in *Vogue* and *Elle* is very different from that in teenage magazines, and a world apart from local newspapers.

Good practice: Art direction

Define your look. Questions to consider are:

- Will the look be classic, fashionable, avant-garde or themed?
- Will the finished effect be the result of a process, say a colouring, cutting or other technique, or created by specific products?
- Will the look have more impact in black and white or colour?
- What clothes and accessories are best suited to the look?
- What image effect are you trying to create – natural, classic, dramatic or romantic?
- Should the photographer have free rein in the creative aspects of lighting, props, camera angles, backdrops and effects?

Putting it together

Once you've decided on the look you're going to go for, start to create your photographic team.

The model

Picking a suitable model can be a tricky task. A common mistake is to choose a pretty girl with unsuitable hair or vice versa; ideally she should have a combination of both. Remember that a conventionally pretty face isn't always photogenic, so study each model's photographic portfolio carefully:

- Look for regular features and bright, clear eyes. Avoid prominent chins and noses, over-full lips or dark circles under the eyes. The skin should be clear (even the most skilful of make-up artists won't be able to disguise completely obvious blemishes), and she should have a long, slim, unlined neck and a good profile to give the photographer maximum scope.
- Ensure the hair suits the type of work you plan to do. Most professional models won't allow you to cut, colour or perm their hair, so your choice needs to be the right length, shade, texture and style. The model must also have the right features to fit your look – a sweet face is no good if you want an aggressive punk image.
- Always use professional models.
- Call a casting and take polaroids of all the girls you like and make notes to refresh your memory later.
- Don't book more than four models for a one-day session – rushed results won't work.
- *Never* cut, colour or perm a professional model's hair (even if she agrees) without checking with her agency first.

A photographic studio

Mahogany

The photographer

Always opt for someone who specialises in hair, beauty or fashion photography. See as many as you can, with portfolios, to check their ideas are in tune with yours. Confirm the booking in writing and brief him/her in detail on the image and 'feeling' you are aiming for.

The make-up artist

A good make-up artist is vital. Bad make-up will ruin a shot. If you can afford it, always use a professional, but don't ask for the impossible. A make-up artist, however good, can't completely change a model's face. Research and brief a make-up artist as you would a photographer.

Clothes and accessories

Decide on the time of year you hope to have the photographs published and bear in mind that most monthly magazines work three months ahead. What type of clothes work best? Obviously this depends on the image you want to achieve and whether you are working with a professional stylist. If you don't want your shots to

Saks Premier Collection

date too quickly then go for neutral fashions that don't scream out a particular season. Necklines should be simple and jewellery effective, but don't overload – if in doubt, leave out.

Plan of action

Think about the designs and put together a storyboard by cutting out images you like from magazines. Once you've decided on the styles, work out how you are going to achieve them. By creating a theme for your collection you'll have more chance of greater coverage.

Teamwork is the key to a successful photographic session, so let those involved know exactly what they will be doing. Remember, studio time is valuable. Do any major hair preparation work before the shoot.

Draw up a list of the equipment and products you'll need, and check them off when packing your session tool kit. The general rule is to take everything – and then add anything else that might come in handy.

On the day

Have a clear idea of the looks you want to create but have in mind several alternatives as back-up. Pay attention to detail and make sure you see a polaroid of every style before the photographer starts snapping in earnest. Picking up on faults not obvious to the naked eye isn't always easy. Those to look out for include gaps in the style, stray hairs on clothes/face, rumpled clothes, pins showing or too much product/make-up.

Be decisive and don't settle for second best. If you're not completely happy with a shot, say so nicely. Always check through the camera; you'll be surprised how different something looks through the lens.

Keep backgrounds simple so as not to distract from the hair. The golden rule is slightly darker for blondes and lighter for darker hair so the shape shows up more clearly. Make sure hair is well lit and the photographer isn't indulging in some fancy lighting effects that show off his artistry rather than yours.

What's the price?

Cost is a four-letter word – so take a deep breath here. If using a top professional photographer and shooting in London, the minimum rates will be £1500 (and the price rises according to the photographer's fame). Then you've got the cost of the studio, models, make-up artist and travel expenses on top. As with most things, it's cheaper outside London. Keep a tight control on budget as costs can easily escalate. Often photographers' quotes only cover their time on the day, so check if heating, lighting and food are on top. Check also film, developing and reprint costs and remember to be clear about how you intend to use your shots. Prices can change depending on whether you use the photographs for one-off editorial, general PR or advertising.

Get the agreed charges in writing beforehand, and don't try to pull a fast one. If you say the shots are for one-off editorial, but use them for PR instead and get found out, you could be in breach of copyright and be sued – and that's expensive.

Getting the size right

Size matters. Individual publications will specify how they prefer to receive photographic material, but those most widely accepted are:

prints – shot on black-and-white or colour film, the best size is 10in × 8in (though 7in × 5in is acceptable).

colour transparencies: medium format 2.25in square or large format 5in × 4in transparencies, particularly if you're hoping for a cover (these films are more expensive). Regular 35mm is also well accepted but these images can sometimes become grainy if blown up fairly big.

Magazines always prefer original transparencies as they reproduce better. However, these can get lost or misplaced, so it's best to get good duplicates to send out and hang on to your originals. The exception here is if your photograph is to be used on a cover. Never send glass-mounted slides. Journalists hate them as the glass always breaks (no matter how carefully packed) and scratches the transparencies, so making the image unpublishable.

Examples of different photo formats

35 mm transparency

60 × 70 mm transparency

Hairdressing competitions

Entering hairdressing competitions can be great fun and a great motivator for staff. It is however, very challenging and requires a lot of personal discipline, dedication and thorough practice in order to achieve the right look that will catch the eye of the adjudicators. Competitions vary enormously between local, regional and national and will also vary in the way that entrants partake. For example, the L'Oréal Colour trophy is a national competition. It is initially shortlisted at regional level by a photographic entry dossier. Entry dossiers are sent out to participating salons early in the new year. The closing date for finished dossiers is early March. After a preliminary judging, selected styling teams are invited to take part in the regional finals, where entrants have to demonstrate their work 'live' in front of a large audience and against the clock. Winners from each of the regions are then invited to take part in the *grand final* in a top London hotel in late spring.

Conversely, NHF competitions at regional levels allow all comers to participate on the competition floor. Finalists from individual regions are then invited to take part at national level. The British Hairdressing Awards (owned and presented by *Hairdressers Journal*) are again a national competition that is shortlisted by photographic entry. In this competition entrants take part in a variety of categories ranging from Regional, Avant Garde, Artistic Team, London and British Hairdresser.

Many hairdressing organisations, colleges and major manufacturers run or sponsor competitions. If this is something that you would like your salon to be involved in, encourage your salon to run an in-house competition first. This is a good way of 'acclimatising' your staff to the pressures of competing.

Good practice

The Hairdressing and Beauty Industry Authority (HABIA) have issued the following tips to help you get started before you step on to the competition floor.

- Watch the trade press for news about when and where competitions are taking place.
- Go along to competitions and watch what happens. See what type of work is successful in competitions and keep an eye on emerging trends and fashions.
- Ask trainers and tutors for advice. Also take advice from people who have entered or know about competitions.
- Read the rules carefully and know exactly what is required.
- Take time to find exactly the right model, one with the right type of hair, the right age and with looks that fit into the competition rules. A beautiful girl with good deportment helps considerably, but if her hairline is not up to scratch she may put you out of the competition.
- Understand that competition work is very different from salon work. Colouring in particular can often be a lot stronger on a competition floor than the salon floor.
- Regular competitors stress the importance of preparation.
- Check and prepare your equipment.
- Take time to find the right model particularly if you are trying to express a specific image or theme.
- Product knowledge and application is imperative. Never attempt to style a model's hair without testing the product's effects on her hair beforehand.
- Practice, practice and practice.

Test Answers

Chapter 1
Answers

Q1	Q2	Q3	Q4	Q5	Q6	Q7	Q8	Q9	Q10
Hazard	True	1 3 6	False	C	False	2 4	First aid	D	True

Chapter 2
Answers

Q1	Q2	Q3	Q4	Q5	Q6	Q7	Q8	Q9	Q10
Catagen	False	1 2 4	True	D	True	2 3	Dermis	C	True

Chapter 3
Answers

Q1	Q2	Q3	Q4	Q5	Q6	Q7	Q8	Q9	Q10
Holding	True	1 2 4	True	D	True	3 5	Baseline	C	True

Chapter 4
Answers

Q1	Q2	Q3	Q4	Q5	Q6	Q7	Q8	Q9	Q10
Velcro	False	2 4 6	True	B	False	1 5	Pleat	B	False

Chapter 5
Answers

Q1	Q2	Q3	Q4	Q5	Q6	Q7	Q8	Q9	Q10
Skin	True	4 5	False	D	False	2 4 5	Red	B	True

Chapter 6
Answers

Q1	Q2	Q3	Q4	Q5	Q6	Q7	Q8	Q9	Q10
Curl	True	1 4 5	True	C	True	1 3	Cortex	C	True

Chapter 7
Answers

Q1	Q2	Q3	Q4	Q5	Q6	Q7	Q8	Q9	Q10
Root	False	3 4	True	B	True	5 6	First	C	True

Chapter 8
Answers

Q1	Q2	Q3	Q4	Q5	Q6	Q7	Q8	Q9	Q10
Credit	False	2 5	False	C	True	2 3	Home care	D	False

Chapter 9
Answers

Q1	Q2	Q3	Q4	Q5	Q6	Q7	Q8	Q9	Q10
Benefits	False	1 3	True	C	True	1 4 5	Eye	C	True

Glossary

accelerator A machine that produces radiant heat (infra-red radiation); can speed up chemical hair processes such as colouring or condition.

access and egress The ways in and out of the building.

acid A substance that gives hydrogen ions in water and produces a solution with a pH below 7.

activator A chemical used in bleaches or some perm lotions to start or boost its action.

albino hair Hair that contains little or no pigment. Albino hair is nearly white or very pale yellow; the condition is usually present at birth.

alkali A substance that gives hydroxide ions in water and produces a solution with a pH above 7.

alopecia Baldness.

anagen The stage of hair growth during which the hair is actively growing.

anterior Towards the front.

antioxidant A substance that prevents or slows down deterioration due to oxidation.

appointment A time and place arranged for a meeting.

aprocine gland A gland whose secretions include a part of the secreting cells themselves (e.g. some sweat glands).

arrector pili The muscles that raise the hair (in humans they are very feeble).

assessment Judging the worth of something or the results of a task; evaluation, appraisal.

assignment A task or a practical activity.

asymmetrical Unevenly balanced, without an equal distribution of hair on either side.

autoclave A device for sterilising items in high temperature steam.

backcombing/backbrushing Pushing hair back to bind or lift the hair using a comb or brush.

backdressing Backcombing or backbrushing.

balance The effect of hair shape on the features of the face and head; even proportions.

baldness traction Hair loss due to harsh physical and chemical treatments, e.g. tight braids and heavy ponytails.

barbering The art of cutting and shaping men's hair.

baseline An initial cutting line from which later cutting lines are established.

basing cream A form of skin protection used when perming or straightening hair.

bleach A substance that removes natural colour; acts first on black pigments, then on brown, red and yellow.

bleaching Removing colour from hair.

block colouring Colouring areas of hair in a way that is intended to enhance the cut style.

blow-drying Drying and shaping hair using a handheld dryer.

blow-stretching Temporary straightening of the hair by smoothing the hair while blow-drying.

blow-waving Waving the hair while blow-drying.

bob cut A hairstyle in which the hair is cut to a level length around the head.

body language Communicating by means of body actions and/or posture rather than words.

brighteners Lightening (bleaching) shampoos or rinses.

canities Hair that is without pigment and therefore grey or white.

case study Examination of a topic as exemplified by a particular event or occasion.

cashier The person responsible for transactions at the point of payment.

castle serrations Reducing areas of a hair section with special serrated scissors.

catagen The stage of hair growth during which the hair stops growing, but the hair papilla is still active.

chemical hair treatment A term that includes perming, colouring or tinting, bleaching, streaking, highlighting or lowlighting, frosting, lightening, permanent straightening.

club cutting Cutting a hair section straight across, producing blunt ends.

cold permanent waving A perming process that does not rely on heat for its activation.

collodion A protective covering used in skin testing.

colour depth Lightness or darkness of hair colour.

colourant Any type of colouring substance used on hair.

colour filling Applying a preliminary colouring of red to hair so that new colour will adhere.

communication The exchange of information and establishment of understanding between two people as, for example, between the stylist and client.

compensation Providing money or services to offset a deficiency and make amends.

complainant Someone who expresses dissatisfaction or a grievance.

compound colourings Mixtures of vegetable and mineral dyes.

computerised Operated automatically using electronic apparatus.

concave Sloping inwards.

concept An idea, impression or thought.

conditioner A product used to correct or improve the state of the hair.

confidential Private information, not for general use.

consultation A process of communication in which the client expresses her wishes and the hairdresser gives advice.

contra-indication A reason why a proposed course of action or treatment should not be pursued because it may be inadvisable or harmful.

convex Sloping outwards.

cornrowing Fine plaits running continuously across the scalp.

creative Individual ability to make a form, shape or style which ideally enhances.

crew cut Short, spiky style with hair standing straight up.

croquignole winding Winding a curl from point to root.

cutting angle The angle at which hair is held and cut.

cutting line The direction in which cutting is made to follow the contours of the head.

cutting method A considered sequence of cutting techniques.

Data Protection Act 1984 Legislation designed to protect the client's right to privacy and confidentiality.

databank A manual or computerised store of data or records.

decolouring Removing synthetic colour from hair.

demonstration A display and explanation of a physical instruction.

depilatory Designed to remove hair.

designer Creator of images.

development time The 'taking time' of a chemical action such as tinting.

diagnose Determine the condition of the hair and scalp.

disclaim To renounce or reject legal responsibility.

discolouration Unwanted colour produced by a chemical.

dreadlocks Long thin plaits.

dressing The forming and blending of hair into a finished shape or style.

emollient A substance used (e.g. in conditioners) to soften and enhance the appearance of hair.

end paper A tissue or wrap used during winding to secure a hair point.

endorsement A signature in confirmation of some statement, affirming that it is true.

eumelanin Black and brown pigment in the skin and hair.

feathering Tapering action using scissor points.

finger waving Forming waves in wet hair using the hands as a comb.

fish hook A point of hair that has been bent back during rollering or winding.

folliculitis Inflammation of the hair follicles; may be caused by bacterial infection.

formative assessment A tool for the regular monitoring and review of students' progress and a means of regular diaglogue between trainee and tutor.

fragilitas crinium Splitting of the hairs at their ends.

franchise Authorisation to sell company goods or services in a specified area.

freehand cutting Cutting without forcing the hair out of its natural position.

French roll A vertical fold of hair, usually on the back of the head.

graduation A sloping variation from long hair to short, or from short to long, produced by cutting the hair ends at a particular angle.

hair extension Real or synthetic fibre added to existing hair.

hair strand A section of hair; a mesh, tress or piece.

HASAWA Health and Safety at Work Act 1974.

heat moulding Shaping the hair while it is softened by heat (e.g. with heated tongs).

historical evidence Evidence resulting from activities that have been undertaken in the past.

host company A company that authorises others to operate, similar to a franchising company but with more direct involvement in daily procedure.

image Likeness, what is seen or portrayed, overall appearance.

incentives Rewards for effort.

incompatible Causing a chemical reaction on mixing; as between a chemical being added to the hair and another chemical already on the hair.

induction The familiarisation process that staff undergo when they first join an organisation (this may include a health and safety requirement).

keratin The principal protein of hair, nails and skin.

lightening Removing colour from hair.

line The line of a style is determined by the directions in which the hair is positioned.

lye The common name for sodium hydroxide.

manually By hand.

melanins The pigments that give colour to skin and hair.

merchandise Goods for sale.

mis-en-pli Putting hair into set.

monilethrix Beaded hair.

movement Variation of the line of a style, such as waves.

negotiation The process of reaching agreement by discussion.

neutraliser A chemical formulation used to return hair to its normal condition after cold perming.

non-verbal communication Means of communication other than words – gestures, facial expressions, stance, and so on.

occipital bone Bone forming the back of the head.

originality New, created for the first time, the ability to be original or inventive.

ornamentation Flowers, ribbons, jewellery and the like worn to enhance the hairstyle.

oxidation Reaction with oxygen, as in the neutralising of a perm.

parietal Bones forming the upper sides of the head.

perimeter The outside line of the hair.

personalising A term which refers to a variety of cutting techniques applied to a style dependent on the client's specific needs.

personality The mannerisms, habits, ways and characteristics of a person – individual identity.

pheomelanin A natural hair pigment.

physiognomy The general appearance of the head and face.

pincurling Forming hair into curl shapes which are held with pins or slips until dried.

porosity The ability to hold moisture.

portfolio A file or folder containing evidence that supports practical activities which have been carried out previously.

postiche A dressed hairpiece.

pre-pigmenting Applying a preliminary colouring of red to hair so that new colour will adhere.

promotion Advertising by way of a publicity campaign.

quality assurance The process by which a desired outcome is guaranteed by means of monitoring and verification.

quality management The establishment and implementation of systems and procedures relating to each function and task.

quality standard Required criteria for a function or part of a function.

recolouring Adding further colouring to hair.

relaxing Reducing the curl or wave in hair.

resources Means of supplying needs (people, stock or facilities).

retouching Colouring regrowth.

reverse graduation A cut in which the top layers are longer than those beneath.

senses The means by which we see, hear, touch, smell and taste.

serrations The saw-like edges of some scissors.

shingling Cutting a short layered style graduating from the nape of the neck.

stabiliser A chemical added to hydrogen peroxide to maintain its strength, for example, phosphoric or sulphuric acid.

straightening Reducing the curl or wave in hair.

summative assessment A means of final evaluation of a trainee's competence against the standards indicated by the stated performance criteria.

symmetrical Balanced by means of an even and equal distribution of hair on either side.

synthetic Artificially made, not natural.

systems Procedures, ways in which things are carried out.

systems manual A book, file or folder displaying the complete system for each aspect of procedure.

tapered Thinner towards the hair points.

tapering Cutting a hair section to a tapered point (i.e. a point like that of a sharpened pencil).

tariff A displayed list of fixed charges.

telogen The period during which a hair ceases to grow before it is shed.

temporal Bones forming the lower sides of the head.

tension The stress or stretch experienced by hair.

texture The feel or appearance of the hair – rough, smooth, coarse or fine.

textured Shaped to take account of the fineness or coarseness of hair, giving lift and fullness.

texturising A term which refers to a variety of cutting techniques.

toning Adding colour to bleached hair.

traction Stress or pull applied to hair.

traction baldness An area of baldness resulting from the stress or pull applied to hair.

training techniques Approaches to training – demonstration, observation, private study, and so on.

transaction The execution of a specific task, together with payment for this task.

trichologist An expert specialising in the treatment of diseases affecting the hair.

void To make invalid.

whorls Hair growth patterns.

Useful addresses and websites

Arbitration, Conciliation and Advisory Service (ACAS)
Head Office
Brandon House
180 Borough High Street
London SE1 1LW
Tel: 020 7210 3613
www.acas.org.uk

Black Beauty and Hair
Culvert House
Culvert Road
London SW11
Tel: 020 7720 2108
www.blackbeauty.co.uk

Caribbean and Afro Society of Hairdressers (CASH)
7 Hinckley Road
London SE15 4HZ
Tel: 020 8299 2859

City and Guilds (C+G)
1 Giltspur Street
London EC1A 9DD
Tel: 020 7294 2800
www.city-and-guilds.co.uk

Commission for Racial Equality
Elliot House
10–12 Allington Street
London SW1E 5EH
Tel: 020 7828 7022
www.cre.gov.uk

Cosmetic, Toiletry and Perfumery Association (CTPA)
Josaron House
5–7 John Princes
Street
London W1M 9HD
Tel: 020 7491 8891
www.ctpa.org.uk

Department for Education & skills
www.dfes.gov.uk

Equal Opportunities Commission
Arndale House
Arndale Centre
Manchester M4 3EQ
Tel: 0161 833 9244
www.eoc.org.uk

Fellowship for British Hairdressing
Peel House
High Street
Tisbury
Wilts. SP3 6PS
Tel: 01747 870310
www.britishhair.org

Freelance Hair and Beauty Federation
8 Willenhall Close
Luton
Bedfordshire LU3 1PY
Tel: 01582 593593
www.fhbf.org.uk

Guild of Hairdressers (GUILD)
Unit 1E
Redbrook Business Park
Wilthorpe Road
Barnsley S75 1JN
Tel: 01226 730112
www.hairguild.org

Hairdressers Journal International
Quadrant House
The Quadrant
Sutton, Surrey SM2 5AS
Tel: 020 8652 3500
www.reedbusiness.com

Hairdressing and Beauty Industry Authority (HABIA)
2nd floor, Fraser House
Nether Hall Road
Doncaster DN1 2PH
Tel: 01302 380000
www.habia.org.uk

Hairdressing and Beauty Suppliers' Association (HBSA)
Bedford Chambers
The Piazza
Covent Garden
London WC2E 8HA
Tel: 020 7836 4008
www.martex.co.uk/hairdressing_and_beauty

Hairdressing Council (HC)
12 David House
45 High Street
South Norwood
London SE25 6HJ
Tel: 020 8771 6205
www.fhbf_org.uk

Hairdressing Employers' Association (HEA)
2nd Floor, Fraser House
Nether Hall Road
Doncaster DN1 2PH
Tel: 01302 380000

Health & Safety Executive
HSE infoline
Tel: 0870 545500
hseinformationservices@natbrit.com
www.hse.gov.uk

Institute of Trichologists
2nd Floor, Fraser House
Nether Hall Road
Doncaster DN1 2PH
Tel: 01302 380000
www.ambernet.co.uk/trichologists

Lifelong Learning
www.lifelonglearning.co.uk

National Hairdressers' Federation (NHF)
1 Abbey Court
Fraser Road
Priory Business Park
Bedford MK44 3WH
Tel: 01234 360332
www.hairco.uk

Qualifications and Curriculum Authority
83 Piccadilly
London W1J 8QA
Tel: 020 7509 3097
www.qca.org.uk

Union of Shop, Distributive and Allied Workers (USDAW)
188 Wilmslow Road
Fallowfield
Manchester M14 6LJ
Tel: 0161 224 2804
www.poptel.org.uk/usdaw

World Federation of Hairdressing and Beauty Schools
PO Box 367
Coulsdon, Surrey CR5 2TP
Tel: 01737 551355

Index